International Relations
of the
Contemporary Middle East

CONTEMPORARY ISSUES IN THE MIDDLE EAST

# International Relations
of the
Contemporary Middle East

A STUDY IN WORLD POLITICS

TAREQ Y. ISMAEL

SYRACUSE UNIVERSITY PRESS

First Edition 1986
92 93 94 95 96 97 98 99   7 6 5 4 3

Library of Congress Cataloging-in-Publication Data

Ismael, Tareq Y.
    International relations of the contemporary Middle
East.

    (Contemporary issues in the Middle East)
    Bibliography: p.
    Includes index.
    1. Near East—Foreign relations. 2. Near East—
Politics and government—1945–   I. Title.
II. Series.
DS63.1.I75 1986   956'.04   86-6049
ISBN 0-8156-2381-X (alk. paper)
ISBN 0-8156-2382-8 (pbk. : alk. paper)

The paper used in this publication meets the minimum requirements of American National
Standard for Information Sciences—Permanence of Paper for Printed Library Materials, ANSI
Z39.48-1984. ∞™

Manufactured in the United States of America

In the memory of
PETER C. CRAIGIE
(1938–1985)
A gentleman, a scholar, and a friend

TAREQ Y. ISMAEL is a Professor of Political Science at The University of Calgary. He is the author of *Governments and Politics of the Contemporary Middle East* (1970); *The U.A.R. in Africa: Egypt's Policy Under Nasser* (1971); *The Middle East in World Politics* (1974); *Canada and the Middle East* (1973); *The Arab Left* (1976); *The Iraq-Iran War: Roots of Conflict* (1982); *Government and Politics in Islam* (1985); and coauthor, with Rifa'at El-Sa'id, of *The Communist Movement in Egypt, 1920–1988* (1990). He is also coeditor of *Canada and the Third World* (1976), editor of *Canadian Arab Relations: Policy and Perspectives* (1984), and editor of *Canada and the Arab World* (1985).

CONTENTS

Tables

Figures

PREFACE

THIS BOOK initially was intended as a revision and updating of my *Middle East in World Politics*, published in 1974. As work progressed, however, it became clear that developments in the Middle East (and in scholarship on the Middle East) deserved—indeed, necessitated—a new approach to the subject, one that placed greater emphasis on regional dynamics, the evolution of external linkages, and the interrelationship between the two in the context of modern world politics. Hence, *The International Relations of the Contemporary Middle East* was born.

The two distinct but intricately related objectives of this volume are represented by its two parts. Part I ("The Regional System") begins by offering a perspective of the region as a unit in international relations (Chapter 1); examines the domestic sources of Middle Eastern foreign policies (Chapter 2); and finally explores the evolution and dynamics of the regional system with emphasis on how the nature of the regional system affects the status, role, and potentialities of the Middle East in world politics (Chapter 3). (While the concepts of systems theory are employed here more for heuristic than epistemological purposes, their effectiveness would seem to suggest greater theoretical significance.)

In Part II ("External Linkages"), the level of analysis shifts to the international arena. The linkages between the region and the principal external actors are examined in a series of case studies. While studies of the international relations of the Middle East generally focus on relations with the superpowers, the systems perspective adopted in this volume suggests that other linkages are significant to the region. Therefore, after examining the Middle East vis-à-vis Western Europe (chapter 4), the United States (chapter 5) and the Soviet Union (chapter 6), similar case studies of China (chapter 7) and Africa (chapter 8) are presented.

In all of these studies, it should be pointed out, the bidirectional nature of the Middle East's contemporary external relations is clearly evident. As Chapter 4 shows, the region's relationship with Western Europe has evolved from one based on imperialism and subordination to a relationship with a more equal footing. As for the United States, its influence in the Middle East has been and continues to be substantial. However, as Chapter 5 reveals, U.S. policy has in large part been shaped by the fact of Israel, a member of the Middle East system. Chapter 6, on the USSR, delineates the existence of this bidirectional influence still further, for despite its superpower status the Soviet position in the Middle East has largely been determined by local and regional developments. Conversely, Chapter 7 shows that China has less interaction with the region and is consequently less affected by events there — although Chinese–Iranian relations remain something of an exception. In Chapter 8, the influence of the Middle East over other, weaker, regional systems is clearly demonstrated in the context of Africa, and in the dynamics of Arab-Israeli competition south of the Sahara.

Many people contributed to make this book possible. I wish in particular to acknowledge the contribution of chapter 5 by Alan R. Taylor, and the coauthorship with me of chapters 3 and 4 by Jacqueline S. Ismael and Rex Brynen, respectively. The latter also collaborated in the revision and updating of Chapter 8, and together with Alex Brynen provided valuable research assistance throughout. Professor Walid Kazziha of the Department of Political Science, American University, Cairo; Prof. Richard Dekmejian of the Department of Political Science, State University of New York (Binghamton); and Dr. Nasif Hitti kindly commented on, and made valuable suggestions regarding, the manuscript — although they, of course, bear no responsibility for the final product. Thanks are also due to Bill Matheson of University of Calgary Communications Media for producing the graphics in this book; to Judi Powell and Cecile Calverley of the Department of Political Science for word-processing the manuscript; and to Ella Wensel, Mary Gray, and Margaret Reed for countless other forms of support.

PART I
The Regional System

INTRODUCTION

The Middle East in Global Politics

THE MIDDLE EAST has long held an important place in world politics. Scholarly writings (and even more so the efforts of Western jour-
nalism) on the area, however, have tended to view the Middle East
through the prism of great power or superpower politics. In this pur-
view, the internal dynamics of the region have been portrayed as being of only secondary importance and concern compared to the goals
of external actors. Indeed, the very term "Middle East" itself betrays
some of this bias, implying as it does the "ethnocentric presumption
that [the region] lies on an international hierarchy topped by the Anglo-
Saxons."[1]

At the outset it is important to note that the term "Middle
East," in addition to suffering from these ethnocentric overtones, suffers also from ambiguity. As far as any general definition is concerned,
there is no clear consensus on what exactly constitutes the Middle
East. Analytically, it has been debated whether the Middle East has
any real explanatory value as a unit of analysis. Middle East analysts
James Piscatori and R. K. Ramazani have written in this connection:

> If the Middle East is a regional system, it is so metaphorically
> —that is, it is *like* a unit with subcomponents in regular interaction.
> "Subsystemic" elements, however, portend to be more revealing of
> how states of the area cooperate with each other, coordinate their
> interests and polities, and disagree with each other. The Middle East,
> already burdened with its own mysticisms, hardly needs the added
> burden of identification with "an almost mystical wholeness."[2]

3

Such an observation comes perilously close to confusing the *relative importance of domestic, regional, and external factors* in Middle East political behavior with the *usefulness of conceptualizations of the Middle East as a regional system*. However, it does point out the dangers of reification, distortion, and even teleology inherent in the latter. An equally valuable warning has been sounded by Oran Young, who once warned that regional conceptualizations are useful only when they are framed in a clear theoretical context and matched with clear analytical goals. To delineate regions solely for the sake of doing so was, in his estimation, analagous to clothing the "naked emperor."[3]

With these caveats in mind, then, we can begin to explore the nature of the region and its position in world politics. Specifically, is the term "Middle East" simply a loose geographic designation for a group of states buffeted in international politics by the big powers? Or can we profitably characterize the area as a discrete political unit in international affairs? If the latter, what is the Middle East's position in world politics? It is to such questions that we now turn.

THE INTERNATIONAL RELATIONS OF THE MIDDLE EAST: A SYSTEMS APPROACH

Although it suffers from many shortcomings — imprecise terminology and conceptualization; excess abstraction at certain times, and counterproductive reification at others; and the absence of a dominant paradigm or even of widely accepted criteria — systems theory provides some useful insights into our questions.[4] The concept of an international political system is, of course, a theoretical construct designed to assist in the analysis of international political behavior. To bring meaning and order to the vast array of information generated by the interaction of states — that is to say, to identify regularities in behavior and to recognize deviations from regularity — we visualize international politics as an adaptive, self-regulating, and self-transforming system of action with characteristics of structure and process. Systems theorists use analogies variously drawn from biology, ecology, physics, and cybernetics to render the concept of system less abstract. For example, we can conceive of the human organism as a physiological system composed of subsystems — nervous system, digestive system, circulatory system, and so on — which can themselves be successively broken down into subsystems, allowing us to focus with ever-

increasing precision on details. We can pass from the gross view of
the human organism to the microview of the cellular system without
losing perspective. Our construct of an international political system
is similar. The international system is the total view of all the action
and interaction taking place at all levels, from the micronational components of foreign policy processes to the supranational character of
the United Nations. The concept of descending levels of systems keeps
the relationships ordered. Thus, in the first instance, a systems approach to the Middle East can be justified on the basis of the clarity
it brings to levels of analyses of the international relations of the area.

For our purposes, we can consider that there are three arenas
of political action—the globe, the region, and the nation-state—that
invite three levels of analysis. In the global arena, the international
system is comprised of the totality of transnational interactions. This
is of course what is commonly understood as "international relations,"
and it tends to be dominated by the interests and actions of the most
powerful nations. In the region, by comparison, the subordinate system is the total interaction of relations within that region. In the
nation-state, finally, the internal system is the totality of relations of
the organizations composing its domestic politics.

Of these three levels of analysis, we know a great deal about
the global and internal systems but comparatively little about subordinate systems and the linkages they provide between the nation-state
and the global arena. Indeed, even the delineation of subordinate or
regional systems is an uncertain business, with criteria ranging from
that of "a relatively self-contained network of political interactions"
between members of a region of limited scope[5] to geographical defini-
tions informed by sensitivity to "consciousness of regional identity,
felt cultural and other affinities, and perceived interdependencies."[6]
The conceptual ambiguity emerges from the fact that a regional system is not necessarily coterminus with the notion of a geographic
region. The composition of a regional system must be defined (if the
system conceptualization is to retain any analytical utility) by a combination of geographic and interaction concepts such that interaction
within the regional system is qualitatively and quantitatively distinct
from interaction outside the system.

The Middle East Regional System

In describing the Middle East as a subordinate system, we are
seeking to identify consistent patterns of interaction that give a

characteristic structure to the internal and external relations of the area. What variables describe the Middle East? Leonard Binder defined the Middle East as the area from Libya to Iran, fringed by Afghanistan, Pakistan, and the Maghreb, noting that common membership in the Ottoman Empire (which left traces of such similar institutions as patterns of patronage, and social networks) was descriptive of the Arab states and Turkey. He also noted the criteria of Islamic culture, pan-Arabism, common language, and ease of communication as related to the systemic quality of the Middle East—although these criteria are not equally relevant for every state in the system.[7]

Do different criteria indicate different groupings of states? Bruce M. Russett, in *International Regions and International System*, posited four variables, in addition to geographic proximity, for operationally defining "region": social and cultural homogeneity, similarity of political attitudes and behavior, political interdependence, and economic interdependence.[8] He utilized factor analysis and related modes of data manipulation for each of his five criteria to allow high correlations on certain factors to form clusters of nations. On sociocultural measures, all of the states previously designated by Binder— that is, those in the area from Libya to Iran, fringed by Afghanistan, Pakistan, and the Maghreb—fell into a common region (Afro-Asia), with the single exception of Israel. However, United Nations voting patterns did not reveal a very homogeneous grouping: Turkey and Iran voted with the Western community: Israel and Pakistan voted with the Latin American group; Afghanistan, Egypt, Syria, Algeria, Iraq, Tunisia, the Sudan, Morocco, and Yemen voted with the Afro-Asians; Lebanon, Jordan, Libya, and Kuwait formed a distinct group (called "Conservative Arabs" by Russett); and Saudi Arabia, finally, fell into no group at all.

A more cohesive appearance takes shape with an analysis of international organization membership data from 1962. Pakistan fell in Russett's Asian group; Turkey was West European by organizational membership, as indicated by its presence in NATO; while Yemen and Afganistan were unclassifiable. Syria, Egypt, Morocco, Libya, Lebanon, Tunisia, Iraq, the Sudan, Israel, Algeria, Jordan, Saudi Arabia, Kuwait, and Iran comprised a single group (although Israel and Egypt also ranked in the Western European groupings). Russett's analysis of trade-pattern data from 1963 also turned up an Arab category, although its members were not all Arab states, nor were all Arab states subsumed in the grouping. It was indicated that Lebanon, Saudi Arabia, Syria, Jordan, Kuwait, Iraq, the Sudan, Egypt, and Libya were closely related by trade. A definite relationship appeared when these states were placed on an index of geographic proximity. Pakistan, Afganistan, the Sudan, and Yemen were marginal on this dimension, with Algeria, Tunisia, and Turkey also somewhat apart from the main group. In terms of proximity to Africa, Asia, and Europe, the other states mentioned by Binder are very similar.

Russett concluded that the Middle East is a distinct (if not highly integrated) region. His results support Binder's estimate, although the boundaries of the region are still vague. Certainly, the scope of any possible regional grouping that could be called the Middle East is limited to North Africa and Southwest Asia, and a certain group of Eastern Arab states is well established as the core of the region.

Louis J. Cantori and Steven L. Speigel, in *The International Politics of Regions: A Comparative Approach*,[9] have advanced a framework for analysis of subordinate systems that incorporates and synthesizes many of the most useful ideas so far posited. They place the patterns of interaction that characterize subordinate systems in comparative perspective by going beyond the idea of regional cohesion to other pattern variables, which structure the analysis of the features and regularities of regional international relations. These are the nature of communications, power relationships, and the structure of relations. Cantori and Speigel further suggest that we employ the concepts of core, periphery, and intrusive sectors of the system, along with the pattern variables, in order to determine the membership of a system and its structure.

These concepts may be summarized as follows: The core may be considered a political center of gravity or focus of international politics within a region, and is thus generally marked by a high level of cohesion and intense interaction. Also, there may be more than one core in a region. The peripheral sector includes those states "which are alienated from the core sector in some degree by social, political, economic, or organizational factors, but which nevertheless play a role in the politics of the subordinate system."[10] The intrusive sector is composed of external-power participation in the affairs of the subordinate system. States operating in the intrusive sector are normally members of other subordinate systems, while peripheral states are not (although they may be marginal participants in two systems).

Utilizing their four pattern variables, Cantori and Speigel define the core of the Middle East subordinate system to include relations among the United Arab Republic, Yemen, Saudi Arabia, Kuwait, Iraq, Lebanon, the Sudan, Jordan, Syria, South Yemen, and the Gulf states. Social and organizational cohesion, reflecting a common history and intense diplomatic activity, provides the criteria for the delineation of the core. (It is largely on grounds of social difference that Israel is excluded from the core.) Although the North African Arab states share many of the elements constituting social cohesion, the pattern is more diffuse, as a result of distinctive experiences during the colonial period and the struggle for independence; consequently, these states participate only nominally in the diplomatic relations of the core. (In point of fact, Cantori and Speigel consider them a separate subordinate system. In their view, the Maghreb has at most a tenuous place in the Middle Eastern periphery.)

In terms of one measure of economic cohesion—real or potential complementarity of economic resources—Cantori and Speigel draw no conclusions for the Middle East; however, they did find a definite relationship when trade, measured in import–export totals, was examined. Little political cohesion could be demonstrated for the Middle East on the basis of the criterion of similarity of regime. The states in the Middle East may be separated into three categories: mobilization systems, military oligarchies, and modernizing autocracies. (By comparison, Europe is dominated by reconciliation systems.) Organizational cohesion—which may tend to promote regional consciousness—is expressed through the League of Arab States, the Council of Arab Economic Unity (CAEU), and the Arab Common Market (ACM). While all three organizations are linguistically exclusive, Cantori and Speigel think it significant that only the Arab League is a trans-core grouping, the CAEU and the ACM being restricted to members of the core. In conclusion, the cohesive elements in the Middle East core sector may be ranked in the following order of strength: social, economic, organizational, and political.

Certain critical comments are in order on the schema of Cantori and Speigel. To begin with, their choice of indicators may not be particularly appropriate to the Middle East. For example, their measure of political cohesion relies upon similarity of internal structure—a view perhaps unduly conditioned by the importance of ideology in the postwar relations of the United States and the USSR. This measure should be balanced by some attention to the foreign-policy goals of the regimes in the area. In addition, the emphasis upon cohesion in defining a core reflects a strong ideological bias towards interactions of a cooperative nature. Such a bias ignores the fact that competitive and hostile interaction can be a significant focus of international politics in a region. Indeed, the composition and nature of the Middle East regional system are different when non-cooperative interactions are given the same weight as cooperative interactions, as we shall see in chapter 3.[11]

Finally, the criteria of organizational unity equate the ACM and CAEU and the League of Arab States, and use the result as one means of distinguishing the core from the periphery. In fact, however, the former two organizations were mere paper agencies and reflected, if anything, the lack of cohesion in the system.

More recent attempts to define the Middle East as a regional system include the work of Jamil Matar and Ali E. H. Dessouki; William R. Thompson; and L. Carl Brown. In their important study of systems in the Middle East (first published in 1979), Matar and Dessouki argue that the concept of a Middle East system reflects more the strategic orientations and objectives of external actors than regional realities.[12] They suggest that the concept implicitly reduces the significance of regionally determined political interaction patterns induced by geography, history and culture, while exaggerating the externally determined political interaction patterns induced by outside forces. This fundamentally distorts an understanding of the patterns in the region. To correct this, they advance the concept of an Arab regional system "which refers to the Arab countries extending from Mauritania to the Gulf whose members are bound by geographic community," culture, and history.[13] The political patterns manifested by these bonds have a phenomenological reality manifested symbolically in the ideology of Arab nationalism.

The work of Thompson provides empirical verification of the existence of an Arab regional subsystem. Thompson defines a regional subsystem as "a relatively regular and intense pattern of interactions, recognized internally and externally as a distinctive arena, and created and sustained by at least two and quite probably more generally proximate actors."[14] He defines this operationally as the number of intergovernmental visits among Middle Eastern heads of state, heads of government, and cabinet-level ministers for the period 1946 to 1975, aggregated into five six-year intervals. While such an indicator does have certain shortcomings—reliance on bilateral interaction; bias toward cooperative activities—it nevertheless validly and reliably reflects "who is relatively salient to whom—which, in many respects, is what the idea of regional subsystems is all about."[15]

In his analysis of this data, Thompson finds that an expanding network of Arab states has maintained a sustained, intense interaction throughout the period; also, both the volume of interaction and the number of actors in the network have increased during the course of the period. Furthermore, throughout the period, inter-Arab

inter-arab & non-arab interaction

interaction has been proportionately greater than interaction with non-Arab states, both inside and outside the area. Finally, he finds that—although the system is relatively fluid over time in terms of structure—the Arab character of the system is consistent.

A still more recent attempt to discern the boundaries of the Middle East system has been made by L. Carl Brown in his *International Politics and the Middle East,* wherein the Middle East (or more accurately, the "Eastern Question System") is defined as the "Afro-Asian lands of the former Ottoman Empire"—that is to say, "the entire Arab world (except Morocco and Mauritania), Israel and Turkey."[16] This definition is derived from a less empirical method than that of Russett, Cantori and Speigel, or Thompson: its delineation is based rather upon the criteria of the history and culture of the region. Nevertheless, it provides the basis within Brown's book for a thought-provoking and coherent examination of the international politics of the region.

Although the methodological approaches and substantive findings of these various studies differ, they all affirm the existence of sufficient grounds for the conceptualization of the Middle East as a regional system in global politics. Even Piscatori and Ramazani, while questioning the usefulness of regional systems study, acknowledge that "geography, culture, and history . . . substantiate the idea of the 'Middle East.'"[17] Chapter 3 will utilize the constructs examined here to explore further the scope and nature of the Middle East regional system.

The Regional System in Global Perspective

Having established the separate identity of the Middle East, we must now place it in the context of international politics as a whole. When, back in 1958, Binder referred to the Middle East as a "subordinate international system"[18] he appears to have had two qualifications in mind: first, that the system was of lesser scope than the total global system; and, second, that less power resided there than in the dominant subsystem of the globe—the U.S.–USSR subsystem. However, this is not to say (and Binder made this very clear) that the subsystem was dominated by the bipolar global system: relations within the subordinate system are by no means entirely a product of great-power relations, although it is true that influence flows more readily from the great powers into the Middle East than in the opposite direction.

The position of the Middle East in the global system is indicated by the power ranking of its members. Here, however, we must be careful to note the limitations of any attempt to weigh regional power. Regional power is never wielded in a unified manner, and is only occasionally coordinated. In the Middle East, regional power has been harnessed only for such issues as the Arab-Israeli dispute and the Iran-Iraq War, and even then has been usually directed inward rather than outward. The distribution of power in the Middle East (and the divisions and polarities that accompany it) are far more important variables affecting the international relations of the region than is any composite measure of regional capability. Furthermore, any attempt to assess power is fraught with methodological difficulties: regional power is dynamic, and is therefore subject to absolute and relative changes. Still, the relative position of the regional system within global politics, and changes in that position over time, do suggest the degree to which the Middle East's external linkages exhibit unilateral or bilateral influence—relations of subordination, dominance, conflict, and cooperation—vis-à-vis other national and regional systems.

One attempt to address this issue has been made by Cantori and Speigel, who assessed state power in the late 1960s. On a composite measure of material and motivational indices, they constructed a seven-level scale descending from primary powers (United States, USSR) to colonies. The three peripheral states of the Middle Eastern system (Turkey, Iran, and Israel) were classed as minor powers—that is, powers of the fourth rank. Of the core states, only the United Arab Republic ranked as a minor power, while seven states fell in the category of regional states and two were microstates—the fifth and sixth ranks, respectively. (Jordan would move down from regional to microstate status if the loss of the West Bank were to prove permanent.) By way of comparison, we may note that Cantori and Speigel identified two secondary powers in the West European core, along with three middle powers and one microstate. Finally, they ranked the Middle East below both Western Europe and Latin America in terms of aggregate power.

It should be pointed out that since that analysis was made, new factors—notably the growth of Middle East oil revenues and the concomitant increase of power—have served to strengthen the global position of the Middle East. Because of these developments, the Middle East has inarguably come to occupy an intermediate position among the regions of the world.

In the mid and late 1970s, a series of attempts to assess regional power was made by Ray S. Cline.[19] Although Cline's power-assessment methodology (and even more so his "politectonic" view of international politics) are open to serious question, his works nevertheless provide some indication of the greater power of the Middle East after the early 1970s. In *World Power Trends*, Cline ranked the Middle East fourth among eleven "zones" on a scale of aggregate perceived power: behind the Soviet bloc, North America, and Western Europe, but ahead of Latin America, sub-Saharan Africa, and other areas.[20]

The Middle East's position within the global system places significant limitations on the freedom of action of its constituent elements. This continues to be true (although to a varying degree) despite the growth of national and regional power in the Middle East vis-à-vis other actors and subsystems—in part because the contemporary global system was constructed in the image of Europe and later modified by bipolar superpower competition. As relative newcomers to an old international game, then, the states of the Middle East are forced to operate under rules and within parameters not of their own making.

This is not to suggest, however, that the states of the Middle East have no choice or influence. Rather, they exercise considerable policy latitude, albeit within certain externally (and internally) defined limits. This position of limited but nevertheless real autonomy within international politics has been carefully explored by Bahgat Korany and Ali Dessouki, who have stated:

> To the majority of international actors, the global system presents an arena of both constraints and opportunities. In the case of Arab countries—as with the rest of the developing or dependent countries—the constraints outnumber the opportunities.[21]

In the present study, we place greater stress on regional and domestic factors in the international behavior of Middle Eastern states than do most studies of the area. Specifically, the subsequent chapters will illustrate that, although the international system does indeed set the parameters of international relations in the Middle East, this fact must be balanced against three critical realities:

> 1. Domestic politics and circumstances define the "discourse" of contemporary Middle Eastern foreign policies. Culture, ideology, economic needs and capabilities, domestic political developments, and the like all play key roles in shaping the international behavior of Middle Eastern actors. When these factors are mobilized in support

of specific foreign policy goals—as they were in Egypt under President Gamal Abd al-Nasser, for example,—major regional (and even global) consequences can result—and while these consequences may be less sweeping than those that involve the big powers, they are nevertheless important. Similarly, when Nasser's successor, Anwar al-Sadat decided to jettison the USSR and embrace the United States, his actions had a major impact both on the region itself and on the East-West competition and balance of power. (Because domestic factors are important, the domestic sources of foreign policy are examined in detail in the next chapter.)

2. Processes and structural arrangements of forces at the regional level are extremely important. When a region is relatively cohesive and united around key issues and/or actors, its ability to resist external pressures and affect other regional systems (and indeed the global system itself) is much enhanced. Hence, in the early 1970s, the relative unanimity of the Arab world on the Palestine issue, and its willingness to coordinate and mobilize its resources—particularly oil resources—in support of this sentiment allowed the Arab states to significantly influence both Western Europe and Africa. In contrast, when a region is internally divided—when multiple power centers and fractious issues arise—the "terms" of its political "trade" inevitably deteriorate. (Because of the importance of these factors, the regional system is more fully explored in chapter 3.)

3. The Middle East occupies an intermediate position in the global system, and as such both receives and exerts influence. Chapters 4 through 8 examine the scope and nature of some significant external linkages of the Middle East—namely, those with Western Europe, the United States, the Soviet Union, China, and Africa.

Throughout this volume, an effort has been made to emphasize the interaction of the domestic, regional, and global levels of analysis, and to show that examination of all three of these is fundamental to any understanding of the international relations of the area. These form three interrelated perspectives, then, from which the reader is asked to view the Middle East in the pages which follow.

NOTES

1. James Piscatori and R. K. Ramazani, "The Middle East," in Werner J. Feld and Gavin Boyd, eds., *Comparative Regional Systems: West and East Europe, North*

America, The Middle East, and Developing Countries (New York: Pergamon Press, 1980), p. 274. For an examination of how ethnocentricism has shaped Western perceptions and the study of the Middle East, see Edward Said's seminal work *Orientalism* (New York: Pantheon, 1978).

2. Piscatori and Ramazani, "Middle East," p. 296. The quotation in the last sentence is drawn from Ernst B. Haas, "On Systems and International Regimes," *World Politics* 27, No. 2 (January 1975): 148.

3. Oran R. Young, "Professor Russett: Industrious Tailor to a Naked Emperor," *World Politics* 21, No. 3 (April 1969): 486–511.

4. For a short but highly readable critique of systems theory as currently constituted see Kenneth Waltz, *Theory of International Politics* (Reading, Mass.: Addison-Wesley Publishing Co., 1979), pp. 38–78. For a more comprehensive (though now somewhat dated) attempt to apply systems analysis to the Middle East one might also wish to see T. Y. Ismael, "The Middle East: A Subordinate System in Global Politics," in T. Y. Ismael, ed., *The Middle East in World Politics* (Syracuse: Syracuse University Press, 1974).

5. Michael Haas, "International Subsystems: Stability and Polarity," *American Political Science Review* 64, No. 1 (March 1970): 101.

6. Werner J. Feld and Gavin Boyd, "The Comparative Study of International Regions", in Feld and Boyd, eds., *Comparative Regional Systems*, p. 4.

7. Leonard Binder, "The Middle East as a Subordinate International System," *World Politics* 10, No. 3 (April 1958): 408–429.

8. Bruce M. Russett, *International Regions and International System* (Chicago: Rand McNally, 1967).

9. Louis J. Cantori and Steven L. Speigel, *The International Politics of Regions: A Comparative Approach* (Englewood Cliffs, N.J.: Prentice-Hall, 1970).

10. Ibid.

11. For examinations of the Middle East regional system with emphasis on conflict rather than cohesion see Michael Brecher, "The Middle East Subordinate System and Its Impact on Israel's Foreign Policy," *International Studies Quarterly* 13, No. 2 (June 1969): 117–139; and Yair Evron, *The Middle East: Nations, Superpowers and Wars* (New York: Praeger, 1975).

12. Jamil Matar and Ali E. Hillal Dessouki, *al-Nidham al-Iqlimi al-'Arabi: Dirsatun fi al-Alaqat al-Siyasiyah al-'Arabiyah*, 4th ed. (Cairo: Dar al-Mustaqbal al-'Arabi, 1983).

13. *Ibid.*, p. 31.

14. William R. Thompson, "Delineating Regional Subsystems: Visit Networks and the Middle East Case," *International Journal of Middle East Studies* 13, No. 2 (May 1981): 213–235.

15. *Ibid.*, p. 219.

16. L. Carl Brown, *International Politics and the Middle East: Old Rules, Dangerous Games* (Princeton, N.J.: Princeton University Press, 1984), p. 7.

17. Piscatori and Ramazani, "Middle East," p. 275. The Middle East is defined by these authors as "excluding Israel, but including eighteen Arab states, Iran, and Turkey".

18. Binder, "Middle East," p. 410.

19. Ray S. Cline, *World Power Assessment: A Calculus of Strategic Drift* (Boulder, Colo.: Westview, 1975) and *World Power Trends and US Foreign Policy for the 1980s* (Boulder, Colo.: Westview, 1984).

20. Cline, *World Power Trends*, pp. 175–177.

21. Bahgat Korany and Ali E. Hillal Dessouki, "The Global System and Arab Foreign Policies: The Primacy of Constraints," in Korany and Dessouki, eds., *The Foreign Policies of Arab States* (Boulder, Col.: Westview Press, 1984), p. 29–30.

Domestic Sources of
Middle East Foreign Policy

WHEN EXAMINING THE FOREIGN POLICIES of the various Middle Eastern
states, it is immediately obvious that there is considerable diversity
in the domestic environments of these countries in regard to history,
economic circumstances, political organization, social structure, and
ideology. In fact, the broad range of variation in foreign policies among
Middle Eastern states is generally explained in terms of this diversity
in domestic environments. A systems perspective, however, suggests
that there are patterns in diversity—patterns of variation that suggest
an element of regularity and predictability in diversity itself. Another
way of seeking to explain the variation in foreign policies among
Middle Eastern states, then, is to examine the patterns of variation
in domestic environments. This chapter seeks to do just that: that
is, to examine some of the more prominent patterns of variation in
domestic environments that are directly linked to foreign policy. True,
in such a brief survey, the full complexity of the linkages between
domestic circumstance and international posture can only be broadly
indicated: only the more striking patterns can be described, to the
neglect of many subtleties and nuances that might have provided a
fuller flavor of international relations. Nevertheless, as the previous
chapter suggested, some of the patterns of variation in domestic environments are directly linked to the systemic nature of the Middle

This chapter is coauthored with Jacqueline S. Ismael, Professor of Social
Welfare, University of Calgary, Calgary, Canada.

East. And these patterns can be highlighted against a backdrop of certain unifying factors.

There are unifying factors in Middle Eastern history, culture, and society that provide a basis for the regularities of behavior observed when comparing these states. The ancient and modern history of the region reveals persistent tendencies to integration. Even in the days of the pharaohs, for example, there was intense interaction (not always friendly) between the Valley of the Nile and Mesopotamia. In incessant competition, the two great centers of civilization in the area brought the other peoples of the region under their suzerainty, and the resultant cultural exchanges created lasting similarities and affinities. The Alexandrian Empire surpassed even the Persian in bringing the Middle East under a single dominion; although fragmentation followed Alexander's death, a cultural unity in hellenism persisted for centuries. The Romans, although losing the far eastern section of the region to the Parthians, swept North Africa and Spain into their great cultural sphere, while the Byzantines retained the eastern sections of the Roman Empire until the rise of Islam: under Muhammad and his successors, the entire Middle East as well as North Africa were brought under Arab rule.

Nevertheless, even when the Arabs were replaced by Persians and Turks as holders of political power; even when the Abbasids lost their grip on their Western domains; even as Islam lost Spain to the Christians (while conquering the Balkans), Arab-Islamic culture — art, architecture, literary forms, language, and script — gave a unified basis to the entire Mediterranean basin. Especially important were the Arabic language, which provided a common means of communication, and Islam, which provided the basis for a common legal and moral system. These facts assume even more salience when it is recalled that, in more recent times, all of the states of the area, excepting only Turkey, Saudi Arabia, and Yemen, have experienced Western rule. Communication has generally been well enough maintained that major intellectual and ideological movements have permeated the entire region.

Upon this basis of common features are overlaid the common problems of underdeveloped states seeking to make a place for themselves in the modern world. Common cultural configurations and parallel economic and political problems provide us with the basis for a generalized model of the relationship of domestic and foreign events. The major linkages will be examined here in three analytically distinct but empirically integral categories: the domestic socioeconomic context, ideology and foreign policy orientation, and the foreign policy process itself.

THE SOCIOECONOMIC CONTEXT

The domestic socioeconomic context within any country affects the foreign policy of that country in a number of ways. Instrumentally, such social and economic variables as population, education, technology, resources, industrialization, and natural wealth form the basis of a nation's capabilities, and consequently delimit its ability to influence the regional and international systems. Motivationally, needs and pressures at the domestic level may require international action, and hence may represent a source of foreign policy objectives. (Alternatively, the domestic social and economic context may set limits on foreign policy aims.)

One aspect of the domestic socioeconomic context of Middle Eastern foreign policies that has recurrently had a major effect on international behavior is the challenge of national development. Although specific circumstances vary widely, economic development remains an imperative for all of the countries in the Middle East. Only if they succeed in expanding production (and enhancing productive efficiency), in industrializing, and in diversifying their primary product economies will the various states be able to meet the needs and expectations of their people, and to lay a secure basis for future well-being. At the same time, the developmental process, in all its forms, involves serious considerations for those undertaking it. Economic development produces social dislocation and strain, most notably in terms of urbanization and the breakup of existing social support networks. It creates new wants and needs, and breeds alienation among large segments of the population as old symbols and institutions change or disappear. Economic development also creates pressure for greater political participation. From the regime's perspective, all of this brings with it the threat of deteriorating political stability.

In addition to these internal dilemmas, there are certain external ones. Historically, the underdevelopment of the Middle East has been, if not entirely caused by, at least exacerbated by external intrusions.[1] In the context of colonial domination in the nineteenth and early twentieth centuries, many areas of the Middle East found the development of indigenous productive forces distorted either by a colonial economy dominated by settlers from the metropole (e.g., Algeria), or by a reorientation and reorganization of production to satisfy European demands for raw materials (e.g., Egyptian cotton). This distortion of local production currents affected all levels of Middle Eastern societies: the Middle East found itself not only politically, but also economically, subordinate to the West. Moreover, this subordination, deeply rooted as it was, did not end with the formal declarations of independence of the 1920s, 1930s, and 1940s. Rather, it persisted, albeit in a slightly different form, and continued to undermine political autonomy. Addressing such subordination, both domestically and internationally, therefore became a prerequisite of any meaningful development. As will be discussed later, nationalist and anti-imperialist ideologies calculated to meet this challenge soon arose in the Middle East.

Perhaps more than any other single commodity or economic sector, the history of Middle Eastern petroleum resources graphically illustrates the problems of development and dependency. The Middle East accounts for more than one-half of the world's currently identified petroleum resources. Western interest in these resources began at the turn of century, when British and other Western oil companies began to scramble for oil concessions in the area. After World War I, complex commercial and diplomatic maneuvering and the consolidation of oil concessions culminated in the establishment of an international oil combine with virtually total control of Middle East oil. By World War II, seven fully integrated companies dominated the petroleum market. These companies not only were joint owners of the various oil-producing facilities in the Middle East, but also — through a skein of complicated contractual and partnership arrangements — mutually controlled every aspect of the exploration, production, refinement, and marketing of Middle East oil.

Only quite limited material benefits accrued to the Middle Eastern countries from the oil cartel's exploitation of their oil resources. It soon became apparent that the oil revenues that Middle Eastern governments were receiving were by no means commensurate with the value of the resources extracted. In fact, foreign governments were often receiving more in the form of tax payments from the oil companies than the producing countries were realizing from oil revenues. In 1950, for example, the Anglo-Iranian Oil Company (AIOC) operating in Iran paid the Iranian government £16,000,000 in oil royalties and taxes, had an after-tax net profit of £33,103,000, and made tax payments to the British government of £50,707,000. Further, while AIOC's profits increased tenfold between 1944 and 1950, Iranian oil revenues increased only fourfold. Such inequities served to heighten the growing tension between the oil companies and the producing countries.

With the rapid influx of Western concepts, techniques, and skills that accompanied the intrusion of two world wars and the burgeoning oil industry, the ranks of an articulate, educated middle class in the Middle East rapidly expanded. This class was impatient with the slow pace of change in their tradition-bound societies and intolerant of foreign domination, and increasingly questioned the terms of the concessions—indeed, the very *nature* of the concessions. Following World War II their main thrust centered on getting better terms from the concessionaires. Endless rounds of negotiations between the governments of the various oil-producing countries and the oil companies had by the mid-fifties achieved better revenue terms for the producing countries. Nevertheless, sovereignty over oil resources still remained in foreign hands. While the governments and economies of many Middle Eastern countries depended on oil revenues,[2] they had no voice in the rate of exploration, exploitation, and production of the resources—the very factors upon which their revenues depended. Nor did they have a voice in the determination of the posted prices used as the basis for calculating revenues, which tended to reflect the costs of oil production rather than its actual market value. All of these factors were under the firm control of the concessionaires, who based their calculations on the profit motive rather than on the economic needs of the oil-producing countries. Such was the essence of the sovereignty issue.

The degree of foreign corporate control over Middle East oil resources was tellingly demonstrated in Iran following World War II. Iranian nationalist sentiment directed against foreign interference in Iranian affairs had been exacerbated by the war, which had brought Russian, British, and American troops to Iran. Following the war, the Tudeh (Communist) Party spearheaded the struggle to regain Iranian sovereignty, and foreign control over oil resources—Iran's main source of revenue—was naturally a primary issue. In 1948, Iran opened negotiations with AIOC, with the aim of regaining its sovereignty over its oil resources. Negotiations failed, and in 1951, under the leadership of the ardent Iranian nationalist, Dr. Mohammed Mossadegh, the Iranian government nationalized its oil resources. Justifying the nationalization before the United Nations General Assembly, the Iranian representative, Nasrollah Entezam, stated: "As you know, oil is the main source of our national wealth. It is therefore proper that we can countenance its exploitation only as a way of ensuring the general welfare of our people."[3]

With the support of their several governments, the oil companies brought the full force of economic, diplomatic, business, and military pressure on Iran. Iranian oil was excluded from the world markets. (The oil companies were able to easily fill the gap simply by increasing oil production in other areas.) Unable to market its oil, Iran was thrown into economic chaos. In 1953, a coup sponsored by the U.S. Central Intelligence Agency threw Dr. Mossadegh out of office and replaced him with the pro-Western Shah Mohammed Reza Pahlavi, who had earlier been forced to flee Iran. In the fullness of time, the oil companies reopened negotiations that concluded with their resumption of control over Iran's oil. It is probably superfluous to add that the Iranian experience made a profound impression throughout the Middle East, effectively demonstrating as it did the awesome power of the oil companies and their control of the world's oil reserves.

Two aspects of the world oil market were responsible for the Iranian failure. First, beginning with the decade of the fifties and running into the decade of the sixties, the supply of oil greatly outpaced demand. When the oil companies and the Western governments allied with them wished to exclude Iran from the oil market, it was a simple matter to increase the production of other wells to compensate for the loss of Iranian oil. Furthermore, the industry was dominated by seven integrated oil companies—the so-called seven sisters—which closely coordinated their marketing and political actions, working together to maintain their complete control of Middle East petroleum resources.

By the decade of the seventies, however, the picture had changed considerably. A plethora of small, highly competitive independent oil companies, anxious to break into the petroleum market, was emerging. In addition, the oil-producing countries themselves had begun to act together in pursuit of their common interests within the framework of the Organization of Petroleum Exporting Countries (OPEC) and the Organization of Arab Petroleum Exporting Countries (OAPEC), formed in 1960 and 1968, respectively. Perhaps most important, continual increases in world oil consumption were by now outstripping production, making oil a more valuable commodity. The international oil business was now a seller's market.

The turning point in the relationship between the oil-producing countries and the oil companies came in 1970 when President Muammar Qaddafi of Libya rejected the prevailing posted price and tax rates for Libyan crude and demanded that both be increased. At first, the companies refused. Libya responded by implementing production cutbacks. Eventually, the companies' dependence on Libyan oil (and the increased competitiveness of the oil market) led the companies to agree, one by one, to the Libyan government's demands.

The Libyan settlement sparked a comprehensive renegotiation of other petroleum agreements in 1971 under the aegis of OPEC. The negotiations were backed by a collective declaration of OPEC members that changes would be unilaterally legislated, and enforced by OPEC-wide boycotts of violating companies in the event that negotiations failed. Within a few months, all other Middle East oil producers had received price and tax increases similar to Libya's. The incident not only effectively demonstrated the dramatic changes in market circumstances and structure, but also removed the check that had been imposed on nationalist aspirations by the Iranian nationalization experience and its aftermath. By mid-1972, Iraq, Libya, and Algeria had nationalized all or major parts of their oil industries, while Saudi Arabia, Kuwait, Abu Dhabi, and Qatar had signed participation agreements with those companies operating in their territories. Furthermore, in 1973–74 and again in 1979, national control over petroleum resources enabled the oil-producing countries to effect major increases in world prices within the framework of the OPEC cartel. As a result, many countries in the Middle East found themselves in a capital-surplus position, as petrodollar earnings continued to grow.[4]

For those Middle East countries with substantial petroleum resources, the "oil revolution" of the 1970s provided the basis for an upsurge in capital-driven development. Other countries in the region, however, were not so fortunate, lacking as they did both petroleum and a resource of equivalent world value. Israel was a partial exception among the non-oil-exporting countries: postwar reparations from the West German government, the value of expropriated Palestinian property, and massive injections of capital from the U.S. government and the Diaspora allowed Israel to pursue a capital-intensive development strategy into the early 1970s. (Since then, however, Israel has found itself in increasing economic difficulties as it strives to maintain a standard of living—and a military establishment—beyond its means.)

Thus, it is possible to differentiate between the "rich" (or capital-surplus) and "poor" (or capital-deficient) states in the Middle East. Yet this is not the only major dimension along which the developmental strategies of Middle Eastern states should be plotted, as even among states in a comparable economic condition there can be fundamental differences as to the manner in which development is fostered. Some states have adopted socialist models of development, while others have inclined to capitalist models. We shall turn our attention to the latter first.

Capitalist Models of Development

The capitalist model of development is, above all, one predicated on capital accumulation and capital-driven economic growth within an environment of capital mobility and market relations. In this view, capital investment leads to a growth in economic productivity, and hence of surplus; this surplus then, constituted as capital, in turn provides the basis for further investment, and so on. Past a certain point, this cycle is believed to become self-sustaining and expansionary, providing the means for achieving ever higher levels of economic development. Because of its emphasis on capital-driven growth, the capitalist model of development places the greatest priority on capitalization of the economy, and on creating and maintaining the market and exchange relations most favorable to capital accumulation.

Adoption of the capitalist model has important implications for the international position of a developing country. Since the domestic economy is, by definition, underdeveloped and undercapitalized, the goal of capital accumulation is generally pursued through integration into the capitalist world market. Reliance on external capital supplies (foreign investment) and the growth of an externally oriented primary production sector (raw material exports) are the two most common manifestations of this integration. Typically, the capitalized sector thus established proves highly adept at capital accumulation, but this capital is then remitted—through debt, the operating realities of multinational corporations, and/or patterns of unequal exchange—to the already developed capitalist countries. Domestic capitalist development thus becomes uneven and stunted: with integration into the world market comes integration (in a subordinate position) into the world division of labor—and dependency. In this fashion, the very quest for integration within the capitalist world market may seduce the developing country into a position of structured underdevelopment.

A second set of effects associated with the capitalist model of development concerns the transformation of internal class forces. With the growth of an externally oriented dependent capitalist sector comes the establishment of a local comprador bourgeoisie. This class, advantaged as it is by the country's dependent relationship, has little incentive to change it. And since its economic power brings with it political influence, its dispositions serve to reinforce economic and political dependency. At the same time, the extension of capitalist production and the capital accumulation process combine to produce severe social dislocation and new inequalities in both wealth and power. These in turn aggravate domestic political instability and social exploitation.[5]

Socialist Models of Development

Socialist models of development reject the social exploitation and external dependency associated with the capitalist model. In place of the former, they advocate the establishment of an equitable and just social order; in place of the latter, they call for self-reliance over dependency as well as for the establishment of a new economic order. Economic growth is still a very important element of the socialist model, of course, but it is accompanied by substantial internal reform, the domestic redistribution of wealth, and the avoidance of a stultifying dependency.

Socialist development in the Middle East has come in a variety of ideological packages, ranging from Labour Zionism to Libyan president Muammar Qaddafi's "Third Universal Theory." Arab socialism, as represented by Nasserism, Ba'athism, and other forces within the Arab New Left, finds its inspiration in the common suffering of the Arab world at the hands of Western imperialism and its local allies.[6] Islamic socialism, on the other hand, draws upon the communal inclinations of Islam, and on its traditional concern with social welfare and justice.[7] However, both Arab and Islamic socialism, although critical of domestic exploitation and favoring some degree of wealth and power redistribution, stress unity—either of the Arab nation or in the case of Islam, *umma* (community) in the face of external political and economic threat. Marxism-Leninism, the official ideology of South Yemen, reverses these emphases: it warns against capitalist imperialism, but places still greater stress on domestic class struggle.

Regardless of its inspiration and tone, however, socialism in the Middle East has typically assumed a statist orientation. It is the state that implements social reform, breaks the power of the dominant classes, and confronts imperialism. One result of this has been a tendency to a burgeoning state sector and bureaucracy in those countries pursuing socialist development, sometimes to the point of administrative immobility, inefficiency, and/or corruption. Also, casting the state (or party-as-state) in the leading role can result in the diminution of personal freedom and—democratic rhetoric and ideals to the contrary notwithstanding—to authoritarianism.

Development Dynamics and Foreign Policy

Using the criteria of rich versus poor and socialist versus capitalist models, it is possible to construct a four-cell typology of development in the Middle East. This is depicted in Table 2.1.

TABLE 2.1

Development Models in the Middle East, 1985*

Model	Rich	Poor
Socialist	Algeria, Iraq, Libya	South Yemen, Syria
Capitalist	Bahrain, Kuwait, Oman, Qatar, Saudi Arabia, United Arab Emirates	Egypt, Djibouti, Israel, Jordan, Mauritania, Morocco, Somalia, Sudan, Turkey, Yemen

*Because of the state of anarchy within Lebanon, it is excluded from this table.

Clearly, this breakdown oversimplifies the diversity of the developmental process in the Middle East. It is important to recognize that there is a wide range of variability within each cell—for example, some poor countries are wealthier than others in the same cell. Similarly, both capitalist and socialist models relate to general principles and goals, so that there can be considerable differences in priorities, strategies, and so forth within the same class. Furthermore, a state's position in the schema is not fixed but may vary. Israel, for example, can be seen as an initially rich country pursuing an initially socialist development model; over time, however, it has become a poor country pursuing an essentially capitalist developmental path. The position of the Islamic Republic of Iran within the schema is even more problematic, and for this reason it has been omitted from the table. In terms of potential, Iran is a capital-surplus or "rich" state. To date, however, the strains of revolution and the demands and dislocations of war have prevented the current regime from exploiting such potential or even articulating clear development goals. Moreover, it is unclear at this point in time exactly what Iran's revolution—which is based upon a return to idealized traditional institutions in the context of contemporary development—may foster in terms of a development strategy.

Nonetheless, once these qualifications have been noted, it is possible to identify certain regularities in the domestic and international behavior of the countries that occupy each cell. For those capital-surplus countries pursuing a socialist path of development, for example, legitimacy is likely to be built on the redistribution of existing wealth as well as on absolute improvements of the standard of living —particularly of the rural poor. Internationally, nationalization of foreign-owned enterprises and a radical foreign policy that challenges the existing global economic order will probably be pursued. Because socialist-oriented regimes tend to see the global environment as a threatening one, economic diversification and self-sufficiency may also be promoted. All of these activities are evident in the foreign and domestic policies of Iraq, Libya, and Algeria—the three "rich" regimes pursuing socialist development in Table 2.1.

In contrast, capital-surplus regimes adopting a capitalist approach to development are likely to place far more importance on absolute increases in societal wealth than on the redistribution of such wealth. Internal legitimacy will be derived from this, as well as from traditional symbols. Domestic policy, although bringing about an improvement in the standard of living, is thus unlikely to include extensive land reform or other measures that would transform the existing socioeconomic structure of society. Internationally, such regimes will favor participation in foreign-owned companies operating within the country, and will therefore seek to participate in—rather than transform—the existing world market. Saudi Arabia provides an example of this sort of developmental approach.

Those capital-deficient regimes seeking to pursue the socialist path of development will find their ability to do so constrained by their lack of resources and capabilities. The redistribution of wealth will be a more difficult task. Because substantial benefits may not be immediately forthcoming, legitimacy must often be forward-oriented—that is, based on the expectation of better things to come (or on charismatic leadership, or ideology) rather than on tradition-alism or contemporary performance. Land reform and the socializa-tion of existing social services may be pursued, but the state's ability to sustain these measures will be limited in the absence of mass sup-port. Internationally, nationalization will be a preferred way of deal-ing with economic dependence, but again the state's ability to adopt this course may be constrained this time by its international weak-ness. Foreign aid will be accepted, but only insofar as it is consonant with revolutionary goals and to the extent it does not threaten to in-crease external dependence. Egypt under Nasser is an example of a "poor" state attempting to further its development through socialist means.

Finally, those capital-deficient countries seeking to develop through a capitalist approach to the problem are likely not to chal-lenge the domestic social status quo, but rather to seek to find means of increasing productivity. Legitimacy is likely to be fostered through appeals to traditional symbols and authority. Since structural changes at the domestic level cannot, by their very nature, be the major source of this increase in productivity, the regime is likely to seek large capi-tal assistance in the form of foreign aid and investment. If the coun-try lacks geopolitical importance or is otherwise unattractive to out-side investors, this sort of assistance may be difficult to secure. In any case, such inflows may have the effect of aggravating existing social inequalities; furthermore, they will tend to increase the dependence of the country in question on the outside world. Egypt under Sadat provides an example of such a developmental strategy.

From the discussion above it ought to be clear that a coun-try's wealth and development model are important variables affect-ing international behavior. It must also be noted that the process of development is a complex internal phenomenon, one that has a dif-ferent impact on different economic sectors in the same country. This latter point is nowhere more clearly illustrated than in the case of the Arab oil producers, whose well-developed and technologically so-phisticated petroleum industries exist beside other economic sectors that suffer from the ills of serious underdevelopment. The result is a paradoxical combination of power and dependency—a combination that has played a major role in shaping the behavior of these states.

IDEOLOGY AND FOREIGN POLICY ORIENTATION

The concept of ideology refers to the relationship between the objective collective experience and the subjective social interpretation of experience. In other words, it addresses the questions of how people interpret the patterns of their everyday lives—the world they experience directly—as well as the world outside the parameters of their own immediate experiences. It is important to note that ideology deals with collective experience and social interpretation, not with individual idiosyncratic experience or personal idiosyncratic interpretation. The concept, then, is based upon the relationship between the patterns of life—political, social and economic—in a society and in the larger world, and the generally accepted interpretations of these patterns within that society.

Viewed from this perspective, ideology may be defined as an interrelated set of assumptions, beliefs, and values concerning human nature and the nature of society that legitimates the patterns of everyday life. Since most of life's everyday patterns in any society are structured by the basic social institutions of that society, the legitimation function of ideology relates to these institutions. The assumptions, beliefs, and values are transmitted through the processes of socialization, education, and social control. They constitute the framework for the interpretation of experiences and the formulation of expectations within the basic social institutions.

So long as the patterns of human experience are congruent with these interpretations and expectations, the assumptions, beliefs, and values that legitimate these patterns remain fundamentally unchallenged. However, as the patterns begin to change, human experience tends increasingly to contradict these assumptions, beliefs, and values, thus initiating the process of ideological change. This process then is directly related to the process of social change—that is, to changes in the patterns of everyday life. And, like social change, ideological change is an uneven process, affecting different segments of the population at different rates. Unlike social change, however, ideological change by definition constitutes a challenge to the legitimacy of basic social institutions and the authority vested in them. In its most manifest form, ideological change constitutes a revolutionary change in the social order—a new set of basic social institutions, and a new set of assumptions, beliefs, and values that legitimate them.

The link between ideology and foreign policy orientation is

based upon the objective historical experience of a society with the outside world, and on the interpretation of that experience by the state. It is the role of foreign policy decision-makers to interpret the outside world to the population—that is, to interpret the relationships of regional and international conditions to the state's circumstances, and to explain the state's actions in the regional and international arenas. Obviously, these interpretations are based upon the legitimation of the most basic political institution—the state—by those people who have the strongest vested interest in maintaining its legitimacy and authority. The assumptions, beliefs, and values embodied in the institution of the state and transmitted by decision-makers about the nature of the state and the nature of the world constitute the ideological basis of foreign policy. The historical foundations of this ideological base are religion and nationalism/anti-imperialism.

Religion

The role of Islam in shaping the foreign policy of Middle Eastern states can be examined in terms of three main periods of development. In the period extending from the seventh to the sixteenth century, Muslim jurists viewed non-Muslim states as falling within the "abode of war" that waited to be incorporated into the "abode of peace": Islam. A Muslim state had the duty to spread the faith, whether by violent or by peaceful means, and especially to strive to ensure that Islamic law and justice be made supreme.

The first clear departure from this concept occurred in 1535 when Suleiman the Magnificent, in a treaty with Francis I of France, agreed to a "valid and sure peace," with each monarch guaranteeing the subjects of the other the protection of certain rights within his respective territory. This event signaled the advent of the second period. Whereas the first was marked by competition and warfare, the second was one of coexistence and moderation. Majid Khadduri enumerates three principles that developed during this second stage: "the separation of religious doctrine from the conduct of foreign relations," the principle of "peaceful relations among states," and "the principle of the territoriality of the law."[8]

It should be noted that the Ottoman Empire was at its apex when Suleiman the Magnificent signed the treaty with France. However, by the seventeenth century, it was being externally checked and challenged by the emerging West and internally dissipated by its own excesses of luxury and abuses of power. By 1917, the process of decline of the Ottoman Empire was completed with its collapse at the end of World War I.

The third significant period in Islam's history vis-à-vis the shaping of foreign policy is marked by the struggle for cooperation among the various Muslim states. The movement began at the end of World War II as the colonial empires began to break up, and the Muslim countries won political independence. Pakistan played a significant role in the movement for cooperation among Muslim states, hosting a number of Islamic conferences soon after its independence in 1947. Further evidence of the growing importance of pan-Islamic themes in postwar Middle East foreign policy is provided by the establishment and/or expansion of a number of transnational and intergovernmental Islamic organizations in the decades that followed: the World Islamic Conference (first convened in 1926); the Islamic Conference Seminar (founded in Jerusalem in 1953); the General Islamic Congress (1955–); the Muslim World League (1962–); the World Islamic Federation; the Afro-Asian Islamic Organization; the International Islamic Organization (1970–); and the Islamic Conference Organization.[9] Of these, the latter has been by far the most important in terms of foreign policy and international relations. Founded in 1969 at a meeting of the leaders of 27 Islamic countries, the Islamic Conference Organization (ICO) has grown into a major international organization with a permanent secretariat, annual foreign ministers' meetings, and conferences of heads of state and government every three years. These meetings (and the organization as a whole) provide a mechanism for discussing and coordinating foreign policy on a broad range of "Islamic" issues, from the Palestine Question to Cyprus and Afghanistan. Some 44 countries, including all 21 members of the Arab League, belong to the ICO.[10]

While these organizational efforts represented a voluntary search by Muslim states for peaceful cooperation, the foreign policy of contemporary Iran reflects the same objective pursued through the opposite means: conflict and coercion. The significant point here is that Islamic cooperation constitutes a basic objective of foreign policy for many Middle Eastern states. Thus, to conclude, the first important period of Islam as a key factor in foreign policy was based on the objective of spreading Islam to non-Islamic lands; the second period, on the objective of coexistence of the Islamic world with non-Islamic lands; and the third, on the objective of cooperation among the states within the Muslim world.

Foreign policy and →

Anti-Imperialism

The concept of anti-imperialism is inextricably linked to nationalism through the historical common denominator of colonialism. In the Middle East, imperialism is almost synonymous with Western influence (although neither Turkey nor Iran would quarrel with the concept of Soviet imperialism). Anti-imperialism has affected the conduct of foreign policy in the Middle East in at least three ways. First, it has often shrouded the relations of Middle Eastern states with the big powers in a miasma of fundamental and profound mistrust. At different times, Egypt, Iraq, Syria, South Yemen, and Algeria have all expressed suspicion of the motives of Western states vis-à-vis the Middle East—a phenomenon commonly described as "anti-Westernism" in the West. Similarly, Iran and Turkey have from time to time distrusted the motives of the Soviet Union. The mistrust and antagonism thus generated have of course compounded existing problems between the states in question.

Second, foreign-policy commitments to anti-imperialism have sometimes set a state on a path of conflict with a Western power. Egyptian support of African and Arab liberation movements during the fifties and sixties, and Libyan support for nationalist movements in Ireland, the Philippines, and elsewhere throughout the seventies are examples of foreign-policy thrust that has created serious tensions in relations with the West.

The third way in which anti-imperialism has affected the conduct of foreign policy in the Middle East is in the development of policies of positive neutralism. First espoused in the Middle East by President Nasser of Egypt in 1955 as a nationalistic assertion of independence in foreign policy, positive neutralism evolved into a two-pronged doctrine of nonalignment in the competition between big powers, and a commitment to establish and represent the interests of the less developed states in international affairs and international forums. (Both objectives can be tempered by flexibility in the pursuit of national interests.) By the mid-sixties, Iraq, Syria, Algeria, Yemen, and Sudan had declared neutralism as the basis of their foreign policies. Neutralism, then, was an important dimension of cohesion in the Arab world in the sixties.

The impact of anti-imperialism on foreign policy has taken different forms at different times. Although these forms are significant, they are not permanent, nor are their effects indelible. What is more significant about them is their indication that anti-imperialism represents an orientation to the world that is uniquely deep-seated in a nation's historic experience.

Ideological Predispositions

It is possible to differentiate between states based upon the ideological foundations of their foreign policy. On the dimension of the nature of the world, a Middle Eastern state's ideological assumptions, beliefs, and values are generally grounded in its historical experiences with the West, since this is the external world that has been most critically involved in the region. Ideological predispositions in foreign policy, then, can be distinguished on the basis of whether the West is interpreted as threatening or nonthreatening to the state. On the dimension of the nature of the state, the primary symbols of the state's legitimacy may be used as a key indicator. The ideological predispositions in foreign policy may be distinguished on the basis of whether the primary legitimacy symbols are religious or secular, as Table 2.2 illustrates.

TABLE 2.2

Ideological Predispositions in Foreign Policy, 1985*

Primary symbols of State Legitimacy	Nature of the World	
	Threatening West	Non-Threatening West
Secular	Algeria, Iraq, Syria, South Yemen	Bahrain, Djibouti, Egypt, Jordan, Kuwait, Mauritania, Qatar, Somalia, Tunisia, Turkey, Yemen
Religious	Iran, Libya	Israel, Morocco, Oman, Saudi Arabia, Sudan

*Because of the state of anarchy within Lebanon, it is excluded from this table.

The colonial experience is central to the world view of those states that view the West as threatening. Not surprisingly, then, a concern about imperialist encroachments on their sovereignty is a characteristic common to their foreign policies. The secular states in this group tend to interpret the state's circumstances in regional and international affairs from the perspective of the international arena generally and the hostile West specifically—that is, they view the West as a causal factor in their affairs of state, both regional and international. To offset this, they seek to establish strong ties with the Soviet Union and East European states. Furthermore, all of the states in this category pursue socialist models of development—a path that, by its very nature tends to make the West more hostile and the socialist states more friendly.

In the regional arena, a common characteristic of the policies of these states is their identification of Israel as an extension of Western colonialism and imperialism. The Arab-Israeli conflict, as a result, is viewed in an international rather than in a regional context. While Syria is the only state in the category that is directly involved in the Arab-Israeli conflict, all of the states in this category view the conflict as the central manifestation of Western imperialism in the region.

The two religious-oriented states in this group—Libya and Iran—view the Soviet Union and East European states as a threat no less than the West. For them, the primary danger is the cultural imperialism of the industrial world, and as a result they attempt to limit political and social interaction with it. However, their economies are heavily dependent upon the importation of industrial goods and services, so that their economic interaction with the feared foreign powers is substantial even though their political rhetoric is hostile. These countries are equally concerned about the imperialist encroachments of all industrial powers, and thus see the international arena—dominated as it is by industrial world politics—as threatening. In addition, both states include strong religious (missionary) orientations in their foreign policies. These two factors—hostility to the international arena and a religious missionary orientation in the regional arena—have made their foreign policies seem adventurous at certain times, irrational at others. Both states are embroiled in conflicts with neighbors, and both interpret these conflicts in terms of a hostile international environment and religious symbology.

All of the states in Table 2.2 that do not view the West as threatening are strongly pro-Western in their foreign policy orientation; consequently, they tend to see the Soviet Union as the threat, rather than the West. Indeed, Turkey, Jordan, Sudan, Saudi Arabia, and Egypt (under Sadat) have all been vehemently anti-Soviet at times. However, of all these states only Turkey has a historical basis for its antagonism. For the others, the negative orientation is more the product of their strong economic and political ties with the West than of their relations with the Soviet Union. All pursue a capitalist model of development and are economically dependent on the West, and their foreign policies are generally aligned with the United States in international and regional affairs. The Arab states in this group tend to view the Arab-Israeli conflict as an area (rather than a regional or international) problem, and to overlook American support for Israel. There are, of course, exceptions to these general tendencies, but on the whole the foreign policies of these states are marked by their pro-American orientation. Furthermore, there are no significant differences in this regard between the secular and the religiously oriented states.

THE FOREIGN POLICY PROCESS

In addition to socioeconomic and ideological factors, domestic influences on the foreign policy of any state can be found in the foreign policy process itself. With regard to the major powers (and especially with regard to the United States), the literature on bureaucratic politics and organizational process, interest groups, political competition, and leadership effects on foreign policy formulation is well developed. Unfortunately, the applicability of much of this work to the developing world is debatable, and few case studies of foreign policy-making in the Middle East (or other developing areas) exist. Indeed, an exhaustive survey of the limited amount of foreign policy literature (in six languages) pertaining to the Middle Eastern countries led two distinguished scholars in the area to remark that the "'underdeveloped study of underdeveloped countries is nowhere more clearly illustrated than in the analysis of Arab foreign policy.'"[11]

Nevertheless, at least two aspects of the foreign policy process can be identified as particularly important in shaping the international behavior of Middle East actors. These are the role of leadership and the apparent triumph of pragmatism in contemporary Arab politics.

Leadership

Most states in the Middle East are characterized by strong, authoritarian leadership; often weak or subservient foreign policy bu-

authoritarian create foreign policy from group of elite advisors

reaucracies; and only a limited foreign policy input from the mass public and non-elite interest groups. Because of this, the perceptions, competence, and style of national leaders play an extremely important role in determining international behavior. This is not to say that institutional factors, or interest groups inside or outside of government, or public opinion, are negligible: such factors are important — indeed, they form the context within which foreign policy decisions are made.[12] Nevertheless, it must be recognized that leadership itself is a very important aspect of foreign policy formation in developing countries — far more so than in many more developed states. The role of political leadership in shaping foreign policy varies from actor to actor, from issue to issue (being more apparent in issues of "high," or security, politics), and from time to time. In the case of Israel, for example:

> . . . where many foreign policy issues are seen to go to the heart of the state's meaning and certainly to the heart of its existence, public participation is active and vocal. The Israeli executive has less policy independence from the public than other regional governments on foreign-policy matters, particularly when the government is a weak coalition. Indeed, the diversity and number of Israeli views as expressed in the Knesset show clear-cut paralyzing characteristics as regards political domains. On military aspects of foreign policy, the executive is granted much greater freedom of action.[13]

Much the same could be said of the PLO. The politicization of the Palestinian population, the dynamics of political and ideological competition between individual Palestinian resistance organizations, and the need to retain both Palestinian support and some semblence of unity has historically limited the initiative and freedom of action of the PLO Executive Committee.[14] Furthermore in a number of Middle Eastern countries (notably Turkey), the army rather than the public represents a major constraint on leadership.

Elsewhere, however, leaders have more latitude. For example, in all the negotiations culminating in the Camp David accords between the United States and Egypt on the one hand and Egypt and Israel (mediated by the United States) on the other, President Anwar Sadat of Egypt acted independently of the Egyptian foreign policy process. Ismail Fahmy, Sadat's foreign minister from 1973 to 1977; Muhammad Ibrahim Kamil, foreign minister from 1977 to September

Sadat of Egypt

1978; and Muhammad Heikal, editor of the Egyptian daily *al-Ahram* and close confidant and advisor of Sadat all report on Sadat's dictatorial and personalized approach to foreign policy making.[15] This occurred despite the fact that Egypt has perhaps the most skilled and professional foreign policy bureaucracy in the Arab world. As a matter of fact, Kamil maintains that Sadat "surprised" his security council and foreign minister with only a verbal notice (that is, no written document) of his plans just twenty-four hours before departing for Camp David.[16]

   The importance of leadership in Middle Eastern foreign policies has a number of implications. For one, it renders policy more subject to the personality and world-view of the chief policy-maker or policy-makers. This is evident not only in the case of Sadat noted above, but even more so in the contemporary foreign policy of Libya under Colonel Qaddafi. Furthermore, as a corollary of the role of leadership, foreign policies may be subject to considerable change with even a peaceful change in national leaders. The differences between Egypt's policies under Nasser and Egypt's policies under Sadat demonstrate how fundamental this change can be. Finally, leadership control over foreign policy, combined with the "ruler's imperative" of regime maintenance, often leads to the use of foreign policy as a means of legitimization for the government or leader in power. Conversely, substantial foreign policy failures (such as the failure of Arab intervention in Palestine in 1948–49) can have a devastating effect on the stability of the regime in power.

The New Pragmatism

   A final aspect of foreign policy-making in the Middle East is what might be described as the "new pragmatism" in Arab politics. In contrast to the 1950s and 1960s, when the Arab states tended to frame their policies in terms of long-term, strategic, ideological goals—Arab unity, anti-imperialism, the liberation of Palestine—the 1970s and 1980s have seen a triumph of realpolitik over vision, and of tactics over strategy. The new pragmatism is best reflected in the process of alliance formation and dissolution, with Middle Eastern alliances having moved from a rigid ideological basis to a flexible, short-term, issue-oriented basis marked by the absence of ideological affinities. Three major developments in the region account for this change.

First, there is pessimism about the attainability of such goals. The massive scale of the Arab defeat in the June 1967 war provided the most penetrating disillusionment, particularly for the confrontation states. In Egypt, the "war of attrition" with Israel along the Suez Canal in 1969–70 underscored the growing skepticism about the ability of Middle East states to successfully pursue such goals, and led to Nasser's pragmatic acceptance of the Rogers plan in August 1970. For the PLO and Syria, dangers of ideologically driven policy were starkly illustrated in Jordan in 1970, when the former was supressed by King Hussein and the latter's intervention in support of the Palestinians was halted by the combination of Jordanian, Israeli, and U.S. pressure. Most recently, Iraq — perhaps the most idealistic of the major Arab states in the 1970s — has been forced by circumstances to forge tactical alliances with the conservative Gulf states, Egypt and Jordan, against Iran, and to seek rapprochement with the U.S. (and with the Western world in general).

A second development contributing to the rise of Arab pragmatism has been the fact of changing leadership. As already noted, leadership plays an important role in Middle East foreign policies. The accession to power in the 1970s of such "pragmatic" Arab leaders as Anwar al-Sadat in Egypt and Hafez al-Asad in Syria (in the latter case, as a direct result of Syria's debilitating experience in Jordan in 1970) thus consolidated the shift to realpolitik in the region.

Oil wealth — and the changing interests and social values it has engendered — form the third set of developments behind the emergence of Arab pragmatism. Ali Dessouki is one of the observers who noted the importance of this:

> In analyzing Arab pragmatism, one cannot overlook the role of oil wealth and its political and psychological impact. Oil created, or helped to create, [a] new set of values and attitudes. New money created new loyalties and new allegiances. In a sense, almost all Arab states have become "oil states", either directly through the possession of oil or indirectly through remittances and financial assistance. The logic of the contemporary Arab state is a rentier one.[17]

With oil wealth has come an emphasis on managerial and technocratic decision-making, and a corresponding shift of emphasis away from "leadership" (in its broadest sense) to "incrementalism." As we will see in the chapter which follows, this shift is one that has had

e of both national foreign policy and
tem.

)TES

he economies of the Middle East cannot pos-
nd variation here. Instead, the reader is ad-
East in the World Economy 1800–1914 (Lon-
An Economic History of the Middle East
University Press, 1982) for two penetrating

ted for 41% of government revenue in Iran,
rly 100% in the Gulf Emirates. See Issawi,

3. Quoted in Tareq Y. Ismael, "Oil: The New Diplomacy", in T. Y. Ismael, *The Middle East in World Politics* (Syracuse: Syracuse University Press, 1974), p. 229.

4. Annual Middle East oil revenues, which had already increased from some $240 million in 1950 to $5,900 by 1970, further increased to $81,000 million by 1975 and to some $162,000 million by 1979. See Issawi, *Economic History*, p. 203.

5. For a case study of the capitalist model of development in the context of a capital-surplus Middle Eastern state, see Jacqueline S. Ismael, *Kuwait: Social Change in Historical Perspective* (Syracuse, N.Y.: Syracuse University Press, 1982).

6. See Tareq Y. Ismael, *The Arab Left* (Syracuse, N.Y.: Syracuse University Press, 1976).

7. Tareq Y. Ismael and Jacqueline S. Ismael, *Government and Politics in Islam* (London: Frances Pinter, 1985), pp. 46–53.

8. Majid Khadduri, "The Islamic System: Its Competition and Coexistence with Western Systems," in Richard Nolte, ed., *The Modern Middle East* (New York: Atherton Press, 1963), p. 153.

9. Ismael and Ismael, *Government and Politics*, p. 132.

10. *Ibid.*, pp. 132–134.

11. Ali E. Hillal Dessouki and Bahgat Korany, "A Literature Survey and Framework for Analysis," in Korany and Dessouki, ed., *The Foreign Policies of Arab States* (Boulder: Westview Press, 1984) p. 9. See also Bahgat Korany, "The Take-off of Third World Studies? The Case of Foreign Policy," *World Politics* 35, No. 3 (1983): 465–87.

12. For a discussion of Third World foreign policy-making that warns against the overemphasis of subjective and psychological factors (and which stresses the importance of the "operational environment") see *International Political Science Review* 5, No. 1 (1984). This entire issue was devoted to "Third World Foreign Policy," and was edited and introduced by Bahgat Korany.

13. R. D. McLaurin, Don Peretz, and Lewis W. Snider, *Middle East Foreign Policy: Issues and Processes* (New York: Praeger, 1982) p. 306.

14. On PLO decision-making see Mohammed Selim, "The Survival of a Non-State Actor: The Foreign Policy of the Palestine Liberation Organization," in Korany and Dessouki, *Foreign Policies* p. 197–240.

15. Ismail Fahmy, *al-Watan al-'Arabi* (London), No. 316, 4–10 March 1983; Muhammad Ibrahim Kamil, *al-Salam al-Dhié* [The Lost Peace], 2nd ed. (London: al-Sharikah al-Suodiyah lil Abhath wa Taswiq, 1984); and Mohamed Heikal, *Autumn of Fury* (London: Andre Deutsch, 1983).

16. Kamil, *al-Salam al-Dhie*, p. 470.

17. Ali E. Hillal Dessouki, "The Crisis of Inter-Arab Politics," *The International Relations of the Arab World 1973–1982*, Joint Research Program Series No. 39 (Tokyo: Institute of Developing Economies, 1983), pp. 149–150. For another view of the rise of Arab pragmatism see Alan R. Taylor, *The Arab Balance of Power* (Syracuse, N.Y.: Syracuse University Press, 1982), pp. 49–72.

Regional Dynamics and
International Relations in the Middle East

As we saw in the introductory chapter, political processes and patterns of interaction at the regional level have an important bearing on the external relations of the Middle East. In other words, the arrangement and operation of the regional system affects not only domestic and regional politics, but also the Middle East's interaction with other regional systems and its general position within the global system. Because of the importance of such factors, this chapter is devoted to an examination of the dynamics of developments at the regional level.

For this purpose, we will use William R. Thompson's definition of a regional system as "a relatively regular and intense pattern of interactions, recognized internally and externally as a distinctive arena, and created and sustained by at least two . . . generally proximate actors."[1] The fundamental aspects of any such system can, for our purposes, be identified as structure, process, and focus. The *structure* of the system can be defined as the dominant patterns of interaction among the states in a region, and *process* as the nature of interaction within these patterns. Alignments, coalitions, fronts, and the like are structural attributes of a region; cooperation, competition, and conflict are dimensions of process.

The degree to which a system is *focused* is the degree to which certain issues dominate regional interaction, forming core patterns within the region. A *core*, then, is a set of patterns interrelated by a focus; hence cores form a major aspect of system structure. The term *core* is, of course, used here in a different sense than that adopted by

Cantori and Speigel and noted in Chapter 1: here, we use it to refer to interactions tied to a dominant issue, rather than to a central group of actors. If a primary focus exists, and if it influences most actors within the system, it is also likely to dominate the external relations of the region. Furthermore, if most actors in the system are oriented towards the issue in a broadly similar way (as in the case of Arab support for the Palestinian cause), the cohesiveness or even integration of the region may be furthered. Conversely, if multiple patterns of intense interaction unrelated by a focus exist within the region, this may have the effect of weakening the cohesiveness of the system, or even fragment the system as a whole. Certain actors, ideologies, or individuals may assume the role of focusing elements, constantly relating events to an issue and hence maintaining the centrality of the focus in question.

Utilizing this model, in this century, three particular arrangements within the Middle East system may be identified. The first, the colonial presystem, extended from the eighteenth century to approximately World War II. The second, the focused system, came into being in the late 1940s and early 1950s, and continued into the 1970s. The final arrangement, that of the contemporary fragmented system, originated toward the end of the 1970s and has continued to the present day. Since it is the last two arrangements that have had the greatest bearing on the recent international relations of the Middle East, the bulk of our examination will be concerned with them.

THE COLONIAL PRESYSTEM

As a part of the Ottoman Empire, the Middle East could be conceived of as a component of a weak, centrifugal, but nevertheless identifiable system centered on Constantinople. The division of the region among European powers in the eighteenth, nineteenth, and early twentieth centuries, however, broke up this weakening system and imposed in its place a structural arrangement determined and operated by external powers. The degree to which this arrangement could be characterized as a genuine "system" is problematic. At an official political level, international politics in the colonial Middle East was directed from London, Paris, and other European capitals. At an unofficial level, much of the social, political, and economic life of the region, although fundamentally affected by colonialism, often ignored or rejected externally imposed borders and channels. Reflecting this paradoxical colonial situation, the conceptual dilemma will be avoided here by calling the colonial Middle East a "presystem"—an arrangement which, though it lacked many systemic qualities, nevertheless represented the basis from which a genuine system would emerge in the middle part of the twentieth century.

Several aspects of the colonial presystem are particularly germane to the study of the contemporary international relations of the Middle East. Since the system was so beneficial to Europe, attempts to maintain it in the face of systemic transformation occupied the colonial powers for much of the twentieth century. As chapter 4 clearly shows, legal integration into the metropole, European advisors, preferential treaties, pro-Western elites, and economic and military domination were all used in an attempt to maintain Europe's position. Indeed, as late as 1956 the two major European colonial powers—Britain and France—unsuccessfully sought to reverse the transformation of the Middle East through direct military intervention at Suez.

Another important aspect of the colonial presystem was the imposition of political and social institutions on the Middle East, some of which would endure up to the present. Colonial powers demarcated colonial boundaries, which became state boundaries after the acquisition of independence, and which accordingly played a major role in shaping national foreign policies. Similarly, the colonial powers created or aggravated many of the regional issues that would later occupy a prominent position in the Middle East system. The Palestine Question is, of course, the most enduring and important example of this.

The nature of the colonial presystem also assured that the struggle for national independence would be a primary struggle for those within the region. Moreover, because European powers were prepared to resist such a development by force, and because Western domination had become deeply ingrained within the social, political, and economic structures of Middle East countries, this struggle would not cease upon the acquisition of a merely formal, legal independence. Rather, the struggle for genuine independence would necessarily involve the ongoing pursuit of domestic as well as regional and international change.

THE FOCUSED SYSTEM

Since independence was a prerequisite of the Middle East becoming a genuine regional system, it was not until after World War II that the attributes of an identifiable Middle East system began to appear. By 1945, the Arab countries of Yemen, Saudi Arabia, Iraq, Egypt, Syria, Lebanon, and Transjordan enjoyed legal — if not in all instances actual — independence. A regional organization, the League of Arab States, came into being that same year. Although the formation of the Arab League had originally been promoted by Britain in the hopes of maintaining regional collective security under its aegis, it failed to perform this function but instead in the fifties provided the basis for greater regional independence and cohesion under the leadership of Egypt.

In the mid-1940s it was unclear exactly what shape the Middle East system would assume. A number of factors mitigated against increased cohesion. The intrusive presence of the European powers remained strong — stronger than that of any single Middle Eastern state, or of any collection of such states. In addition, no clear regional leader had yet emerged. Egypt, Iraq, Saudi Arabia, and even Transjordan competed for this role — a competition further exacerbated by traditional rivalries between Egypt and Iraq, and between the Hashemites and the Saudis.[2] Finally, the generally pro-Western orientation of the ruling elites of various Middle Eastern countries (many of whom owed their positions to the former European colonial powers) inhibited the ability of regional leaders to act in ways contrary to the interests of the colonial powers.

Three related, historically sequential developments altered this situation: the Palestine Question, the Palestinian diaspora, and the Israeli occupation of Arab territory following the 1967 Arab-Israeli war. Palestine, of course, had long held a special place in the Arab consciousness: its geographic, historic, and religious significance predated modern Arab nationalism by more than a millennium. It was a country at the crossroads of the Arab world, a land bridge between the Arab East and the Arab West whose territory figured prominently in centuries of Arab history. It was, finally, above all else the land of Jerusalem, a site holy to Muslim, Christian, and Jewish Arabs alike.

In the interwar period, Palestine gained a new significance as a symbol of colonialism and of resistance to it. Events in Palestine embodied the essence of the Arab struggle for independence and self-determination. Because of this, the concept of Palestine was raised as a banner by the many groups throughout the Arab world attempting to rally support for their fight against Western imperialism. In Iraq, for example, the Palestine issue provided a major basis for nationalist agitation against British domination in the 1930s. Similarly, in Egypt the Palestine cause provided a major impetus for the expansion of the Muslim Brotherhood during the same period. Thus, well before 1948 Palestine was the transcendent issue of the area, crystallizing as it did all the perceived injustices of colonial rule.

After 1948, of course, the creation of Israel and the resulting displacement and dispossession of more than three-quarters of a million Palestinians immeasurably heightened the importance of the Palestine Question. Palestine, and the Arab struggle for its liberation, were issues that came to influence profoundly almost all aspects of regional politics.

The 1967 Arab-Israeli War finally moved the Palestine Question still higher on Arab agendas. The scale of the Arab defeat in the conflict underscored the need for coordinated Arab action and even greater levels of Arab commitment. The loss of territory on the Golan Heights, on the West Bank, and in the Sinai and Gaza Strip led Syria, Jordan, and Egypt to devote overriding attention to the Arab-Israeli conflict, and to spare few efforts in attempts to secure similar attention to the conflict from other actors in the region. The addition of 300,000 Palestinians to the number already displaced from historic Palestine added still further urgency. In the aftermath of the 1967 war, a non-state actor—the Palestinian resistance movement—was catapulted to the forefront of Arab politics, particularly after the movement assumed control of the Palestine Liberation Organization (PLO) in 1968–69. It thereafter acquired a stature in the Arab world equivalent to or even in some cases greater than that of many state actors in the region, and in many ways replaced the progressive Arab regimes in the vanguard of Arab nationalism and radicalism.

System Structure

As discussed below, by 1970 these developments led to the evolution of the Middle East system into a highly organized, almost rigid structure. Figure 3.1 is a schematic representation indicating the key patterns in the structure, and the relationships of the various system actors to these patterns. As the figure indicates, there were two dominant centers or cores of interaction in the region. The first of these was the *Arab-Israeli conflict core*, composed of Egypt, Syria, Jordan, Israel, and—through the Palestine Liberation Organization and the various Palestinian resistance groups—the Palestinians.[3] For Israel and the Palestinians, of course, the issue at stake was fundamental.

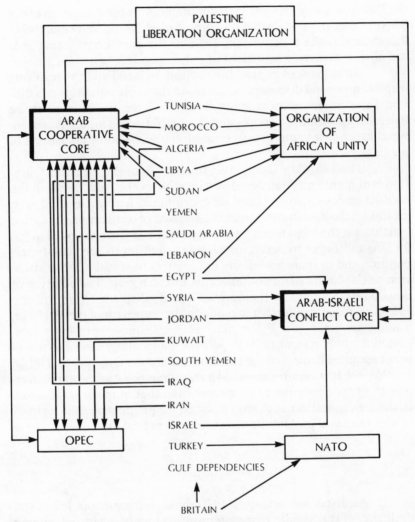

FIGURE 3.1
Middle East Regional System, 1970

For the Arab confrontation states, historical, cultural, religious and political factors rendered the Palestine question important through the 1948 and 1956 wars; the 1967 Arab-Israeli War and the Israeli occupation of the West Bank, Gaza Strip, Sinai, and Golan Heights raised the issue to one of overriding national importance. Other Arab states were peripheral to this core in the sense that their interaction in the conflict was not based on direct military confrontation. However, some Arab states—notably Iraq, Saudi Arabia, Kuwait, Libya, and Algeria—had considerable involvement in the issue (despite their geographic and political distance from it), and virtually all of the other Arab states showed some degree of interest.

Military action—the Arab-Israeli wars of 1948, 1956, 1967, and 1973; border raids; Palestinian guerilla activity; the 1969–70 "war of attrition" between Egypt and Israel—was the most spectacular form of interaction within the conflict core. Nevertheless, certain non-military actions—Arab-Israeli diplomatic competition in world capitals and the forums of international organizations; the Arab economic boycott and the Arab oil embargos of 1956, 1967, and 1973–74—were also important. In terms of both its composition and interaction, the Arab-Israeli conflict core remained relatively stable from 1948 to the late 1970s.

The second dominant center of interaction within the regional system was the *Arab cooperative core*, composed of the official bilateral and multilateral relations between Arab states, as well as nongovernmental agencies and popular organizations across Arab states. The League of Arab States, formed in 1945 with seven members (increasing to 14 members by 1970, and to 21 by 1978), and the Organization of Arab Petroleum Exporting Countries (OAPEC) formed in 1968 were the most important formal organizations addressing multilateral relations within the core.[4] They were complemented by the existence of councils of Arab ambassadors in every major foreign capital, as well as by Arab caucuses in the United Nations and other international agencies.

Arab heads of state (summit) conferences, initiated in January 1964 and convened irregularly thereafter in response to crisis, constituted another significant pattern of Arab cooperative interaction.[5] So too did the regular bilateral and multilateral meetings held between Arab cabinet ministers of various portfolios, including foreign affairs, justice, health, housing, development, and education. Furthermore, as noted in chapter 1, a careful examination of the nature of high-level intergovernmental visits within the Middle East reveals a clear pattern of intense political interaction between Arab states in the period 1946–1975.[6]

The establishment and operation of national and multilateral Arab aid agencies throughout the 1960s and 1970s can be viewed as yet another manifestation of the Arab cooperative core. These agencies functioned to redistribute wealth from the oil-rich to the poorer Arab states on a regional basis—a significant development in the history of inter-Arab economic cooperation. The Kuwait Fund for Arab Economic Development, established in 1961, was the first such agency, and remains the largest regional fund. The Arab Fund for Economic and Social Development, established in 1968, did not actually become operational until 1972. The Abu Dhabi Fund for Arab Economic Development, set up in 1971, was followed by the Saudi Fund for External Development in 1974. The Iraq Fund for External Development and the Arab Monetary Fund subsequently joined the group. Between 1963 and 1974 such agencies disbursed bilateral and multilateral development loans to Arab countries with a value in excess of $507 million. For the period 1975–1980 the total rose to over $6.6 billion.[7] The total of all inter-Arab economic assistance, including funds bilaterally disbursed outside of the major development agencies, was much higher still. Doubtless, some of this increase was attributable to growing capital surplus on the part of the Arab oil-producing states, but it was also a clear manifestation of Arab cooperative activity.

Finally, and perhaps most dramatically, another pattern of Arab cooperative core interaction emerges from the repeated attempts of many states in the area to realize some degree of Arab unity. The formation of the United Arab Republic in 1958 was the most conspicuous attempt, enduring as it did for more than three years. Other, less successful, examples are the tripartite federal union of Egypt, Iraq, and Syria in 1963; the Iraqi-Egyptian union of 1964; the Egyptian-Sudanese-Libyan federation of 1970; the federation of Arab Republics (Egypt, Libya, and Syria) of 1971; the Egyptian-Libyan and North Yemen–South Yemen unity agreements of 1973; the 1974 Arab Islamic Republic (Libya-Tunisia); the Syrian-Jordanian Supreme Command of 1975; the Syrian-Egyptian United Political Leadership of 1976; and the Syrian-Iraqi unity agreement of 1979.

George Lenczowski has identified four major issues that have fostered the development of these instruments of cooperative interaction: issues related to the struggle against imperialism; issues involving Israel and Palestine; issues of cooperation and coordination in oil affairs; and issues related to the resolution of inter-Arab conflicts and disputes.[8] However, the issue of Arab unity must be added to this list. While Arab unity itself has remained implausible in theory and unworkable in practice (as illustrated by the catalog of unsuccessful unity experiments above), the issue has been one of the most powerful political symbols in the Arab world in the twentieth century, and constitutes the focus of the Arab cooperative core. Indeed, every Arab country's constitution enshrines the goal of Arab unity in some form as a cardinal responsibility of government.

Pan-Arab groups and political parties (most notably the Ba'ath, the Arab Nationalist Movement, the Nasserites, and the New Left groups) formed a nongovernmental, transnational dimension of the cooperative core. Pan-Arab professional and academic associations, as well as business, labor, educational, sports, and cultural organizations (such as the Union of Arab Chambers of Commerce, the Union of Arab Universities, the Union of Arab Artisans, the Union of Arab Broadcasters, the Arab Literary Union, and so forth), all represented manifestations of Arab cooperative interaction within the focused system.

The Palestine Liberation Organization, created by the first summit conference of Arab heads of state in January 1964 as the official representative of the Palestinians, has played an important role in both cores, as indicated in Figure 3.1. By 1969, the PLO had become the umbrella organization of the Palestine resistance movement, a powerful force in the Arab world in the aftermath of the 1967 Arab-Israeli war. In 1974, the Rabat Arab Summit Conference declared the PLO to be "the sole legitimate representative of the Palestinian people."[9] That same year the PLO won Observer status within the United Nations, and throughout the 1970s the organization received the diplomatic recognition of a growing number of states around the world.

While the PLO was a product of the Arab cooperative core, it would become an independent actor in the region and the international arena after 1967. Nevertheless, it maintained a strong direct tie with the core through its representation in the League of Arab States and its agencies, and through its direct bilateral relations with core members. Most significant, the PLO by 1970 had operational bases in Jordan, Syria, and Lebanon, and headquarters in Cairo. At the same time, the PLO maintained an armed struggle with Israel, and—through its international political activities—internationalized the Palestinian issue. Thus, the PLO constituted one of the strongest links between the two cores—a strength that helps explain Israel's unremitting attempts to literally wipe out the PLO.

In addition to the existence of the two cores, the structure of and interaction within the Middle East system was shaped by certain extrasystemic linkages, including those represented by the Organization of Petroleum Exporting Countries (OPEC), the Organization of African Unity (OAU), and the North Atlantic Treaty Organization (NATO). As Figure 3.1 shows, OPEC was directly tied to the Arab cooperative core through the overlapping membership with OAPEC. This direct core tie made OPEC a significant external organization linkage, whose significance was reflected in the importance of oil in domestic, regional, and international politics (as discussed in other chapters). The Organization of African Unity was also tied directly to the Arab cooperative core through overlapping membership. As such, Africa is the only contiguous geographic region of the world that is linked so directly with the Arab system. (The significance of Africa as a regional linkage is addressed in chapter 8.)

NATO was connected with the region through Turkish membership in the alliance and through Britain's continuing control of the Gulf dependencies. The former reflected Turkey's peripheral role in the region (indeed, from a systems perspective its inclusion is more a matter of geography and history than of an analysis of contemporary interaction patterns), while the latter reflected the remnants of colonial and imperialist domination of the Middle East. In 1971, the Gulf dependencies became independent states, members of the League of Arab States and OAPEC, thus joining the Arab cooperative core and dramatically changing the configuration of power in the Gulf.[10]

Several extrasystemic organizational linkages not indicated on Figure 3.1 should also be mentioned, since they were products of and reflected dynamics within the system to be discussed shortly. The Afro-Asian People's Solidarity Organization, for example, was an international, nongovernmental organization with the aim of combating imperialism and colonialism in Africa and Asia. It was organized in 1958 and headquartered in Cairo. Most of the popular and nationalist groups and movements of the Arab world were represented in it, along with those of Africa and Asia. The organization provided a forum for expanded nongovernmental interaction and the cooperation of progressive groups across Africa and Asia throughout the 1950s and 1960s. The Islamic League, a nongovernmental religious body dedicated to spreading Islam (and consequently combating secularism), was organized in 1962 and headquartered in Mecca. By the 1970s many Islamic groups in the Arab world as well as Africa and Asia were represented in it—27 countries in all.

The Organization of the Islamic Conference was established in 1972 as a formal structure for regular and intense interaction of the governments of Islamic countries. Summit conferences met every three years and foreign ministers annually. With every Arab state a member by 1976, this international organization featured a strong tie with the Arab cooperative core.[11]

The structure of the Middle East system was defined by the relationship between the two cores. All of the patterns represented in the Arab cooperative core were founded around the issue of Arab unity. The Arab-Israeli conflict core, while involving only four states directly, nevertheless provided a focus for the entire structure. This derived from historical experiences of the Middle East and reflected the significance of the Arab-Israeli conflict in the region, manifested in the central role of Arab nationalist ideology in focusing the system around this issue and relating it directly to the issue of Arab unity.

Arab Nationalism: A Focusing Element

Every region of the Arab world had its own experience with imperialism in the course of the nineteenth and twentieth centuries, and from these experiences emerged a discrete ideology: Arab nationalism. In its origin, Arab nationalism represented diverse and segmented ideologies emerging from the equally diverse and segmented Arab world as new classes rose to the fore in different areas in the nineteenth and twentieth centuries, offering visions of a new Arab reality. These visions were shaped by specific historical experiences within the great cultural expanse of that world, and reflected the diversity of experiences and potentials for change within that world. Religious, petit bourgeois, and tribal ideologies, among many others, all contributed to the "Arab Awakening," and provided the dominant ideology in various places during various historical periods. Underriding all these ideologies, however, was the vision of an Arab world — a world bound together by language, history, and geography, and destined to achieve a new political reality. It is the consistency of this vision that we identify as Arab nationalism, whose ideology has taken shape under the impact of an imperialist exploitation that has, in effect, progressively homogenized the Arab experience.

The struggle for political independence spearheaded by early Arab nationalists had neither unified the Arabs nor made them masters of their own houses: the control of Arab destiny had merely shifted from Istanbul to various Western capitals. It appeared then that those Arab nationalists had betrayed the essence of Arab nationalism —the struggle for true freedom, true unity—for a superficial political independence that protected the power and privilege of the entrenched elites behind the facades of Western democratic institutions. Within a decade of the Palestine defeat, however, these facades were dismantled by coups in Egypt (1952), Syria (1954), and Iraq (1958), and were severely challenged in every other Arab country where they existed.

Gamal Abd al-Nasser effectively articulated the unique relationship between Palestine, imperialism, and Arab unity to the Arab masses, and within a few years of the Egyptian revolution Nasserism was a powerful political force in the Arab world. As an ideology, it represented the contemporary expression of Arab nationalism that manifested the resistance of the Arab people to external intrusions into their world. Within this context, the Palestinian struggle symbolized the Arab struggle, since imperialist exploitation of the Arab world had its profoundest impact on Palestine. As a result, Palestine developed as the central political issue of Arab nationalism generally and of Nasserism particularly. For not only does Palestine proclaim the failure of Arab regimes to meet the supreme challenge—the challenge of national survival—but it also signifies the necessity of Arab unity in a hostile world. Ideologically, then, the struggle for Palestine is intertwined with the quest for Arab unity, and Nasserism articulated this fact for the Arab people more effectively than any other doctrine before it.

Thus, within the ideology of Arab nationalism as articulated by Nasserism, the Arab-Israeli conflict is seen to be closely associated with the intrusion of Western powers into the Middle East. Israel itself represents the most manifest outcome of this intrusion: the colonization of Arab land and the political alienation of an entire Arab people. It is in this context that Nasser evolved Egypt's role as a vanguard Arab nation leading the struggle for Arab independence and unity against powerful external forces allied by regional reactionary regimes. Egypt's assumption of this role was made possible not only by the subjective appeal of Nasserism to the Arab world, but also by Egypt's objective status as the central and most powerful of the Arab states.[12] Although the power of Israel and its Western supporters (especially the United States) severely limited Nasser's ability to advance his objectives within the Arab-Israeli conflict core, the twin factors of ideology and capability enabled him to shape substantial aspects of the contemporary pattern of inter-Arab interaction. The Arab co-operative core assumed its structure and role in this context.

It was Egypt under Nasser that led the challenge to the participation of Arab states in Western alliance systems (the Baghdad Pact, 1955; the Islamic Pact, 1966), articulated the doctrine of positive neutrality in the Arab world, and established relations with the Soviet Union as a counterbalance to Western influence through aid and trade. As a result, the nature of external intrusion into the Middle East changed in this period as U.S. policy shifted from a reliance on regional alliance systems as its primary regional strategy to a dependence on bilateral relations with particular states (Israel, Jordan, Saudi Arabia within the conflict and cooperative cores; Iran in the periphery). At the same time, the domination of Western intrusion was counterbalanced by the introduction of the USSR as an actor in the core, also through bilateral relations (first with Egypt, then Iraq, and finally Syria). By 1965, U.S.–Soviet competition for influence in the cores through bilateral relations with member states constituted the most significant form of external intrusion into the region.[13]

It was Egypt under Nasser that fostered the growth of the Arab cooperative core. Under the influence of Nasser and fueled by the potent political force of Arab nationalism, the League of Arab States was transformed into a platform for the official expression of Arab solidarity against the forces of imperialism and colonialism. Arab nationalist sentiment, as reflected in the power of pan-Arab political groups generally and in Nasserism specifically throughout the Arab world, effectively forced even the most conservative, Western-oriented regimes to align themselves with Egypt, at least publicly, on such issues as Palestine, the Suez Canal, the Sinai war, the Dhafor rebellion, the British-Yemeni conflict, the Aden protectorate, Algeria, and the Israeli boycott.

System Dynamics

What the growth of the Arab cooperative core in the thirty years following World War II indicates in terms of a systems perspective is that patterned cooperative linkages continued to expand among the Arab countries in spite of fundamental differences and persistent conflicts among them. These linkages reflected a consistent perception among Arab leaders of common problems that could not be resolved independently, and encouraged a concerted push towards cooperation in solving these problems. This commonality of interests was evident despite the significant ideological, economic, political, and social differences among the various Arab states. One of the most significant characteristics of the growth of the core was its consistent effort to bring external influences under control, and thereby to reduce the impact of external powers on the course of Middle East destiny.

This paralleled the tide of political transformation within Arab states that swept out the traditionalist regimes set up by colonial administrations as puppet or client governments, replacing them with nationalist regimes strongly opposed to foreign interference. In fact, by 1970, half of the Arab states were governed by revolutionary nationalist regimes, and traditional monarchies remained in only five states: Saudi Arabia, Jordan, Morocco, Kuwait, and Oman. And these monarchies feared for their survival against the force of the nationalist tide — a fear that made them more dependent on supportive external alignments and at the same time forced them to compromise with nationalist sentiment. While the core forced them to be more radical in their responses to regional issues, they in turn forced the core to be more moderate in its collective responses.

By 1970, with Egypt in the role of a vanguard Arab nation and Nasserism as the dominant expression of Arab nationalism, the Arab-Israeli conflict core and the Arab cooperative core were fully integrated in an essentially dialectical relationship. The 1967 Arab-Israeli war had brought this relationship to the fore by intensifying the inherent contradictions of the structure. The most apparent contradiction was the U.S. role in the conflict core both as Israel's main ally and as an important influence in neighboring Jordan. Another contradiction between the cooperative and conflict cores was revealed by Jordan's brutal attack upon and expulsion of the Palestine Liberation Organization in September 1970. The relationship between Saudi Arabia and the United States on the one hand, and U.S. support for the 1967 Israeli aggression and continued occupation of Arab lands in its aftermath on the other, was also a manifestation of the contradictions between the conflict and cooperative cores.

Nasser's strategy of counterbalancing opposing forces relied on the contradictions implicit in the dual role played by conservative regimes in both cores. Caught between the forces of Arab nationalism on one hand and their strong ties with the United States on the other, these regimes were in effect forced to participate in the cooperative core to protect their own interests. The thrust of Nasserism in structuring the system was to exploit the contradictions of their position, and thus force their increased participation in the cooperative core. (Their role was to enforce the moderation of the cooperative core.) Nasser's rapprochement with Saudi Arabia and Jordan, and his acceptance of the Rogers plan (see chapter 5) in exchange for a collective front against Israeli aggression and continued U.S. support for it, were evidence of the dialectic between conservative regimes and Arab nationalist forces.[14]

The focused system emerged as a result of the problems left behind by colonialism: the political, social and economic fragmentation of Arab society; an aggregation of weak national governments dependent upon external powers; an ever-increasing subpopulation of Palestinian refugees; and an expansionist Israeli state. The dominant patterns of cooperation and conflict evolved in the post–World War II period from the efforts of national governments to deal with these problems as they threatened the sovereignty, legitimacy, and/or capability of the state itself. The ideology of Arab nationalism generally and of Nasserism in particular helped to focus the system by mobilizing the Arab people in a common struggle to overcome these problems and control their destiny.[15] The focus resulted in the increasing integration of the dominant patterns of cooperation and conflict in a dialectical relationship, with the result that by 1970 the system was fully structured around the integration of the two cores.

By increasing Arab cohesion—that is, by enhancing the probability of concerted Arab action on common problems—the power of the Arab states under this system was essentially aggregated at both the regional and international levels. Concerted Arab action in the October 1973 Arab-Israeli War and the Arab oil embargo of 1973–74 illustrated the impact that the arrangement of the regional system could have on regional and extra-regional relations. During the peak of systemic focus and cohesion in the early 1970s, the Arab world found itself able, by virtue of that cohesion, to exert significant influence on the policies of external actors. In Africa, for example, Arab policy succeeded, both bilaterally and multilaterally, in displacing a not inconsiderable Israeli influence and securing African support for the Palestinian cause. (Much the same thing occurred in Asia.) In the developed world, the relative cohesion of Arab countries facilitated their pursuance of linkage politics. The Arab economic boycott of Israel, the oil embargo, and the Euro-Arab dialogue all demonstrated this growing ability. In a different vein, the cohesion fostered by the two closely integrated foci of the system facilitated regional cooperation on different international issues. Such cooperation was particularly evident in 1971–74, when united action succeeded in breaking the power of the multinational oil companies in the Middle East and bringing about a transformation of the global petroleum market.

This is not to suggest that, even at its most cohesive, the Arab world represented a unified force either regionally or internationally; such would be a gross distortion of reality, for the political divisions among Arab states remained (and remain) profound. It is appropriate to note, however, that the Palestine Question and the self-examination and cohesion that it promoted did play a major role in limiting external influence in the region after World War II. Furthermore, the focus and cohesiveness of the Arab world in the early 1970s brought about an improvement in the Arab world's bargaining position, collectively and individually, on a broad range of issues.

THE DECADE OF THE SEVENTIES: FRAGMENTING FORCES

In the 1970s, several developments set in motion certain significant changes within the regional system. The first of these was the disappearance or weakening of the focusing elements of the system: Nasser, Nasserism, and Egypt's vanguard role among Arab states. All of these factors had worked to concentrate the attention of regional actors on the Arab-Israeli issue, and their decline presaged a decline in the degree of integration of the cooperative and conflict cores. Weakening support for the PLO on the part of several Arab governments also tended to reduce the integration of the two cores. At the same time, subregional or localized focal issues arose, thus further hastening the fragmentation of the system. Finally, economic developments in the Middle East (and in the world as a whole) brought about major changes in the distribution of capability within the region, and hence changed both structure and process in the regional system. While short-term Arab cohesion could still be maintained on some occasions—most notably during and immediately after the 1973 Arab-Israeli War—the long-term trend was toward division and fragmentation.

The death of Egyptian President Gamal Abd al-Nasser on 28 September 1970 may indeed have marked the initiation of this process. With Nasser gone, the region lacked the popular, charismatic leader who could continue to focus Arab nationalist forces. Nasser's successor in Egypt, President Anwar al-Sadat, did indeed continue

Nasser's effort to maintain inter-Arab cohesiveness in the face of Israel for the first few years following Nasser's death; however, he lacked Nasser's pan-Arab appeal. More important, he set Egypt on the path of unilateral settlement with Israel after the 1973 Arab-Israeli War, a process that culminated in the Egyptian-Israeli peace treaty of 1979. In effect, the second focusing element in the system—Egypt's vanguard role—disappeared therewith.

In part, Sadat reoriented Egypt's position in the Arab-Israeli conflict because he believed that other states would follow his lead; in part, because he had a narrower view of Egypt's national interests than his predecessor; and in part because of his generally pro-Western orientation.[16] Regardless of his motives, however, Sadat's actions had a profound impact on the region. Although at first it appeared that, in opposition to Egypt's moves, a new, reactive Arab cohesion might be forged (such as that evident at the 1978 Ninth Arab summit conference in Baghdad, where twenty Arab League members condemned Sadat's policies and took action against Egypt), this did not in fact happen. Instead, Nasser's death and Egypt's subsequent defection removed what had been linchpins of the focused regional system.

The weakening of the final focussing element—Nasserism—both reflected and hastened the decline of pan-Arab ideologies during this decade. Practically speaking, Nasser's death deprived Nasserism of its charismatic core. The man was a particularly important element of the doctrine's appeal, as Nasserism had failed to create any meaningful organizational structure whereby it might be perpetuated.[17] At an ideological level, the appeal of pan-Arabism was diminished by disillusionment with its ability to provide effective solutions to the major problems of Arab society. In Syria, for example, the rise to power of Hafez al-Asad in 1970 and further losses on the Golan heights in 1973 encouraged the subordination of Ba'athist ideology to the imperatives of national interest. Iraq, too, found itself forced to adopt an increasingly pragmatic approach after the Iranian revolution in 1979, and particularly after the outbreak of the Iran-Iraq war in 1980.[18]

As the 1970s progressed, the PLO's function of integrating the conflict and cooperative cores was seriously weakened by external and internal difficulties. "Black September" (the suppression of the PLO in Jordan in the autumn of 1970) was the first of these difficulties, and probably the most extreme example of the efforts of Arab governments to control and manipulate the Palestinian resistance. Saudi Arabia and the Arab Gulf states, which had large numbers of Palestinians in their labor forces, clamped rigid controls on their political activity. Syria, too, significantly reduced the freedom of action of its large refugee population. The PLO was additionally weakened by internal dissension over matters of strategy and objectives (the formation of the Rejection Front, 1974–); by external interference by certain Arab states in its internal affairs, manifestly in the Lebanese Civil War (1975–); and by serious conflicts with Syria (1976–77), Egypt (1977–), and Iraq (1978). The PLO's growing difficulties during the 1970s came as no surprise as a product of the Arab cooperative core, situated in an integrating role between this and the Arab-Israeli conflict core, it was only natural that it would suffer as Arab cohesion declined. This, in turn, further encouraged the fragmentation of the system.

Thus, throughout the decade, the elements that had kept the regional system focused on the Arab-Israeli dispute and Arab unity declined in effectiveness, and as a result the integration of the cooperative and conflict cores declined. At the same time, new issues were arising. In North Africa, Moroccan-Mauritanian occupation of the Western Sahara in 1975, and the ensuing war between these countries and the indigenous Polisario guerrilla movement (supported by Algeria and Libya), became an important issue. In the Horn of Africa, Ethiopian-Somalian tensions exploded into the Ogaden War in 1977–78. Arab countries in the area became increasingly concerned with this and other conflicts. (Somalia and Djibouti joined the Arab League in 1974 and 1977, respectively.) In the Gulf, the Shah of Iran promoted himself in the hegemonic role of the "policeman" of the area after the British withdrawal in 1971, occupying three Arab islands and raising new concerns for the Arab Gulf states in the process. Tensions increased still further in the Gulf after the Iranian revolution of 1979, and especially with the start of the Iran-Iraq War the following year.

Since all of these issues diverted attention from the Arab-Israeli conflict, Israeli policy actively sought to exacerbate them. Israel extended aid to the Kurdish rebels in Iraq in the early 1970s;[19] to various Lebanese militias after the eruption of the Lebanese Civil War in 1975;[20] to Ethiopia;[21] and even to the Islamic Republic of Iran following the deterioration of Iranian-Iraqi relations.[22] Perhaps the best (and most ironic) example of Israel's policy of inflaming regional issues that diverted attention from the Arab-Israeli conflict came in 1976 during Syrian-PLO fighting in Lebanon. According to PLO sources, at that time Israel deliberately allowed arms and ammunition to reach the PLO so as to prolong its resistance to Syrian intervention, and hence prolong the Lebanese Civil War.[23]

Finally, it is important to recognize that all of the developments above were occurring in the context of real changes in the distribution of power among Middle East states. The extension of national sovereignty over oil production and the rising price of oil in the 1970s led to a massive influx of capital to the oil-producing states. At the same time, Egypt under Sadat proved unable to sustain Egypt's role of leadership in the Arab world. The net effect was a shift in the Arab balance of power whereby Egypt was weakened, the oil-producing states strengthened, and no one actor could lay claim to leadership by right of greatest capability.[24] As a result ". . . in the 1970s the Arab world moved into an era of multiplicity of centres of influence, dispersion of capabilities and sharing of power. Egyptian centrality was weakened and no other state seemed fit to take its place."[25] This, coupled with the disappearance of Nasser from the Arab stage, rekindled competition for the leadership of the Arab world and further hastened its fragmentation.

THE FRAGMENTED SYSTEM

The outcome of such changes in the 1970s was the fragmentation of the Middle East system, as depicted in Figure 3.2. Its most fundamental characteristic is a profusion of conflicts unrelated to or by a central focus. While much of the structure of the focused system remains essentially intact, it has nevertheless lost its central focus around the Arab-Israeli conflict and Arab cooperative cores. The proliferation of subregional or localized centers of intense interaction fragment the cohesion of the system. The only pattern discernible in the structure is one of general locations or geographic areas of activity: the Red Sea area, the Gulf area, and North Africa are the three locations or centers of new activity.

What we described here as the Red Sea area is a territory that embraces Egypt, Sudan, Somalia, Djibouti, the two Yemens, and Saudi Arabia from the Middle East region, and Ethiopia from outside the region—in other words, the states bordering the Red Sea and the Horn of Africa. The area is depicted in Figure 3.2 by the Ogaden War between Somalia and Ethiopia. Not indicated, but just as significant from the area perspective, are a number of local conflicts: civil war in Ethiopia, insurgency in southern Sudan, the occasional tension between the two Yemens. These crises have been exacerbated by widespread famine and refugees fleeing war and hunger. The area, in other

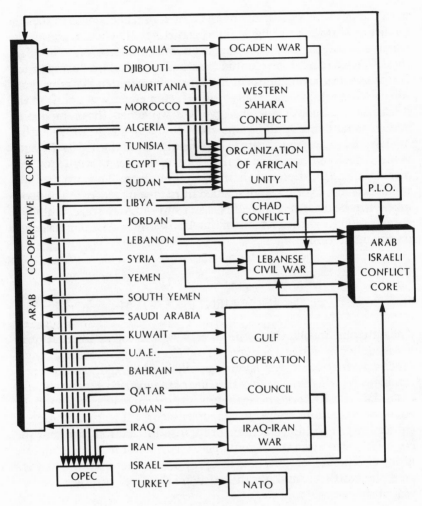

FIGURE 3.2
The Middle East Regional System, 1985

words, is a tinderbox of human and natural disaster. While no focus has emerged that interrelates these problems, the level of activity in the area has become intense and has involved regional as well as extraregional actors. Such developments as Arab League support for Somalia in its conflict with Ethiopia; support from Saudi Arabia, Iraq, and the Gulf States for various elements of the Eritrean guerrilla movement; the March 1977 Taiz Conference on the Red Sea, sponsored by Yemen and attended by South Yemen, Sudan, and Somalia; and the August 1981 Aden Treaty Tripartite Alliance (Aden Pact) linking South Yemen, Ethiopia, and Libya all reflect the increased activity in the area. Finally, Ethiopia and South Yemen have extended port privileges to the Soviet Union; Somalia and Egypt have granted similar rights to the United States, and France retains a significant military presence in Djibouti—thus raising the grim spectre of cold war competition in this volatile area.[26]

The Gulf area embraces Iran, Iraq, Saudi Arabia, and the smaller Gulf states: Kuwait, the United Arab Emirates, Bahrain, Qatar, and Oman. It is represented in Figure 3.2 by the Iran-Iraq War and the Gulf Cooperation Council. While the outbreak of the Iran-Iraq War in 1980 had been preceded by a decade of volatile relations between the two countries,[27] it was the Iranian Revolution of 1978–79 that dramatically intensified the level of political activity within the area. The commitment of Iran's revolutionary leaders to export the Islamic revolution was an important catalyst to this activity. Largely because of this threat, all of the Arab states of the Gulf rallied behind Baghdad in its war with Iran, providing substantial economic aid to Iraq—about ten billion dollars a year between 1980 and 1984.[28] The formation of the Gulf Cooperation Council (GCC), an alliance of the noncombatant Arab Gulf states precipitated by the war, introduced a very cohesive group into the regional political arena. The GCC coordinates the internal and external security of its members, in addition to promoting cooperation on a broad range of other political and economic considerations. It commonly acts as a bloc in regional and international organizations. The group is dominated by Saudi Arabia, and has served to considerably increase Saudi Arabia's local, regional, and international power. Finally, the war has polarized the political differences among Arab states, with Libya and Syria supporting Iran while Saudi Arabia, the smaller Gulf states, Jordan, and Egypt support Iraq.

The North African area encompasses Libya, Tunisia, Algeria, Morocco, and Mauritania, as well as the Polisario guerrilla movement fighting for the independence of the Western Sahara.[29] The common membership of these states in both the Arab League and the OAU reflects their unique position in the regional political arena. In the focused system, the center of gravity of the regional system was the Mashreq (Arab East). The North African states, being geographically and politically separate from the Mashreq, remained largely aloof from this center—peripheral, that is, to the dominant issues and patterns. In the fragmented system, however, the intense patterns of interaction that have emerged in the area assume greater significance in regional politics. While the Western Sahara and Chad conflicts are the most prominent features of interaction in the area, they themselves are but manifestations of the intensity of political activity. Recent years have seen a host of cooperation, friendship, and even integration agreements on educational, economic, and political levels among Maghreb (Arab West) states. While many of these have been quickly forgotten or rendered obsolete within a matter of weeks, "[by] any standard of measurement, the diplomatic activity among North African states . . . has been remarkable."[30] Moreover, these intense interaction patterns have been complemented by a Maghreb unity focus in the emerging cooperative interaction patterns, explicitly expressed in the constitutions of Tunisia, Algeria, and Morocco.

As noted earlier, despite the establishment of a multiplicity of localized interaction centers the two cores central to the focused regional system—the Arab-Israeli conflict core and the Arab cooperative core—have remained intact, albeit modified and no longer transcendent. Because of the fragmentation of the Middle East in the 1980s, the scope of the Arab-Israeli core has narrowed considerably, now representing a substantial part of the foreign policies only of those actors directly involved: Israel, Syria, Jordan, Lebanon, and the PLO. The attention of the other states in the region has been diverted to localized centers of activity. The Lebanese situation has, since the mid-1970s, become as much an arena for this conflict as an actor in it, although the various subnational political groups and forces in that country might be regarded as such.

As a result of the diminution of the core (and especially as a result of Egypt's marginalization from the conflict as a direct result of the Camp David process), the balance of power has substantially shifted in Israel's favor. As the size of the subsystem diminishes, Israel's relative power vis-à-vis the remaining actors increases. This was graphically illustrated during Israel's 1982 invasion of Lebanon, when Israel invaded an Arab country and beseiged an Arab capital with little interference from other Arab states. Israel's subsequent direct and proxy occupation of southern Lebanon has followed a similar pattern, with resistance to Israeli occupation arising not from the Arab world as a whole but rather from the local population. The narrowing of the Arab-Israeli core has also bolstered the position of Syria, which has become the major actor on the Arab side since Egypt's defection in the late 1970s, and which has assumed a predominant role in Lebanon. Finally, the fragmentation of the system has been manifest in serious splits in the PLO. These splits culminated with a Syrian-backed revolt against PLO Chairman Yasser Arafat in 1983, and have continued into 1986.

In effect, then, the Arab-Israeli conflict appears to have been reduced to a localized conflict in the fragmented system—simply one of the many in the area. The appearance is deceptive, however. As chapter 2 indicated, unlike any of the other conflicts, the twentieth century of the entire region is bound up in the Palestine Question: it is the most enduring pattern in the region. Finally, it is the only conflict that has not only engaged the cultural psyche of the Arab people, but has done so for an extended period of time. The conflict, in other words, has deep historic, cultural, and political roots in the region, and is directly related to its systemic nature. As such, its course or pattern of interaction directly imprints upon the regional and international relations of the Middle East regional system. In a sense, it is a microcosm of the system.

The viability of the Arab cooperative core can be seen in the continued operation of all of the patterns of the core outlined earlier. Egypt's expulsion notwithstanding, the League of Arab States has continued to function, and indeed plays a important political, economic, and social role in the Middle East. Similarly, the level of Arab developmental aid to other Arab (and other developing) countries has grown dramatically since the 1960s and 1970s. Of the $20.4 billion in aid disbursed by Arab development agencies between 1962 and 1984, $11.7 billion (or 57.2 percent) was granted after 1980. Of this aid, over half (51.2 percent) was given to Arab countries, principally Jordan ($1.3 billion), Morocco ($1.1 billion), Tunisia ($1.1 billion), and North Yemen ($1.1 billion).[31] In the 1980s, inter-Arab development aid has thus totaled about $1 billion per year.

Still more evidence of the vitality of an Arab cooperative core is provided by the persistence of Arab unity experiments. Since 1980 these have included unification agreements between Syria and Libya (1980), Libya and Chad (1981), and Libya and Morocco (1984); integration agreements between North and South Yemen (1982) and Egypt

and the Sudan (1982); the Maghreb Treaty of Friendship and Cooperation between Algeria, Tunisia, and Mauritania (1983); and the Pan-
Arab command of Algeria, Libya, South Yemen, and Syria (1985).

The fact that the Arab cooperative core has continued within
the Middle East regional system does not mean that it has not undergone severe strains, however. These strains were apparent, among other
places, at the 12th Arab Summit Conference in Fez (November 1981),
where disagreement over the so-called Fahd peace plan forced the ad-
journment of the summit until September 1982. This was the first
time that Arab leaders had ever found it necessary to take such a step.
Since that date, disagreement over the Iran-Iraq War, the PLO, and a
host of other issues has prevented the holding of a full Arab summit;
indeed, when Morocco attempted to convene a summit in August 1985
the meeting was boycotted by Algeria, Lebanon, Libya, South Yemen,
and Syria. Still (and despite this lapse), a myriad of other less spectacular forms of Arab cooperative interaction occur every day—bilaterally and multilaterally, formally and informally.

CONCLUSION

The fragmented, localized nature of the contemporary Middle East
has had a substantial effect on the international relations of the region. The fragmentation of the contemporary system has weakened
the ability of the Middle East to resist external intrusion. As chapter
5 shows, clear evidence of this has been provided by the growth of
a U.S. political and military presence in the region in the 1980s, start-
ing with President Carter's enunciation of the so-called Carter Doctrine in January 1980, which declared the Gulf to be an area of vital
interest to the United States, wherein it was prepared to intervene
with force, if necessary. In keeping with this doctrine, the United States
has created a Rapid Deployment Force for regional intervention; has
tried to create a parallel force with the Jordanian army; and has acquired or upgraded military facilities or rights in Morocco, Egypt,
Oman, Bahrain, Somalia, Kenya, and the Indian Ocean (Diego Gar-
cia). Whereas in the 1950s the Baghdad Pact, the Eisenhower Doctrine,
and CENTO were largely unsuccessful in installing a Western security framework in the region in the face of regional opposition capa-
bly led by Nasser, the fragmented system of the 1980s has made such
a task much easier.

System fragmentation has served to facilitate the expansion of external influence in another way. Because the number of actors involved in any one area is limited, the relative power of an external actor within that area is strengthened. Like the United States, France has been a beneficiary of this effect in the Gulf, where it now plays a significant political and economic role (see chapter 4).

The impact of regional fragmentation on the international relations of the Middle East has also been very apparent with regard to the Arab world's ability to influence the policies of other regions and powers. As will be shown in chapter 8, division in the Arab world has been accompanied by a weakening in African support for the Arab position in Palestine. As will be shown in chapter 4 with regard to Western Europe, division in the Arab world has allowed many European powers to avoid the issue of Palestine (and indeed other regional issues) altogether, and to concentrate instead on narrow commercial interests. In both cases, another regional actor—Israel—has been the beneficiary. The decline of regional cohesion has also served to undermine the interregional economic and political dialogues established in the 1970s. Both the Arab League–Organization of African Unity "Afro-Arab Dialogue" and the Arab League–European Community "Euro-Arab Dialogue" have been frozen in the 1980s.

NOTES

1. William R. Thompson, "Delineating Regional Subsystems: Visit Networks and the Middle East Case," *International Journal of Middle East Studies* 13, No. 2 (May 1981): 213.

2. On rivalry between Egypt and Iraq in the context of postwar Syria, see Patrick Seale, *The Struggle for Syria: A Study of Post-War Arab Politics 1945–1958* (Oxford: Oxford University Press, 1965).

3. Lebanon's membership in the core is somewhat more difficult to determine; although it had been directly involved in the Palestine War of 1948, and although it was the target of an increasing number of Israeli raids in the late 1960s and 1970s, its weakness and less strong Arab orientation meant that it was only marginally involved in most core interactions. Indeed, when it was involved in core interactions, such involvement was often unintentional or even unwilling (e.g., the growing Palestinian presence in Lebanon and the Israeli punishment strikes that the Palestinians attracted).

4. For a list of the specialized agencies of the League and joint projects of OAPEC, see Yusif A. Sayigh, *The Economics of the Arab World: Development Since 1945* (London: Croom Helm, 1978), pp. 692–693.

5. Arab Summit Conferences have been held in January 1964 (Cairo); September 1964 (Alexandria); September 1965 (Casablanca); August–September 1967 (Khartoum); December 1969 (Rabat); November 1973 (Algiers); October 1974 (Rabat); October 1976 (Cairo); November 1978 (Baghdad); November 1979 (Tunis); November 1980 (Amman); November 1981/September 1982 (Fez). An attempt to hold an Arab Summit Meeting in Casablanca in August 1985 was boycotted by Algeria, Lebanon, Libya, Syria, and South Yemen.

6. Thompson, "Delineating Regional Subsystems," pp. 213–35.

7. Mitsue Osada, "Basic Data on the Arab World," in Ali E. Hillal Dessouki, ed., International Relations in the Arab World 1973–1982, Joint Research Program Series No. 39 (Tokyo: Institute of Developing Economies, 1983), pp. 227–229.

8. George Lenczowski, The Middle East in World Affairs, 4th ed., (Ithaca, N.Y.: Cornell University Press, 1980), pp. 749–751.

9. "Resolution on Palestine Adopted by the Seventh Arab Summit Conference," Journal of Palestine Studies 4, No. 3 (Spring 1975): 177–178.

10. I have argued elsewhere that these changes in the Gulf's role in the regional system, together with other structural realignments in the system, are closely related to the outbreak of the Iraq-Iran war. See Tareq Y. Ismael, "The Iraq-Iran Conflict in Regional Perspective: A Systems Approach," in William L. Dowdy and Russell B. Trood, eds., The Indian Ocean: Perspectives on a Strategic Arena (Durham, N.C.: Duke University Press, 1985).

11. See Tareq Y. Ismael and Jacqueline S. Ismael, Government and Politics in Islam (London: Frances Pinter, 1985), pp. 133–134.

12. Paul Noble has attempted to measure the distribution of demographic, cultural and communications, military, and economic capability in the Arab East in the mid-1960s and mid-1970s. Although space is inadequate to give a full explanation of his methodology, his findings are worth repeating. For the mid-1960s, Noble's assessment of power distribution among Eastern Arab states are:

Demographic Capabilities: Egypt (53.0% of total); Iraq (14.0%); Syria (11.5%); Lebanon (7%)

Cultural and Communications Capabilities: Egypt (63.5%); Iraq (10%); Syria (10.0%); Lebanon (6.5%)

Military Capabilities: Egypt (48.5%); Iraq (19.5%); Syria (15.5%); Jordan (8.0%)

Economic Capabilities: Egypt (29.0%); Kuwait (25.0%); Saudi Arabia (14.0%); Iraq (11.5%)

From Paul C. Noble, "The Arab System: Opportunities, Constraints, and Pressures," in Bahgat Korany and Ali E. Hillal Dessouki eds., The Foreign Policies of Arab States (Boulder, Colo.: Westview Press, 1984), pp. 52–55.

13. See chapters 5 and 6.

14. On the inter-Arab rivalry during this period see Malcolm H. Kerr, The Arab Cold War: Gamal 'Abd al-Nasir and His Rivals, 1958–1970, 3rd ed. (London: Oxford University Press, 1971).

15. See chapter 2 for a discussion of the impact of ideology on Middle Eastern foreign policies.

16. For a more detailed discussion of Sadat's policies see David Hirst and

Irene Beeson, *Sadat* (London: Faber and Faber, 1981). See also the account of Sadat's close advisor and confidant, Mohamed Heikal, *Autumn of Fury* (London: Andre Deutsch, 1983), and the memoirs of Sadat's foreign ministers: Muhammad Ibrahim Kamil, *al-Salam al-Dhié* [The Lost Peace], 2nd ed. (London: al-Sharikah al-Suodiyah lil Abhath wa Taswiq, 1984), and Ismail Fahmy, *al-Watan al-Arabi* (London) No. 316, 4–10 March 1983, p. 24.

17. Jacqueline S. Ismael, "Nasserism," in Tareq Y. Ismael, *The Arab Left* (Syracuse, N.Y.: Syracuse University Press, 1976), pp. 78–91.

18. Tareq Y. Ismael and Jacqueline S. Ismael, "Iraq's Interrupted Revolution," *Current History* 84, No. 498 (January 1985): 29–31, 39.

19. See Edmund Ghareeb, *The Kurdish Question in Iraq* (Syracuse, N.Y.: Syracuse University Press, 1981), pp. 142–145.

20. See Lewis Snider et al., "Israel," in Edward P. Haley and Lewis W. Snider, eds., *Lebanon in Crisis* (Syracuse, N.Y.: Syracuse University Press, 1979).

21. Peter Schwab, "Israel's Weakened Position on the Horn of Africa," *New Outlook* 20, No. 10 (April 1978): 21–25, 27.

22. *New York Times*, 22 August 1981.

23. Abu Iyad, *My Home, My Land: A Narrative of the Palestinian Struggle* (New York: Times Books, 1981), p. 193.

24. Noble's assessment of capability distribution in the Arab East in the mid-1970s reflects this shift in the Middle East balance of power:

> *Demographic Capabilities:* Egypt (51.0% of total); Iraq (12.5%); Syria (11.0%); Saudi Arabia (7.0%)
>
> *Cultural and Communications Capabilities:* Egypt (50.5%); Iraq (16.0%); Syria (9.5%); Lebanon (8.0%)
>
> *Economic Capabilities:* Saudi Arabia (32.5%); Kuwait (15.5%); Egypt (13.0%); Iraq (9.0%); United Arab Emirates (9.0%)
>
> *Military Capabilities:* Egypt (34.0%); Syria (27.5%); Iraq (17.5%); Jordan (6.0%)

Egypt's average across these four categories drops from 48.5% (mid-1960s) to 37.1% (mid-1970s). (Noble, "Arab System," pp. 58–60.)

25. Ali E. Hillal Dessouki, "The Crisis of Inter-Arab Politics," in Dessouki, ed., *International Relations*, p. 137.

26. International Institute of Strategic Studies, *The Military Balance 1984–1985* (London: IISS, 1984), pp. 57, 74.

27. See Tareq Y. Ismael, *Iraq and Iran: Roots of Conflict* (Syracuse, N.Y.: Syracuse University Press, 1982).

28. *Le Monde* (Paris) 23 September 1984.

29. Despite its geographic presence in North Africa, Egypt's traditional and contemporary orientation of its foreign policy interest to the east and south and its alienation from the Arab world since the late 1970s mean that it cannot, from a systems perspective, really be considered a part of the area.

30. John Damis, "Prospects for Unity/Disunity in North Africa," *Arab-American Affairs* 6 (Fall 1983): 39. On the other hand, this increase in intra-Maghreb interaction has been balanced by the greater Maghreb-Mashreq interaction brought about

by the transfer of the League of Arab States headquarters from Cairo to Tunis, and by the activist foreign policies of Algeria and Libya. Such developments have served to inhibit the fragmentation of the Maghreb from the regional system.

31. *Middle East Economic Survey*, 18 March 1985, p. B4; ibid., 6 May 1985, p. B5.

PART II
External Linkages

Western Europe and the Middle East

It has been said that world politics was born in the Mediterranean basin. For thousands of years before the birth of the modern European state system and its extension throughout the globe, the cities, regions, peoples, and empires of Mediterranean Europe and the Middle East interacted with one another. Such contact has continued to the present—sometimes peacefully, in the form of cultural and economic exchange; at other times less peacefully, in the form of political conflict, economic exploitation, war, conquest, and armed resistance. Today, while European–Middle Eastern relations may have something less than their once profound significance, interaction between the two regions remains a highly important feature of global politics.

In this chapter we will focus upon Western European–Middle East interaction as a dynamic and interregional process, a process conditioned not only by the perceptions, interests, and actions of individual national foreign policies but also by the changing structural characteristics of the European and Middle East regional economic and political systems. In particular, we will show how the interregional relationship has, since the late seventeenth and eighteenth centuries, evolved in a series of identifiable stages, from an "imperialist" phase (ending ca.1920), through a half-century of declining European power (ca.1920–1971) and a brief decade of "Europolicy" and interregional collective dialogue (ca.1971–1980), to a contemporary stage characterized

This chapter is coauthored with Rex Brynen, Doctoral Fellow in the Department of Political Science, University of Calgary, Calgary, Canada.

by a renewed bilateralism in European foreign policies, and in general a triumph of European commercial interests over active diplomacy and political engagement. We will examine the conditions under which each of these historical stages operated and evolved. Finally, in a brief conclusion, we will examine the extent to which current conditions suggest future continuity or change in the pattern of European–Middle East relations as evident in the first half of the 1980s.

THE IMPERIALIST ERA

Although Europe and the Middle East may have interacted throughout recorded history, the "modern" history of European involvement in the Middle East dates only from the late seventeenth and eighteenth centuries, when the Ottoman Empire—hitherto the dominant power in the region—entered its long downward period of decay. Expansionist and industrializing European powers became increasingly concerned with the fate of Ottoman territories, and the "Eastern Question"—the question of who would get what with the eventual dismemberment of the "sick man of Europe"—came to the fore. It was at this point in history that the imperialist phase of European–Middle East relations can be said to have begun.

In the early days of the Eastern Question, the nature of European policy toward the Ottoman Empire and the Middle East remained qualitatively similar to that which had been pursued in earlier days. Russia and Austria continued to press the Ottoman Empire's Balkan possessions; France maintained its traditional support for Turkey; Britain paid but little attention; and the lesser European powers were either unconcerned or insignificant. Meanwhile, the technological (and hence military) gap between Europe and Turkey widened.

The nature of European activity in the Middle East changed dramatically in 1798, however, when Napoleon and some 40,000 French troops landed in Egypt in the hope of severing British communications with India. The French, while militarily successful against the Mameluke governors of Egypt, ultimately came to grief in the face of British naval superiority in the Mediterranean and Ottoman resistance in the Levant. Napoleon returned to France (without his army) in 1799, and by 1801 what remained of the French Army in Egypt had surrendered. Even so Napoleon's abortive Egyptian campaign had a major impact on the region, transforming the nature of the Eastern Question in at least three important respects. First (and most immediately), Napoleon's actions brought about a substantial British involvement in the region, and although British troops were withdrawn from Egypt within a few years of the French surrender, Britain had gained an abiding interest in the Middle East — an interest made manifest in its acquisition of Malta at the Congress of Vienna in 1815. Second, the campaign in Egypt underscored the weakness of the Ottoman Empire, and its vulnerability not only to incremental encroachment on its periphery but also to lightning thrusts at its non-European possessions. Thus, Napoleon's invasion presaged a new form of European penetration of the region. Third and finally, the presence of French troops in Egypt (and more generally, the display of European power that the Egyptian campaign represented) stimulated the interest of Middle Eastern leaders and intellectuals in European technology and society: the easy success of French arms over the Mamelukes emphasized the need for political, social, and military reform in the Ottoman Empire, whose reigning military system was based on a quasi-feudal social system. The eighteenth century thus saw efforts at Middle East "modernization," with such autonomous regional rulers as Muhammad Ali of Egypt and Ahmed Bey of Tunisia showing a frank interest in the knowledge of the West. The Ottoman Empire itself embarked on a major period of (generally unsuccessful) internal reform — the "Tanzimat" of 1839–1876.

None of these reforms and reactions, however, were sufficient to halt the accelerating pace of European interest in and penetration of the Middle East. And as Harry Howard notes in *The Middle East in World Politics*, the particular policies and priorities of the major European powers varied.[1] In the West Mediterranean, France sought to preserve commercial and cultural interests in the region that dated back to the Crusades. Britain sought to guarantee a line of communication to India, and (until Anglo-Russian rapprochement and increasing German influence in Constantinople rendered the policy obsolete) to maintain the Ottoman Empire as a buffer against Russian expansionism. Austria-Hungary was primarily interested in extending its hegemony in the Balkans, and in opposing Russian influence there. Russia sought to gain control of Turkish European and Asian territories through the domination or division of the Empire, so as to strengthen its position on the Black Sea and guarantee access for itself from the Black Sea to the Mediterranean through the Turkish Straits. Finally, Imperial Germany, after its unification in 1870–71, sought to extend its influence through the political and economic penetration of the Ottomans, rather than through military confrontation.

Similar to oil from
Coal = imbrichent
M.E. imbrichent

In the Arab Gulf, too, Britain's primary concern was with safe-guarding India. Later, however, this interest was conjoined with an additional concern: From the time the British navy began to switch from coal to oil around the turn of the century, the access to secure sources of oil had become an increasingly important concern of the British government. To this end, in 1914 it purchased a 51 percent share of Anglo-Persian Oil Company stock. Anglo-Persian held an oil concession that covered all of Persia except for five northern provinces. In Iraq, likewise, Britain acquired a 75 percent control of the Turkish Petroleum Company, which held a concession over Mesopotamian oil granted by the Ottoman government. Nevertheless, the acquisition of oil supplies never became a major much less an overriding determinant of Britain's Middle East policy. As Edward Haley has noted, the "desire to control the region's oil followed rather than initiated the intrusion of British power into the Middle East. Even if oil had never been discovered in Persia or Iraq . . . the general direction of British policy in the Middle East would have been the same."[2]

In the Maghreb, the extension of European influence was spear-headed by France. In 1830 Charles X of France unsuccessfully attempted to divert domestic political opposition to his regime by noisily occupying the nominally Ottoman city of Algiers and its environs. The next several decades were dedicated to expanding French control of the area in the face of a local opposition that was not fully overcome until 1881. France also engaged in the intensive colonization of Algeria, a drive given voice by Governor Thomas Bugeaud when he declared in 1840 that "wherever there is fresh water and fertile land, there one must locate *colons* without concerning oneself to whom these lands belong."[3] In 1848, in support of this policy, Algeria was formally reconstituted into three overseas departments of France itself.

France further enhanced its position in North Africa in 1881 and 1904 with protectorates in Tunisia and Morocco, respectively.[4] Here, however, no attempt was made to integrate the newly acquired lands into the metropole: rather, local sultans were permitted to coexist with a dominant French administration. Spain also acquired a protectorate in southwest Morocco in the early 1900s, and in 1911 Italy—anxious not to be left behind in the European scramble for African and Middle Eastern colonies, and also recognizing North Africa as a possible outlet for excess population—invaded Libya, the only part of the region not yet occupied by a European power. The following year it was formally ceded to Italy by the Ottoman Empire.

And so, impelled by the geostrategic importance of the region, by the spur of national rivalries and conflicting economic interests, and by the power vacuum left by the Ottoman Empire's slow but terminal decay, the European powers committed considerable attention to the Eastern Question. Indeed, as Table 4.1 shows, the century between the end of the Napoleonic Wars and the onset of World War I saw almost every major European power gain some significant possession in the region.

TABLE 4.1

European Penetration of the Middle East, 1815–1914

1815	Congress of Vienna; Britain acquires Malta
1828–29	Russo-Turkish War
1830–	French occupation of Algeria
1839–	Britain occupies Aden
1853–56	Crimean War
1856	Suez Canal concession granted to French engineer
1860	France intervenes in Lebanon
1869	Suez Canal opens Britain signs treaty with Trucial Oman and gradually extends influence in the Arab Gulf
1875	Britain purchases Egyptian shares in Suez Canal
1877–78	Russo-Turkish War
1878	Treaty of Berlin, in which Ottoman Empire loses many of its Balkan possessions Cyprus ceded to Britain
1881–	French protectorate in Tunisia
1882–	British occupation of Egypt
1896–98	Anglo-Egyptian reconquest of Sudan
1899	Anglo-Egyptian condominium in the Sudan Secret British protectorate in Kuwait
1902	Berlin-Baghdad Railway Agreement
1904	Anglo-French Entente (Britain recognizes French influence in Morocco)
1907	Anglo-Russian agreement divides Persia into spheres of influence
1911–	Italian conquest of Libya
1912	French and Spanish protectorates in Morocco

While the Ottoman Empire attempted to resist these incursions, some of its "subjects" actively sought closer links with Europe in an attempt to bolster their own local autonomy. Both Muhammad Ali of Egypt and the Maronite Christians of Lebanon, for example, saw in France a useful ally in the mid-nineteenth century. Similarly, in the aftermath of the Young Turk Revolution of 1908, when the new rulers of the Ottoman Empire sought to strengthen it through a program of political centralization and "Turkification," some Arab nationalist leaders turned to Britain for assistance. Thus, during the Eastern Question period of Europe–Middle East relations, a pattern of local actors seeking to "internationalize" regional conflicts by appealing for external assistance became firmly established.

World War I and the Middle East

In the years between the Young Turk Revolution and the onset of World War I, it was Germany, rather than Britain or France, which gained the greatest influence in Constantinople. The reason for this is quite obvious: Germany was unique among the major European powers in having refrained from occupying large portions of formerly Ottoman territory. Also, Germany had evinced a willingness to assist in the economic and military modernization of the Empire. Given this, it came as no surprise, in August 1914, that Turkey's sympathies lay with the Triple Alliance, and that by November of that year the Empire was formally at war with Britain, France, and Russia.

The ensuing military operations in the Middle East, although clearly secondary to the battles of the Western and Eastern fronts in European eyes, had nevertheless considerable military and political significance. In particular, Britain's campaigns in Mesopotamia, Arabia, and the Levant had a critical bearing on the postwar disposition of these territories. In Mesopotamia, British and Indian forces had by 1918 captured most of the region between Mosul and the Arab Gulf. In Arabia, Sherif Hussein of the Hejaz reached an agreement with Britain whereby the latter promised to support postwar Arab independence. In exchange, Sherif Hussein declared war against his former Ottoman rulers on 5 June 1916, an event that has subsequently become somewhat famous as the "Arab Revolt."[5] Thereafter, Arab irregular forces not only drove Turkish troops from much of the Hejaz but also, under the command of Hussein's son Faisal, harassed them in inland Syria and Palestine as well. At the same time, British forces in Egypt fought their way along the Mediterranean coast into Palestine and Syria. Jerusalem was captured on 11 December 1917, and on 1 October 1918 British and Arab forces simultaneously entered Damascus. A few weeks later, on 31 October, an armistice brought Turkish military resistance to an end.

With the end of the war, the question of what was to become of the Ottoman Empire's Middle Eastern territories arose. A number of competing claims were advanced—by Arab nationalist leaders, by adherents of the Zionist movement, and by the victorious allied powers themselves. It is interesting to note that such questions were not raised (or at least, not seriously entertained) with regard to North Africa, where victorious France, Italy, and Britain had "acquired" their territory before the outbreak of general hostilities in 1914. There, colonial control continued unmodified.

For their part, Arab nationalist leaders demanded immediate Arab independence, recalling the wartime promises made to Sherif Hussein by the British High Commissioner in Egypt, Sir Henry McMahon. Great Britain had pledged to support such independence in the area bounded by the 37th parallel to the north, the Persian border to the East, the Arab Gulf emirates to the south, and the Mediterranean to the West, excluding only "the districts of Mersina and Alexandretta" and those "portions of Syria lying to the west of Homs, Hama, and Aleppo."[6] (It was the fulfillment of this pledge that the Arab delegation led by Emir Faisal sought at the Versailles Peace Conference in January 1919.) The Zionist movement, on the other hand, sought Allied support for the establishment of a Jewish national home in historic Palestine. They too could point to wartime promises, in the form of the Balfour Declaration of November 1917 in which the British government, anxious to maximize Jewish support for the war effort, undertook to support the "establishment in Palestine of a national home for the Jewish people . . . it being clearly understood that nothing shall be done which may prejudice the civil and religious rights of existing non-Jewish communities in Palestine. . . ."[7] (A Zionist delegation also attended the Versailles Peace Conference.)

Finally, France and Britain continued to nurse their territorial ambitions in the area. During the war they had, along with pre-revolutionary Russia and Italy, made a number of secret agreements relative to the partitioning of the region among themselves at war's end. The most significant of these agreements was based on negotiations betwen Britain's Sir Mark Sykes and France's Georges Picot in 1915–16. Under the terms of the Sykes-Picot Agreement of 16 May

1916, Britain was to gain control of southern Mesopotamia and the ports of Haifa and Acre in Palestine, while France was to get the coastal regions of Syria and those areas of Turkey north and northeast of this coastal strip. The remainder of Palestine was to be internationalized, with remaining territories to be divided into French and British spheres of influence.[8] Of course, such ambitions flew in the face of wartime Allied propaganda in support of democracy and self-determination, and they were formally opposed at the Versailles Peace Conference by the United States. More important, they were clearly at odds with the wishes of the populations of these regions, who demanded independence and self-government.

The Mandate System

The eventual "solution" to the problem posed by these conflicting claims was the mandate system of the post–World War I period. In theory, the Class A mandates established in the Middle East after the war were designed to foster progress toward eventual independence under the temporary tutelage of a European power itself under League of Nations supervision. Britain and France, however, saw the mandate system as a mechanism for establishing and maintaining a colonial foothold in the region, while simultaneously giving the appearance of adherence to the principle of national self-determination. In any event, as we shall see, the mandate system proved unequal to the task of maintaining European domination of the Middle East in the face of irresistible nationalist sentiment in the region.

At the San Remo Conference of April 1920, the mandates for the Middle East were assigned: France, with continuing cultural and commercial interests in the East Mediterranean coast, received the mandate for Syria; Britain, with interests in the Arab Gulf and Suez Canal areas, received the mandates for Iraq and Palestine. The latter mandate, submitted to the League of Nations in 1922 for ratification, explicitly recognized the promises made by Britain in the Balfour Declaration.

In Syria, France was faced with the immediate problem of enforcing its mandatory authority, for while French troops had begun deploying along the coastal region in 1919, the Syrian hinterland remained under the de facto control of Faisal and Arab nationalist forces. Furthermore, in March 1920 a Syrian National Congress declared Faisal to be the king of an independent Syria. This led General Gouraud, commander of French forces in Syria, to dispatch an ultimatum to Faisal on 19 July demanding that he recognize the French mandate. Faisal eventually acceded, but not fast enough for Gouraud. French troops marched on Damascus, defeating a small Arab force to enter the Syrian capital on 25 July.

Having effectively conquered Syria, France split the region into smaller units that would facilitate colonial rule. On 1 September 1920 the mandated territory was divided into four "states", with separate administrative regions being set up in the areas of Greater Lebanon, Damascus, Aleppo, and Latakia. In 1922 a Druze Muslim region, Jebel Druze, was created out of the "state" of Damascus. A few years later, on 1 January 1925, Aleppo and Damascus were united as Syria. Thereafter, separate constitutions were drawn up for Lebanon and Syria, and political institutions based on the French model, with a president chosen by an elected National Assembly, were created. In spite of this, French control remained firm. French High Commissioners manipulated elections, and imposed or suspended constitutions at will; French troops remained in the area; French experts dominated the bureaucracy; and France controlled the railways, banks, and utilities as well as ruled directly in the districts of Latakia and Jebel Druze. Finally, both the Lebanese constitution of 1926 (Article 30) and the Syrian constitution of 1930 (Article 116) formally recognized France's position as the mandatory power.

During this period, France managed (despite a Druze-led insurrection in 1925–26) to successfully stifle most nationalist resistance. By 1932, however, demands for independence in the Syrian Chamber of Deputies had reached irresistible proportions. These demands, colored as they were by Britain's granting of independence to Iraq in 1932, led France to agree to open Syrian-French negotiations on ending the mandate. After four years, these negotiations resulted in the conclusion of a treaty between France and Syria on 9 September 1936. Under its terms Syria was to become independent within three years, although France would retain substantial military rights in Syria as well as economic ties. A similar treaty was signed with Lebanon on November 13. In the end, the threat of war in Europe led to neither treaty being ratified by France, and with the outbreak of war in September 1939 they were rendered academic.

In Palestine, meanwhile, Britain faced even thornier problems, due to the conflicting promises to Arabs and Jews that had been made during World War I. Even before Britain's assumption of the Palestine mandate, the Zionist movement pressed Britain to fulfill its pledges to transform Palestine into a Jewish national home, demanding unrestricted Jewish immigration and settlement. Not surprisingly, the Arab population of Palestine, which constituted more than 90 percent of the total at the end of the war, opposed Zionist claims on their country and demanded that their right to self-determination be honored. Moreover, Britain's mandatory obligations and foreign policy interests were unclear. In the first case Britain had, in the Balfour Declaration and Palestine mandate, undertaken to simultaneously transform Palestine into a Jewish national home and safeguard the civil rights of the existing population—clearly an impossible task, since the goals were mutually exclusive. In the second case, Britain was torn throughout the mandate years by the demands of an influential Zionist lobby and those of an anti-Zionist and geostrategically important Arab world.

Thus, British policy in Palestine was from the beginning confused, and conflict was inevitable. Major anti-Zionist riots occurred in 1920 and 1921. In 1922, colonial secretary Winston Churchill issued a memorandum in which the British government declared that henceforth Jewish immigration would be limited to the "economic capacity" of the country. Nevertheless, Jewish immigration continued to rise (to some 34,000 persons per year in 1925), and major violence erupted again in 1928–29. In October 1930 the British government issued a White Paper on Palestine. In combination with the Hope-Simpson Report on Immigration, Settlement, and Development that accompanied it, the White Paper noted the negative impact of large-scale Zionist settlement on the Palestinian Arab population and recommended restrictions on Jewish immigration and land acquisition. This in turn resulted in a storm of protest from the Zionist movement, with the result that by early 1931 Prime Minister Ramsey McDonald had publicly reinterpreted the White Paper in a manner more acceptable to Zionist expectations.

Jewish immigration continued, then, with the Jewish population of Palestine growing to 16–17 percent of the total by 1931, and accelerating still faster in the mid-1930s under the stimulus of rising anti-semitism in Europe. This trend, coupled with the British government's obvious unwillingness or inability to meet Palestinian Arab demands, served to increase the radicalism of the latter and culminated in armed attacks against the British authorities and against Jewish settlements during the "Palestine Revolt" of 1936–39. By the time the insurrection was finally suppressed by the British in the autumn of 1939 as many as 5,000 Palestinian Arabs had been killed, with many thousands more wounded or in detention.[9]

The Palestine Revolt did lead to some political change, however. In 1937 the Peel Royal Commission, formed to examine the causes of the dispute, found that "irrepressible conflict has arisen between two national communities within the narrow bounds of one small country. About 1,000,000 Arabs are in strife, open or latent, with some 400,000 Jews. There is no common ground between them."[10] The Commission recommended that Palestine be partitioned. Two years later the British government, faced with the growing likelihood of a war in Europe (and therefore wishing to maximize its support in the Arab world), adopted a new and different policy. In its 1939 White Paper, Britain undertook to limit Jewish immigration to 75,000 over five years, with further immigration after that contingent on Palestinian Arab approval. The British also promised the eventual independence of a unified Arab state tied to Britain by treaty. Palestinian leaders, however, continued to demand immediate independence and self-determination, while Zionist leaders not surprisingly condemned the new White Paper.

Matters were very different in those areas of the mandate east of the Jordan River. Under the terms of the Palestine Mandate, Britain was authorized to detach Transjordan and administer it separately.[11] Later, in February 1921, forces under Faisal's brother, Emir Abdullah, entered Transjordan from the south on their way to Syria, where he hoped to reinstate his brother's rule. Wishing to avoid conflict with France, Churchill sought to deflect Abdullah from his course by offering him the emirate of Transjordan, an offer that Abdullah accepted. Two years later the British High Commissioner for Palestine, Herbert Samuel, indicated to Abdullah that Britain was willing to grant independence to Transjordan provided a constitutional regime was established and a preferential treaty signed with Britain. On 25 May 1923, Abdullah duly declared Transjordan to be "independent," and on 20 February 1928 an Anglo-Transjordanian treaty was concluded. Under its terms Britain reserved the right to approve the appointment of foreign advisers, the budget, and several categories of legislation. Britain also retained control over much of Transjordan's defense, foreign relations, and resource exploitation. Neither Abdullah's declaration of "independence" nor the 1928 treaty, therefore, put an end to Britain's mandate over the territory. Genuine independence was not to come until March 1946 when Britain, under the terms of a new treaty, finally relinquished its authority.

OVERVIEW: RELATIONS IN THE IMPERIALIST ERA

The period that began with the Eastern Question at the turn of the eighteenth century and lasted until the San Remo Conference of 1920 has been described here as the imperialist phase of European–Middle East relations. During this time, a widely accepted imperialist paradigm, variously defined as "destiny," "the white man's burden," the *mission civilisatrice*, or the competition for "a place in the sun," provided the ideological context for European colonial expansion in Africa and Asia. This expansion was encouraged not only by this world view, however, but also by the imperatives of political competition in Europe and by the economic need for raw materials, markets, and investment opportunities for the capital accumulating in rapidly growing European capitalist economies. It is clear in retrospect that imperialist expansion was both self-perpetuating and self-defeating. It was self-perpetuating in the sense that inter-European competition for colonies accelerated the colonial process, most notably in North Africa. Imperialism also provided its own motivation in that the strategic need to defend existing territories (e.g., British India) required the acquisition of additional territory (e.g., the Suez Canal and British Egypt), which in turn spurred the acquisition of still more territory (British Palestine). At the same time, imperialism was self-defeating in that it was a policy limited ultimately by the availability of unconquered territory, and insofar as it necessitated the subjugation and dominance by a foreign power of indigenous populations that could not be expected to tolerate such circumstances in perpetuity. Moreover, imperialism brought with it the extension of capitalism and the growth (often from a preexistent social elite) of a new local bourgeoisie, who sought to expand their power within the context of a capitalist, Western-oriented but independent political system. As a result of these factors and their synthesis, the imperialist framework began to break down in the Middle East soon after the allocation of mandates in 1920—slowly at first, and then with increasing speed.

Despite its subsequent breakdown (discussed below), the imperialist era did have a fundamental and lasting impact on the nature of the Middle East: at the very least, the subordination of the Middle East to the European system guaranteed that some aspects of the later would be indelibly imprinted on the region. This was evident not only in the spread of capitalism and modern productive techniques to the Middle East, but also in the adoption (or imposition) of many political institutions and concepts from the metropole. The unity of the

Middle East, once a tenuous fact within the tangled framework of the Ottoman Empire, was torn asunder, artificial borders, and later the European state system, were established that formalized the division of the region among the colonial European powers. This is not to say that the Middle East became a mere reflection of the dominant European system: such a transformation was beyond the ability of Europe, despite the most strenuous efforts in French Algeria and Italian Libya. Furthermore, it was obvious even then that the peoples of the Middle East retained their distinctive character throughout the imperialist era, contributing much more from within to the emerging Middle East system than was imposed upon them from outside. Still, the imperialist phase of European involvement in the Middle East did play a major role in shaping the contemporary political, economic, and social structure of the region, with consequences that endure to the present day.

THE DECLINE OF EUROPEAN INFLUENCE

Neither Syria-Lebanon nor Palestine-Transjordan had fully escaped mandatory control by the onset of World War II, although there was evidence of a clear drift toward replacing mandates with preferential treaties — that is, of replacing direct with indirect control — in these areas. In mandated Iraq and British-occupied Egypt, however, independence came before 1939, albeit an independence that remained strongly qualified by British influence. Nevertheless, it was here that the decline of European power, although gradual, was most evident.

Britain's assumption of a mandate for Iraq in the spring of 1920 had been accompanied by a full-scale uprising in the country. It took Britain nearly a year and a half and some 2,500 casualties before the last major opposition to its mandatory authority was suppressed. The scope and intensity of such resistance led Britain to revise its strategy for dealing with Iraq and other Middle East territories: A pro-British ruler would be installed, and tied to Britain by preferential treaty. (As we have already seen, Abdullah performed such a role in Transjordan.) In Iraq, Faisal — who had been ejected from Syria by the French — was the obvious candidate, and after being approved by 96% of the population in a British-run referendum, he was crowned king of Iraq on 23 August 1921.

The history of the decade following Faisal's accession to the throne was one of gradual relaxation of direct British control. In 1922, an Anglo-Iraqi Treaty was signed in lieu of a formal League of Nations mandate. Under its terms Britain was given the right to appoint advisers, assist the Iraqi army, advise on economic and foreign affairs, and protect foreigners. In the face of nationalist agitation for independence, additional Anglo-Iraqi treaties were concluded in 1926 and 1927—each of which gave Iraq somewhat greater autonomy. Finally, a new treaty, signed on 30 June 1930 and ratified the following year, granted Iraq independence. In exchange, Iraq agreed to a 25-year alliance with Britain, on-going foreign policy consultation between the two governments, exclusively British training and supply of the Iraqi armed forces, and British use of "all facilities . . . including railways, rivers, ports, aerodromes and means of communication" in the event of war.[12] Pursuant to the treaty, Britain sponsored Iraq's entrance into the League of Nations on 3 October 1932.

A similar process took place in Egypt. As early as 1920 a British investigatory commission recommended that Egypt be granted independence, with British interests to be guaranteed by an Anglo-Egyptian treaty. In 1921 Egypt was officially informed that Britain was prepared to grant it the "national prerogatives and the international position of a sovereign state" on these conditions. The following year, however, unable to reach an agreement with the Egyptian government, Britain unilaterally terminated the protectorate and recognized Egyptian independence. At the same time it retained absolute discretion over four areas: "(a) the security of the communications of the British Empire in Egypt; (b) the defence of Egypt against all foreign aggression or interference direct or indirect; (c) the protection of foreign interests in Egypt and the protection of minorities; (d) the Sudan".[13] In practice, Egypt's real independence took many long years to win. Intermittent and inconclusive negotiations between the British and successive Egyptian governments dragged on through the 1920s and early 1930s, during which time Britain retained control of Egyptian territory through the presence of influential advisers at all levels of the Egyptian government and through military *force majeure*. Nationalist demands for Egyptian sovereignty grew ever more powerful, and nationalist attacks against British soldiers and other personnel became common.

By the mid-1930s, however, British and Egyptian alarm at the growing power of European fascism (dramatically demonstrated by Italy's 1935 invasion of Ethiopia) led both sides to reenter negotiations with greater flexibility and determination, and on 26 August 1936 an

Anglo-Egyptian Treaty was signed. The treaty (and its accompanying notes) provided for an alliance between the two countries, with Britain to defend Egypt and Egypt to provide communication facilities to Britain in the event of war; retention of the British naval base at Alexandria for eight years, and the deployment of a British garrison of 10,000 in the Canal Zone until both parties agreed that Egypt was itself capable of guarding the canal; the evacuation of other British military and police personnel; and Egyptian military and immigration access to the Sudan. Britain would also train and advise the Egyptian armed forces. The treaty, although of indefinite duration, would be subject to revision (although not abrogation) after twenty years.[14] Britain also agreed to support Egyptian candidacy for the League of Nations, and on 26 May 1937 Egypt was formally admitted into that body.

North Africa, where the colonial population generally made up a larger percentage of the total (and where, as a consequence, European control was more firmly established), was an exception to this pattern of transition from direct colonial administration to indirect control through preferential treaties and the entrenchment of local pro-Western rulers and elites. Certainly, indigenous tribal opposition did continue. In Morocco, French (and Spanish) troops engaged in "pacification" operations until 1934, with the fiercest resistance coming from the Rif tribes in the 1920s. In Libya, the Sanusi religious order engaged the Italian occupiers in intermittent guerrilla warfare into the 1930s. Even more important, the interwar years saw the emergence of growing opposition to colonial rule from young, alienated Arab intellectuals and professionals and from the nascent working class. It was these individuals who established the basis of a new nationalist opposition in Algeria, Tunisia, and Morocco. Nevertheless, European rule in North Africa remained firmly in place in the years prior to World War II. The more than 800,000 European *colons* in Algeria pressed for closer integration of that country within the French Republic, while simultaneously opposing the extension of civil and democratic rights to the local population. In Libya, Italy's fascist government embarked on a program of intensive colonization beginning in 1938, and on 9 January 1939 the Libyan provinces of Tripoli, Misurata, Benghazi, and Derna were formally made a region of Italy itself. At its peak in 1940, the Italian population of Libya numbered more than 110,000 persons.[15]

A final aspect of European–Middle East relations that must be examined at this stage is oil. As direct European control of Middle

East territories began to relax in the interwar period, oil concessions and oil company privileges became an important mechanism for solidifying Western influence over the foreign and domestic policies of Middle Eastern countries, particularly in the Gulf. With petroleum exploitation and government revenues dependent on a small number of very powerful Western oil companies—companies whose position was usually defined in the small print of contractual agreements and treaties negotiated when the colonial countries were at their most powerful, and which could count on the support of their home governments as well as each other in the event of any attempt to change the status quo—the countries of the Middle East had very little in the way of real independence.

Nevertheless, oil continued to be generally regarded as a valuable byproduct, rather than as a primary mechanism or objective, of European diplomacy. Before the outbreak of World War II, the Middle East was of only relatively minor resource importance, producing in 1938, for example, only 15 million tons of crude oil—less than 6 percent of the world supply. Even Britain, with the most extensive Middle East oil interests of any European nation, was receiving only 22 percent of its oil supplies from the Middle East, as compared to 57 percent from the Western hemisphere.[16]

The Impact of World War II

With the outbreak of war in September 1939, the Middle East assumed considerable strategic significance for the Axis and Allies alike, and several important military campaigns took place in the region. The most important of these was in North Africa, which represented the major battleground for the armies of the Western Allies and those of Germany and Italy from the fall of France in June 1940 until the collapse of Axis forces in the area in May 1943. There was also conflict in Iraq, where British, Indian, and Transjordanian forces overthrew the short-lived pro-Axis regime of Rashid Ali in May 1941, and in Syria and Lebanon where British and Free French forces wrested control from the Vichy authorities in the following month. In addition, Iran was occupied by Allied troops from August 1941 until the end of the war, with forces being deployed in northern Iran and Iraq to guard against a possible German breakthrough in the Caucasus, and massive quantities of lend-lease war materiel passing to the Soviet Union through the area. German (and to a lesser extent, Italian) military strategy during the war aimed at seizing the Suez Canal and the Middle East oil fields, and at interrupting British communications with India by means of a pincer movement directed across North Africa on the one hand and through the Caucasus on the other. The Axis also sought to undermine the French and British position in the Middle East through the encouragement of certain Arab nationalist elements. British and Allied strategy, for its part, was designed to safeguard Mesopotamia and the Suez Canal, and eventually to clear North Africa of Axis troops preparatory to an assault on southern Europe itself.

As might be expected, Arab attitudes toward the combatants were mixed. Much of the established Arab leadership and elite, having achieved wealth and power through their accommodation with Britain and France during the interwar years, favored the Allies. Their sympathies were tempered (up to 1943), however, by the fear that the Axis powers would triumph in the conflict, and that as a result any open collaboration with Britain would prove costly in the end. At the same time, there was a considerable body of nationalist sentiment—encouraged, of course, by Axis propaganda—that welcomed the war as a blow to French and British colonialism, and which thus opposed any Arab assistance to the Allied war effort. Britain responded to this challenge by seeking the support of moderate Arab nationalists while simultaneously suppressing its more radical or pro-Axis manifestations. (As already noted, the 1939 Palestine White Paper represented one application of this strategy. It succeeded in quieting much of the anti-British sentiment among Palestinian Arabs, while the Zionist movement in general confined its opposition to peaceful verbal protestations, for fear that more militant action would inhibit the war against fascism.)[17] In Iraq, nationalist resentment against Britain led to the 3 April 1941 coup by former Prime Minister Rashid Ali al-Gailani. Although Rashid Ali sought Axis support for his short-lived regime little was forthcoming, and by the end of May his rebellion had been crushed by British military action. Subsequent Iraqi governments were far more favorable to Britain, and on 16 January 1943 Iraq became the first Arab country to formally declare war against Germany, Italy, and Japan. In Egypt, Prime Minister Ali Maher and his successors, although honoring the minimum stipulation of the 1936 Treaty, resisted British pressure to formally enter the war. This position continued even after Italian and German troops entered Egyptian territory in 1940–41, and some Egyptian officers (notably, former Chief of Staff General al-Masri) exhibited unequivocal pro-Axis sympathies. Britain responded by forcing King Farouk to appoint a government more in line with British wishes in February 1942. In Syria and Lebanon, Britain and the Free French under General de Gaulle initially pledged themselves to Lebanese and Syrian independence, and indeed in the autumn of 1941 the independence of both countries was duly proclaimed. However, the French delayed handing over real power while strengthening their own military position in the area, provoking considerable nationalist agitation. Riots erupted, and on 29 May 1945 French forces bombarded Damascus in an attempt to stifle nationalist opposition. Britain, alarmed by such developments, ordered de Gaulle to desist or to expect British military intervention. De Gaulle acquiesced and on 7 July 1945 France recognized the independence of both Syria and Lebanon.

The Second World War thus hastened the end of direct European involvement in the countries of the Middle East. Not only were the colonial powers severely weakened, but nationalist sentiment was reaching new heights. Because of this, the decade 1945–55 saw the continual weakening of French and British influence in the region, a process that culminated in their ill-fated gamble at Suez in 1956. The other European colonial powers—Italy and Spain—also saw their Middle East presence permanently altered.

La France Outre-Mer

With the independence of Syria and Lebanon in 1945, France's direct control over Middle Eastern territories was reduced to Tunisia, Morocco, and Algeria. Here, as in the Levant, the war had served to intensify nationalist demands while at the same time weakening France's prestige and power. In Morocco, the Istiqlal party was formed in 1944 to press demands for independence. Sultan Muhammad V also actively called for independence, actions which led French authorities to (temporarily) depose him in 1953. This move served only to heighten nationalist sentiment, and France was ultimately forced to grant Morocco independence on 2 March 1956. In Tunisia, the neo-Destour party of Habib Bourguiba pressed for the establishment of a sovereign state, albeit one "tied to France by a freely negotiated treaty which guarantees the latter its strategic, economic and cultural interests."[18] Amid growing violence in the 1950s, France eventually agreed to grant Tunisia autonomy in 1955, followed by independence on 2 March 1956.

The situation in Algeria was very different. Algeria, unlike

Morocco and Tunisia, was not merely a protectorate but rather a department of France whose national liberation French governments were willing to oppose if necessary by military force. France had extensive economic interests in Algeria, and more than 100,000 Algerian workers labored in French factories. Major oil and natural gas reserves discovered in Algeria in the mid-1950s were believed to be sufficient to satisfy all of France's needs into the foreseeable future. Most important, more than 900,000 of Algeria's nine and a half million inhabitants were of European extraction (1954). Successive French governments would not give up Algeria easily, nor would the *colons* and their metropolitan supporters of *Algerie française* let them.

As already noted, Algerian nationalist demands for autonomy or independence had intensified during the 1930s, and had been given added impetus by World War II. In February 1943 an Algerian delegation led by liberal nationalist Ferhat Abbas published the *Manifeste de Peuple Algerien*, which demanded equality for Muslims in Algeria; a few months later, a supplement called for the establishment of an Algerian state through legal means. Both the Vichy and the Free French governments rejected or ignored such demands, but the divided nationalist movement temporarily united behind the manifesto. On 8 May 1945, VE Day celebrations in the Algerian town of Setif boiled over into a nationalist rally, which in turn erupted into a clash between authorities and the demonstrators. In the riots and violent government and *colon* repression that followed, more than a hundred Europeans and several thousand Algerians died.

As a result of the Setif massacres, the Algerian nationalist movement once more fell into disarray. The French, in an attempt to ameliorate Algerian grievances, introduced legislation in 1947 that set up an elected Algerian assembly with local powers. In practice, however, the elections to the Assembly (already structured to give a disproportionate voice to the *colons*) were characterized by widespread fraud.

After several years of relative calm, Algeria exploded into war on 1 November 1954 with simultaneous attacks against military and economic targets by the newly formed *Front de Liberation Nationale* (FLN). French Premier Mendès-France responded by declaring that "the Algerian departments are part of the French Republic. . . . Between them and metropolitan France there can be no conceivable secession."[19] Under both Mendès-France and his successor Guy Mollet, French troop strength in Algeria was increased, and attempts were made to fully implement the 1947 statute. Violence and counter-violence on the part of the FLN, the French armed forces, and the *colon* population continued to escalate as the FLN consolidated its position as the leading Algerian nationalist movement.

The FLN's war of liberation was strongly supported by President Gamal Abd al-Nasser of Egypt, who lent verbal, political, and material backing. The extent of this support became starkly evident in October 1956 when a ship carrying some 70 tons of arms and ammunition from Egypt to the FLN in Algeria was intercepted by the French. Because of Egyptian assistance to the FLN (and also because of Nasser's nationalization of French interests in the Suez Canal area in July 1956), French Premier Mollet likened him to Hitler and Mussolini, and it was in the belief that Nasser's downfall would weaken or even extinguish the Algerian revolution that France eventually intervened with Britain at Suez in the autumn of 1956.

Moreover, because of Egyptian policy, many French leaders supported Israel's cause in the Arab-Israeli conflict. Among leftist politicians, this sympathy was reinforced by the perception that Israel was a socialist country—a "pioneer country socializing itself."[20] France supplied substantial quantities of arms to Israel in the early and mid-1950s, and joined Britain and the United States in the Tripartite Declaration of May 1950, in which the three powers announced their opposition to the use of force in the Arab-Israeli dispute and their support for the territorial integrity of Israel.

Britain: Twilight of Empire

Britain's interests in the Middle East were more extensive than those of France, and with the end of the war it became clear that Britain hoped to continue to exercise a preponderant role in the region. A major element of its strategy to do so could be seen in its attempts to foster a British-influenced league of Arab states. (Such an Arab League did in fact emerge during the war, consisting of Iraq, Syria, Lebanon, Transjordan, Egypt, Saudi Arabia, and Yemen.) Britain also sought, through its wartime support for Syrian and Lebanese independence, to weaken the French presence in the region. In practice, however, the war-weariness at home, the rise of the superpowers, and the strength of Arab nationalism combined to prevent Britain from maintaining its power in the Middle East. Diplomatically, British Middle Eastern policy floundered in Palestine and Egypt, and ultimately came to grief in the Suez debacle of 1956.

In Palestine, Britain emerged from the war still faced with the competing, irreconcilable demands of the Palestinian Arab majority and the Zionist movement. The Arabs, pointing to their majority status, refused to discuss anything less than independence and self-determination, while the Zionists sought increased Jewish immigration and eventual Jewish statehood—a position that U.S. President Truman supported. Britain at first responded to this situation by attempting to involve the United States more closely in the Palestine Question, hoping that in so doing it would force the United States to adopt a more "realistic" and helpful position. When this strategy failed, Britain—unable (and unwilling) to impose its own settlement of the issue—turned the fate of Palestine over to the nascent United Nations on 14 February 1947. When the United Nations General Assembly eventually voted to partition Palestine on 29 November, Britain declared that such a policy was unworkable in the face of Palestinian Arab objections, refused to participate in its implementation, and reaffirmed its decision to terminate the mandate and withdraw its forces on 14 May 1948. Britain refrained from being drawn into the Arab-Zionist clashes that occurred in the months leading up to the scheduled date of partition, or into the war that followed the declaration of the State of Israel and the intervention of the armies of Lebanon, Syria, Transjordan, Iraq, and Egypt.[21]

This first Arab-Israeli War proved disastrous for the Arab Palestinians. All of Palestine, save only a portion of the West Bank of the Jordan occupied by Transjordan (and later annexed) and a coastal strip around Gaza occupied by Egypt, were conquered and incorporated into the State of Israel. Some 770,000 Palestinians either fled or were driven from their homes in what was now Israel.

Events in Palestine also proved disastrous for European and Western influence in the Arab world. The loss of a territory so intimately a part of the Arab world's historical, cultural, and religious heritage and identity in the face of an essentially Western movement —Zionism—and with the apparent complicity or open involvement of Western powers served to intensify Arab anti-imperialism. The West's position in the Middle East was seriously damaged. Britain recognized Israel after the conclusion of armistice agreements in 1949, and resumed arms shipments to Arab states shortly afterwards. Along with France and the United States, Britain also took part in the Tripartite Declaration of 1950.

In Iraq, the Anglo-Iraqi Treaty of 1930 remained in force, although nationalist opposition to its terms was such that Britain was unable to negotiate its renewal. In its place, however, Iraq's pro-Western Prime Minister Nuri al-Said sought to join Turkey and Pakistan (linked by defensive treaty since April 1954) in a Northern Tier defense pact. Iraq signed a defense agreement with Turkey in February 1955, and in April Britain joined the Turkish-Iraqi alliance while simultaneously cancelling the 1930 treaty. In October Iran also joined, and in November the members of the "Baghdad Pact" held their first meeting in Baghdad. Throughout this period Iraq endured bitter criticism from the new government in Cairo as well as from Saudi Arabia for concluding alliances outside the League of Arab States. Additionally, the Baghdad Pact was unpopular among the Arab masses, who saw it as an indication of subservience to Western interests. When Britain and Iraq tried to enlist Jordan's participation in the pact in 1955–56, the popular backlash was such that it forced Jordanian King Hussein to dismiss the British commander of the Arab Legion, Lt.-General John Bagot Glubb, from his post on 1 March 1956 in an effort to mollify nationalist sentiment.

In Egypt, the scope of the defeat in Palestine intensified anti-British and nationalist feelings and seriously undermined the stability of the regime. It was in such a context that Egyptian leaders sought to reduce Britain's military privileges under the 1936 Anglo-Egyptian Treaty and gain control of the Sudan. When negotiations failed to win such concessions, Egypt announced in August 1951 that it intended to unilaterally abrogate the 1936 treaty. Britain, supported by the United States, attempted to salvage some military presence in the area through securing Egyptian participation in a regional defense pact. Egypt refused, and on 15 October the Egyptian Parliament unanimously agreed to abrogate the treaty. When Britain refused to depart from the Canal zone, however, the level of anti-British violence and of British reprisal escalated, becoming intense. Then, to add to the turmoil, a group of "Free Officers" led by Gamal Abd al-Nasser overthrew the monarchy on 23 July 1952. In 1954 the new government signed an agreement with Britain providing for British military evacuation of the Canal zone within twenty months and an end to the 1936 Anglo-Egyptian Treaty. Britain was, however, given the right to reenter Egypt in the event of an attack against Egypt, Turkey, or any other member of the Arab League defense agreement.[22]

Soon thereafter, however, Egypt's relations with the West underwent a sharp deterioration, primarily because of Nasser's steadfast opposition to the Baghdad Pact. In December 1954 and again in January 1955, Egypt used the League of Arab States — originally designed, ironically enough, as an instrument of British Middle Eastern policy—as a forum for mustering opposition to the pact. In February 1955 a major Israeli raid against Gaza led Nasser to request arms supplies from the West; when the United States and Britain refused him, he turned to the Soviet bloc and in September concluded a momentous arms deal with Czechoslovakia. In October, in response to both the Baghdad Pact and the military threat of Israel, Egypt formed joint commands with Syria and Saudi Arabia, and a year later a joint Syrian-Jordanian-Egyptian military command was set up under Egyptian auspices. In March 1956, Jordan's dismissal of Glubb and the riots that accompanied British Foreign Minister Selwyn Lloyd's visit to Bahrain, were attributed by Britain to Egyptian machinations—for by this time, British Prime Minister Anthony Eden had come to identify "the growing influence of Nasser with his anti-Western ideology and collusion with Soviet Russia" as the major threat to British interests in the Middle East.[23]

For Britain as for France, the final straw came in July. On 19 July the United States, angered at Nasser's friendly relations with the Soviet Union, withdrew its offer of funding for Egypt's Aswan High Dam. Britain also withdrew a similar offer. On the 26th, an angry Nasser responded by nationalizing the Suez Canal and declaring that its revenues would be committed to the dam project. Although Nasser guaranteed compensation to stockholders and freedom of navigation to canal users, Britain and France (the major stock-owning countries) were incensed. According to Eden, Nasser's move was a strategic threat to all of Western Europe:

> The continuing supply of fuel, which was a vital source of power to the economy of Britain, was now subject to Colonel Nasser's whim. The oilfields of the Middle East were then producing about 145 million tons a year. Nearly 70 million tons of oil had passed through the Suez Canal in 1955, almost all of it destined for Western Europe. Another 40 million tons of oil reached the ports of the Levant by pipelines running through the territories of Egypt's then allies, Syria and Saudi Arabia. More than half of Britain's annual imports of oil came through the Canal. At any time the Egyptians might decide to interfere with its passage.[24]

Eden, like Mollet, likened Nasser to another Hitler.[25] He concluded that Nasser's overthrow was essential to safeguarding British interests and preserving British influence in the Middle East.

The Suez Crisis

On 29 October 1956 Israel, claiming as *causus belli* guerrilla raids from Egyptian territory, invaded the Gaza Strip and Sinai and rapidly advanced across the latter toward the Suez Canal. The following day Britain and France demanded that both Israel and Egypt cease fighting and withdraw to a line ten miles on either side of the Canal. When Nasser rejected this clearly inequitable demand, British and French forces struck: air raids were launched against Egyptian targets on October 31, and on November 5 French and British paratroops attacked and captured Port Said and Port Fuad preparatory to a general advance along the Canal.

Officially, the actions of Britain and France were emergency measures motivated by concern for the safety of navigation through the Canal. In fact, however, they were part of a coordinated British-French-Israeli strategy designed to topple Nasser and weaken Egyptian power. For Britain and France, of course, Nasser's nationalization of the Suez Canal represented a direct threat. In addition, Britain saw Nasser as a general challenge to British policy (particularly to Western security arrangements) in the region, while France had reason to fear him as the major external supporter of the Algerian liberation struggle. For its part, Israel was motivated not only by a desire to halt Egyptian-sponsored guerrilla raids, but also by the hope that military action would both secure free Israeli navigation in the Gulf of Aqaba and bring about the downfall of a leader who had done much to strengthen the unity and harden the resolve of the Arab world.

As early as 3 August, France and Britain had begun to explore the possibility of joint military action against Egypt in response to the nationalization of the Canal. The French had approached Israel in early September and had found that it would be willing to invade Egypt, thus providing the necessary pretext for Anglo-French intervention. On October 14 the idea had been broached to Eden. He was receptive, and two days later talks between Eden, Mollet, and their respective foreign ministers were held in Paris. On October 24 the three countries signed a secret agreement at Sevres committing themselves to the plan. A second agreement between France and Israel committed France to deploy aircraft and naval forces in support of Israel during the conflict.

The actual military operations failed to achieve the aims of the planners, however: British and French action proving insufficient to bring about Nasser's downfall or to reestablish European control of the Canal Zone. Moreover, their actions and the Israeli attack which "provoked" them lacked the support of the United States and were strongly opposed by the Soviet Union. Faced with these grim facts (and with Nasser's resilience), Britain, France, and Israel were forced to back down, and on November 6 a ceasefire went into effect. British and French forces, which had advanced only 23 miles south of Port Said, were withdrawn from Egypt by December, and in March 1957 Israel finally relinquished control of the Gaza Strip to Egypt.

The Retreat from East of Suez

For Britain, the Suez intervention had precisely the opposite effect from that intended. For one thing, Egypt, Syria, and Saudi Arabia broke off diplomatic relations. Also, immediately following Anglo-French intervention Nasser blocked the canal (and hence any movement of oil through it), while on November 3 the Syrian army stopped the flow of oil from Iraq to the Mediterranean through the Iraqi Petroleum Company pipeline. As a result, two-thirds of Western European oil supplies were interrupted, forcing Europe to temporarily fill its needs elsewhere. As for Nasser, far from being removed from power he had gained considerable prestige and influence as a result of his successful resistance to the tripartite attack. Consequently, his revolutionary message of anti-imperialism, neutralism, Arab nationalism, and Arab unity swept through the Middle East. In Iraq, this groundswell led to the overthrow of the pro-Western regime on 14 July 1958 and the effective collapse of the Baghdad Pact.

Britain did continue to exert some direct presence in the Middle East for a few more years: British paratroops were airlifted to Jordan in July 1958 to bolster King Hussein's rule; troops were briefly deployed in Kuwait in 1961 to deter an Iraqi invasion; and British forces remained in Aden until 1967 fighting a rearguard action against nationalist forces. Still, these actions were the last of their kind, and in January 1968 Prime Minister Harold Wilson announced the government's intention to withdraw from east of Suez by the end of 1971. Britain could no longer bear the costs of its far-flung military and political presence; moreover, decolonization of the British Empire had narrowed Britain's strategic interests to Europe and the North Atlantic. In November 1971 Britain terminated its protectorates in the Arab Gulf (encouraging Iran to capitalize on the withdrawal of British power from the area by seizing the islands of Abu Musa and Greater and

Lesser Tumbs). With the British withdrawal the United States assumed an increasing military role and presence in the Middle East. Indeed, when King Hussein faced another threat to his rule in September 1970 it was American and Israeli rather than British offers of support that saved his regime.

Paradoxically, the British military retreat from the Middle East helped it to regain some of the prestige and influence it had lost in 1956. Economic links with Middle Eastern countries expanded, and Britain became a significant supplier of military equipment to Saudi Arabia, the Gulf States, and Jordan. Diplomatically, Britain played a significant role during and after the 1967 Arab-Israeli War. A British resolution (Resolution 242) on the principles of a "just and lasting peace" in the Middle East was unanimously approved by the United Nations Security Council in November 1967, and was subsequently accepted by Egypt, Syria, Jordan, and—with reservations—Israel.

De Gaulle's Middle East Policy

Like Britain, France also failed to achieve its objectives at Suez. With the exception of Lebanon, all independent Arab countries broke off diplomatic relations, and France too was subjected to an interruption of its Middle East oil supplies during the crisis. The war in Algeria continued, as did Egyptian assistance to the FLN—the Suez crisis serving only to buoy the morale of the insurgents. In February 1958 the attempts of yet another French government to legislate reforms concerning the administration of Algeria and the civil and electoral status of Algerians led to bitter opposition from the *colons*, culminating in a *colon* "insurrection" in Algiers on May 13. Such political instability paved the way for the assumption of power by General de Gaulle on June 1.

Once in power, de Gaulle's initial concern was with the consolidation of the Fifth Republic, and his Algerian policy was far from clear. In a broadcast on 16 September 1959, however, he first mentioned the importance of Algerian "self-determination." This provoked a second revolt in Algeria by the *colons* and their military supporters in January 1960, which de Gaulle withstood. In April 1961, elements in the French Army in Algeria attempted a putsch, which was also unsuccessful.

By this time international pressure on France to reach an Algerian settlement had become intense, while at home the French public grew increasingly impatient with the costly and bloody war. Accordingly, in May 1961 talks between the French government and the FLN were held at Evian. These discussions, although inconclusive, paved the way for a second round of negotiations in March of the following year, leading to the so-called Evian Accords of March 19, whereby the two parties agreed to a ceasefire and France agreed to recognize Algerian independence. Voters in France and Algeria subsequently approved the agreement by an overwhelming majority, and on 3 July 1962 Algerian independence was officially proclaimed.[26]

De Gaulle's settlement of the Algerian conflict marked the beginning of a major shift in French policy in the Middle East, a shift that reflected the change in France's status from a colonial power attempting to maintain hegemony to a postcolonial nation seeking international relations of a more balanced and cooperative nature. France did continue to supply Israel with arms, and de Gaulle publicly referred to Israel as a "friendly and allied state."[27] At the same time, however, de Gaulle was trying to improve cultural and economic relations with the Arab world, particularly after 1962 when diplomatic relations were gradually reopened. By the end of the 1960s France had become the second largest supplier of goods to the region, while some 90% of French oil imports flowed from Arab sources.[28] Amid rising Arab-Israeli tensions in the summer of 1967, France supported Israel's claim to free navigation in the Gulf of Aqaba and more generally its "right to exist."[29] Simultaneously, de Gaulle warned that neither the Egyptian blockade nor the removal of the United Nations Emergency Force from the Sinai was grounds for war. When hostilities did break out on June 5, France condemned Israel's aggression and called for a ceasefire.

After the war France supported Resolution 242 in the Security Council. France also expressed concern with the increasing number of Israeli raids against Lebanon in the late 1960s. Following an Israeli attack on Beirut airport in December 1968, de Gaulle announced the suspension of arms shipments to Israel and the Arab confrontation states (excluding Lebanon itself). This suspension was continued by de Gaulle's successors, Georges Pompidou and Giscard d'Estaing. However, France did sell Mirage fighter aircraft to Libya in 1970, despite Israeli fears that they would be transferred to Egypt. That same year Israel pirated from Cherbourg five gunboats that had been ordered by the Israeli navy, but whose delivery had been held up by the arms embargo.

Italy, Spain, and West Germany

The decolonization of Italian and Spanish North Africa, while clearly of less international importance than the decline and transformation of British and French policy in the same region, was nevertheless a significant development in postwar European–Middle East relations. For the former countries, as for Britain and France, decolonization marked the end of direct domination over Middle Eastern territories and the beginning of a shift to bilateral diplomatic, economic, and cultural interaction on a new, more cooperative basis. (West Germany, of course, had no Middle Eastern territory to decolonize. Its growing interest in the area was primarily motivated by economic considerations and, in the case of Israel, feelings of guilt and the pinch of reparations relative to the Nazi holocaust that consumed European Jewry before and during World War II.)

The Second World War dealt a severe blow to Italian colonization in Libya, both physically and politically. Nevertheless, postwar Italian governments, while renouncing all claims to former Italian colonies, hoped to salvage at least a trusteeship over the area. The United States, Britain, France, and the Soviet Union, however, were unable to agree among themselves as to the disposition of the territory, and in 1948 the issue was referred to the United Nations. A last-minute proposal to divide Libya into Italian, British, and French trusteeships was defeated by Soviet and Third World votes in the General Assembly, and on 21 November 1949 the General Assembly approved the formation of a united and independent Libya. In 1956 the two governments finally reached an agreement regarding Italian property rights in Libya, the legal status of Italian colonists, and other outstanding decolonization issues. The Italian community slowly declined in number as many returned to Italy.

In 1959 major oil reserves were discovered in Libya. Following the Libyan Revolution in 1969, the new Libyan government of Col. Muammar Qaddafi announced on 22 July 1970 that Italian properties would be confiscated in compensation for the costs of colonialism and the ravages of World War II, and Italians in Libya were given three months in which to leave the country.

Spain terminated its protectorate over Morocco in 1956, with General Franco recognizing Moroccan independence on April 7. On 1 April 1958, Spain and Morocco reached an agreement on the transfer of Southern Morocco from Spanish to Moroccan control. The decolonization of the Spanish Sahara took somewhat longer, as Spain's lingering colonial dream (to say nothing of the area's important phosphate resources and off-shore fishery) made the Spanish government reluctant to part with the area. In January 1958, in an attempt to avoid United Nations discussion of the fate of Spanish colonial territories, Spain reclassified them as provinces. However, this did not stop the international organization from passing a series of resolutions beginning in December 1965 calling for the decolonization of the Spanish Sahara. After 1973, the Spanish government bowed to the pressure and embarked on a gradual program of self-rule for the region with a goal of eventual independence. However, in November 1975, as Franco lay dying and in an atmosphere of intense diplomatic pressure generated by King Hassan II of Morocco's "Green March," Spain partitioned the Spanish Sahara between Morocco and Mauritania. Such annexation was resisted by the local population, and the sustained guerrilla war that resulted continues to this day.[29]

Although its immediate postwar involvement in the region was minor compared with that of Britain, France, Spain, and Italy, West Germany also showed interest in the Middle East after World War II, as mentioned above. From the 1950s on, Germany pursued two simultaneous policies in the region: first, it sought to expand economic links with the Arab countries; second, it sought to atone for the Nazi persecution of European Jews through support for Israel. Some $1 billion in reparation payments were paid by the West German government to Holocaust survivors in Israel—a flow of capital that played a major role in Israel's early economic development. Germany also began the selling of arms to Israel, and in 1965 it was revealed that a number of U.S.-built M-48 tanks had been transferred by Germany to Israel at the request of the Unites States. 1965 also saw the establishment of diplomatic relations between the two countries.

West Germany's support for Israel, however, served to undermine its attempts to forge strong economic links with the Arab world, and in 1965 the establishment of West German–Israeli diplomatic relations and the revelation of Germany's role in the arms transfers mentioned above created a major breach. West German policy toward Israel was condemned by the League of Arab States in March 1965, and a number of Arab countries, including Iraq, Saudi Arabia, and Egypt, broke off diplomatic relations with West Germany for several years. West Germany was among those nations subject to the ineffectual Arab oil embargo of 1967.

West German relations with both Israel and the Arab world improved during the 1970s, although the presence of Palestinian groups in Germany and the 1972 Black September attack against Israeli athletes at the Munich Olympics provided an irritant to both German-Israeli and German-Arab relations. Generally, West Germany sought to depoliticize its involvement in the Middle East, avoiding any entanglements in the Arab-Israeli dispute that might jeopardize its expanding economic activity in the region. Germany's postwar involvement in the Middle East typified the emergence of new European linkages, associations based not on the remnants of empire but rather on a more symmetrical basis—deriving, that is, not from the desire to maintain an existing position, but rather from the desire to establish a new one.

Middle East Oil in a Changing World

In the aftermath of World War II one feature of the Middle East—its vast petroleum resources—gained increasing importance in Western European eyes. Postwar industrialization led to a worldwide demand for oil and gas that increased at an average rate of 7.8% after 1950. European demand increased even more sharply, from 414 thousand barrels per day in 1940 to 1198 thousand in 1950 to 3,848 thousand by 1960. The Middle East itself became an increasingly important source of this oil for the world in general and for Western Europe in particular. Before the Suez Crisis of 1956, some 78% of Western Europe's oil imports came from the Middle East.

Still, the structure of the world petroleum market remained highly favorable to Western interests. Seven fully integrated multinational oil companies—one British, one Dutch, the rest American—dominated all aspects of pricing and production, and in some cases paid more in taxes to their home governments than they paid in royalties to the oil-producing countries. When the domination of these companies and the pricing and revenue structures associated with them were challenged by Middle Eastern countries (as they were in Iran in 1951–53, for example), the companies could count upon the support of their home governments. Furthermore, despite increasing consumption, the worldwide supply of oil continued to run ahead of demand into the 1960s. This not only kept prices relatively low but also bolstered the bargaining power of the companies and consumers. In short, it was a buyer's market.

This situation began to change in the late 1960s, when world oil demand began to equal, and then to exceed, supply. In Europe alone, consumption climbed to 12,450 barrels per day in 1970—an amount equivalent to over ten times 1950 levels. At the same time, the oil-producing countries banded together to form the Organization of Petroleum Exporting Countries (OPEC) in 1960 and the Organization of Arab Oil Exporting Countries (OAPEC) in 1968 in an effort to alter through collective action the prevailing market structure. As discussed in chapter 2, such developments, coupled with the emergence of numerous small oil companies anxious to break the existing oligopoly, led to a revolution in the oil market in 1970–72 whereby the countries of the Middle East successfully gained control over oil pricing and production. Thus, as the 1970s arrived, a final link subordinating the Middle East to Europe and the West was showing signs of fundamental change.

Overview: Decline and Withdrawal

In contrast to the imperialist phase of European–Middle East relations (and as a direct result of it), the period roughly between 1920 and 1971 was one of declining European influence in the Middle East, characterized by the withdrawal of the European military and administrative presence there. The very elites whose position had been established or bolstered by the colonial powers in the earlier phase were the first to seek political autonomy, and—however much Hussein, Faisal, Nuri al-Said and the Wafd may be viewed with suspicion by a contemporary generation of Arab nationalists—it is undeniable that they played a major role in ending direct colonial rule and facilitating ever greater degrees of local independence. The first British preferential treaties negotiated in Transjordan and Iraq with such nationalists in the 1920s soon had a ripple effect, stimulating demands for the same in Syria, Lebanon, and Egypt, and leading to the establishment of a looser, more indirect form of European influence that would endure until after World War II.

Later in this second phase of modern West European–Middle East relations, World War II marked a turning point in national emancipation for a variety of reasons. First, it severely weakened the colonial powers, including their control over the Middle East. Second, wartime and postwar industrialization increased world demand for Middle East oil, altering the strategic value of the area in Western eyes and ultimately precipitating a transformation of the entire relationship between the oil companies and consuming nations on the one hand, and the oil-producing countries on the other. Last, the war and its aftermath saw accelerated industrial development in the Middle East itself. This in turn fostered the growth of an Arab intelligentsia and professional and working classes. These enjoyed greater political consciousness than had been the case among the traditional peasantry and tribal elements, and they were more successful in organizing and carrying out nationalist agitation. The armies of the newly independent Arab states often provided a further training ground and arsenal for the pursuit of nationalist aspirations, and the army was often the avenue that this new, more radical nationalist leadership would follow to gain power.

Palestine provided an important and spectacular rallying point for all Arab nationalists, simultaneously embodying the very essence of the colonial relationship (foreign control, the denial of independence and autonomous development) and striking at the heart of the Arab world's cultural identity and national conciousness. Indeed, it was the shock of Palestine that ultimately laid bare the limitations of the old (bourgeois nationalist) regimes, and triggered the transformation of the Middle East system and the emergence of new, radical anti-imperialist regimes in Egypt (1952), Syria (1956), and Iraq (1958). Nasser's role in advancing transformation throughout the Middle East system was very important—a role that was correctly perceived (although unsuccessfully attacked) by Britain, France, and Israel at Suez.

What was the European response to such developments—to this growing challenge to their position in the Middle East? At first, having found the opposition to direct control too great to suppress, Britain and France sought accommodation with the established nationalist elite through preferential treaties. After the war, however, the emergence of a new nationalist element threatened even these indirect mechanisms of foreign control, at the same time that the decolonization of other regions—British India, French Indo-China—made the Middle East less important as a colonial line of communication and created another global ripple effect of decolonization.

Up until the Suez Crisis of 1956 both Britain and France sought to stem the nationalist tide through economic embargo (the Iranian oil nationalization, discussed in Chapter 2, is an example), alliance arrangements (the Baghdad Pact), and military force. After Suez, however, both countries were spent as dominant forces in the Middle East, and while some fighting continued (Algeria, Aden) the remainder of the 1950s and 1960s were generally a period of measured withdrawal. By 1971, with the British withdrawal from the Arab Gulf, West European–Middle East relations were entering a new era, one based on economic interaction and diplomacy between sovereign units rather on domination, occupation, and control. Furthermore, this interaction soon took on a multilateral rather than bilateral guise as the European Community and the League of Arab States assumed the responsibility for transforming the relationship into a truly interregional one.

WESTERN EUROPE AND THE MIDDLE EAST IN THE 1970s

With the absence of any dominating European presence in the Middle East (except in Djibouti), relations between Western Europe and the Middle East could be reordered on a new, more cooperative, and better balanced basis. This process was well established before October 1973, as evidenced by the foreign policies of post-Algeria France and West Germany in particular, and on a multilateral level by the European Communities' (EC) unpublicized attempts to draw up a unified position on the Middle East conflict in 1971. However, it was the 1973 Arab-Israeli War that triggered the major change in interregional relations. When war between Israel and its Arab neighbors erupted again on 6 October 1973, the reactions of West European nations were mixed. Spain, for its part, expressed support for the Arab cause. French Foreign Minister Michel Jobert noted France's preference for a "peaceful and negotiated" settlement to the conflict, but also questioned whether Arab efforts to regain territories occupied by Israel could really be considered as an act of aggression.[31]

Britain proved highly reluctant to comment on the rights and wrongs of the conflict; generally speaking, the government confined itself to calls for a ceasefire and expressions of hope that a peace settlement could be achieved based on Security Council resolution 242. Britain did declare an embargo on arms shipments to the combatants on October 10—a decision that according to the Times (London) 17 October 1973 was condemned as pro-Arab both by Israel and by many British backbenchers. Britain also denied the United States the use of British facilities for the latter's military resupply of Israel. Italy, Austria, Belgium, and West Germany adopted a concerned but neutral position on the conflict, and when the West German government learned that the United States had been loading military equipment on Israeli ships at Bremerhaven, it lodged a formal diplomatic protest

and stressed its "strict neutrality" in the war. Denmark and the Netherlands, on the other hand, openly declared their support for Israel and
accused Egypt and Syria of aggression, while Portugal allowed the
Azores to be used in American resupply operations. On October 13
the then nine members of the European Communities (EC) issued
a joint communique calling for a ceasefire and efforts toward a negotiated settlement of the Arab-Israeli conflict based on Security Council resolution 242.

The Oil Embargo

In formulating their positions on the October 1973 Arab-Israeli
War, virtually every European nation was forced to take into account
the changes in the world petroleum market that had taken place in
recent years. As we have seen, in the early 1970s a number of Middle
East countries asserted domestic control over their national petroleum
resources. At the same time, Western Europe's dependence on Middle East oil had grown dramatically: by October 1973, Europe was im-
porting some 80% of its oil from the Middle East, with all but 20%
of that flowing from Arab countries. Finally, the general growth in
world energy demands had resulted in a shift of economic power
from the consumers to the producers, as oil supplies no longer ex-
ceeded oil demand. In 1956 and again in 1967, interruptions of Arab
oil supplies had only a minimal impact on Western nations, because
of oversupply and the general Western domination of petroleum production (and of the petroleum-producing countries). Now, however,
the extension of national sovereignty over Middle East petroleum
resources, coupled with the importance of Middle East oil to Western
European energy requirements and the lack of excess global petroleum supplies, put the Arab countries for the first time in a position
to use the "oil weapon" effectively against Israel's supporters in the
Arab-Israeli conflict.

Well before the outbreak of hostilities in October 1973, Arab
oil producers had discussed the possible effectiveness of an oil embargo as a means for furthering the liberation of Israeli-occupied Arab
territories. On 17 October these discussions were transformed into
practice when Saudi Arabia, Kuwait, Iraq, Libya, Algeria, Egypt, Abu
Dhabi, Bahrain, and Qatar announced that they would cut oil production by 5% per month until Israel withdrew from the occupied territories. Later, on November 4, the Organization of Arab Petroleum

Exporting Countries (OAPEC) decreed a 25% production cut. Arab oil producers also embargoed all oil supplies to the Netherlands and the United States as a protest of their support of Israel, while Britain and France were exempted from production cutbacks because of their apparent sympathy to the Arab cause. Iraq went a step further by nationalizing U.S. (October 7) and Dutch (October 21) interests in the Basrah Petroleum Company.

The Netherlands, heavily reliant on oil imports from the Middle East, was severely hit by the embargo, and emergency restrictions on and rationing of what energy supplies remained were immediately put into effect. Moreover, most other European nations (particularly West Germany and Belgium) were seriously affected, since much of their oil supply was routed through Rotterdam and Dutch refineries. In any event, those countries with sufficient energy—notably Britain and France—were reluctant to anger their Arab oil suppliers by assisting the Netherlands, and a major diplomatic rift opened up within the EC as a result. The embargo lasted until March 1974, and during this period the price of oil increased nearly three-fold—not because of the embargo per se, but because of a collective decision by members of the OPEC cartel.

The embargo had a significant effect on the energy policies of Western European nations and the EC, and—as will be discussed below—the search for energy security became a major area of concern in European capitals after 1973. The embargo also had a significant impact on the formal positions of European nations regarding the Arab-Israeli dispute. Meeting in Brussels on 6 November 1973 in the midst of the crisis, the foreign ministers of the Nine passed a resolution on the Middle East conflict that was widely regarded at the time as signalling a tilt toward the Arab view. The statement, while calling for negotiations on the basis of Security Council resolution 242, was significant in stressing the "need for Israel to put an end to the territorial occupation which it has maintained since the 1967 conflict" and its recognition that "the legitimate rights of the Palestinians must be taken into account in the establishment of a just and lasting peace."[32]

Subsequently, foreign ministers from the Sudan, Algeria, and Tunisia and a minister from the United Arab Emirates traveled to a Common Market summit in Copenhagen to inform EC leaders that, while their common position was encouraging, greater support for the Arab cause was desirable. At that time, the Nine issued a statement calling for "negotiations with oil-producing countries on comprehensive arrangements comprising cooperation on a wide scale for the economic and industrial development of these countries, industrial investments, and stable energy supplies to member countries at reasonable prices."[33] European statements played a part in OAPEC's decision to exempt all of Europe except the Netherlands from the planned December 1973 production cutbacks. On December 25 OAPEC further announced that the flow of oil to Europe would be increased by 10% in January.

The Euro-Arab Dialogue

The Brussels and Copenhagen declarations of 1973 marked the beginning of what was subsequently called the "Euro-Arab dialogue" between the EC and the Arab world. This dialogue came into being formally on 31 July 1974 when a one-day meeting between the President of the European Commission, the acting President of the EC Council of Ministers, and the President and Secretary-General of the League of Arab States produced an agreement on preliminary work aimed at establishing an institutional structure for continued discussion on a variety of economic, technological, social, and cultural issues.[34] Because Arab petroleum policy was formulated and coordinated through OPEC, energy issues were not included among the topics for discussion.

During the following months, political difficulties arose which threatened the future of the Euro-Arab dialogue. For one thing, the United States opposed some aspects of the dialogue when it was first announced, fearing that European initiatives on energy and the Arab-Israeli conflict would interfere with its own diplomatic activities. Difficulties also arose because of European objections to the PLO's participation in the dialogue on the Arab side. Finally, EC negotiation of a preferential trade agreement with Israel (concluded on 11 May 1975) placed a strain on EC-Arab relations. Because of such difficulties, the first meeting of the General Committee of the Euro-Arab Dialogue did not occur before December 1974 as originally planned, but not until May 1976, in Luxembourg. By that time, U.S. concerns had diminished, and the question of PLO representation had been resolved by the so-called Dublin formula of February 1975 whereby the Nine proposed that the dialogue avoid discussion of political issues and that delegations be homogeneous and regional. PLO delegates subsequently participated in the dialogue as members of a unified Arab League delegation.[35]

In addition to meetings of the various specific committees of the Euro-Arab dialogue, the General Committee met in June 1976 (Brussels), February 1977 (Tunis), October 1977 (Brussels), and December 1978 (Damascus). During this period, EC-Arab trade increased dramatically. EC exports to the Arab countries rose from $8.65 billion (or 6.7% of all extra-EC exports) in 1973 to $40.97 billion (15.8%) in 1979. Arab exports to the Nine similarly increased, from $14.91 billion in 1973 to $55.58 billion six years later. By 1979, imports from and exports to the EC accounted for over one-third of all Arab trade.[36] Preferential trade and cooperation agreements were signed with all the Mediterranean Arab states (except Libya) and Jordan in 1976–77. Moreover, as Arab petroleum revenues multiplied in the aftermath of the 1973–74 increases in world oil prices, Europe became a primary target of petrodollar investment. By the end of 1979 Arab private and state deposits in European banks alone stood at approximately $106 billion.[37]

While the Euro-Arab dialogue and the Mediterranean trade policy adopted by the European Communities in October 1972 played a major role in the expansion of economic interaction between the two regions, other factors were also important. In particular, increases in petroleum prices and petrodollar-induced import demand served to increase the value of EC-Arab trade. Moreover, as the 1970s progressed, it became apparent that the Euro-Arab dialogue suffered from serious shortcomings. The exclusion of contentious energy and political issues from the formal structure of the dialogue, for example, served to limit its utility to its European and Arab participants, respectively. At the same time, the Arab side encountered great difficulty in forming a unified regional stance on many issues, and often found themselves at a disadvantage when faced with highly skilled and tightly coordinated European delegations. By late 1979, the Camp David negotiations had rendered the problem of Arab unity insurmountable, and in April 1980 the Arab League requested that the dialogue be suspended.

Western Europe and the Palestine Question

As already noted, the 1973 Arab-Israeli War and the oil embargo associated with it combined to encourage the beginning of a significant shift in European positions on the question of Palestine. The Brussels declaration of November 1973 signaled the beginning of a new, unified, multilateral European approach to the issue within the structure of the EC. Such an approach reflected Europe's increased desire to boost its diplomatic stature and pursue a coordinated European foreign policy distinct from that of the United States—a desire that had been evident in the Community for many years before the 1973 war, and which had found expression in the Davignon Report on European political cooperation of 1970. Furthermore, a "Euro-approach" to the Middle East had the added advantage of allowing individual EC members to occasionally decouple thorny political issues from their bilateral economic dealings with Israel and the Arab world, thus facilitating the latter. The Euro-Arab dialogue, although not formally addressing the Palestine issue, did allow the League of Arab States to impress its importance upon their European counterparts. This was particularly evident at the end of the 1978 Damascus meeting of the General Committee, when the Arab delegation warned that the progress of future discussion would be closely tied to European acceptance of the PLO as the sole legitimate representative of the Palestinian people. In addition, it is reasonable to assume that the increased European-Arab interaction fostered by the dialogue also served to increase the salience of the Arab-Israeli conflict in European capitals.

As the 1970s progressed, the EC produced a number of important statements on the Arab-Israeli dispute. In June 1977 a meeting of the EC council of ministers in London released a communique in which they affirmed their belief that any solution to conflict in the region must take into account "the need for a homeland for the Palestinian people," and that all parties must participate in any negotiations.[38] 1978 saw French, Irish and Dutch troops participate with EC blessings in the United Nations Interim Force in Lebanon (UNIFIL), deployed in southern Lebanon after the Israeli invasion of March. The next year, following the conclusion of the Camp David accords, the EC issued a number of statements that combined cautious support for the American-sponsored agreement with continued emphasis on the need for a comprehensive settlement of the Arab-Israeli dispute that recognized the legitimate rights of the Palestinian people.

It was in 1980, however, that the EC issued its most important statement on the question of Palestine. The Venice Declaration of 13 June 1980 saw the assembled leaders of the Nine declare that "the time has come to promote the recognition and implementation of the two principles universally accepted by the international community: the right to existence and to security of all States in the region, including Israel, and justice for all peoples, which implies recognition of the legitimate rights of the Palestinian people."[39] They also declared that all countries in the region were entitled to live in peace within secure and recognized borders; that the Palestinian people must be allowed to exercise its right of self-determination; that all parties (including the PLO) must be involved in negotiations; and that Israel should withdraw from the territories occupied since 1967. They condemned Israeli settlements in the occupied territories, rejected unilateral changes of the status of Jerusalem, and called for all parties to renounce the use of force. Finally, they announced that they had decided to make the contacts necessary to further the EC initiative — an oblique reference to the PLO.

EC Statement on the Middle East, 13 June 1980, "VENICE DECLARATION," quoted from *Bulletin of the European Communities* 13, no. 6 (1980): 10–11:

1. The heads of State or Government and the Ministers of Foreign Affairs held a comprehensive exchange of views on all aspects of the present situation in the Middle East, including the state of negotiations resulting from the agreements signed between Egypt and Israel in March 1979. They agreed that growing tensions affecting this region constitute a serious danger and render a comprehensive solution to the Israeli-Arab conflict more necessary and pressing than ever.

2. The nine Member States of the European Community consider that the traditional ties and common interests which link Europe to the Middle East oblige them to play a special role and now require them to work in a more concrete way towards peace.

3. In this regard, the nine countries of the Community base themselves on Security Council Resolutions 242 and 338 and the positions which they have expressed on several occasions, notably in their Declarations of 29 June 1977, 19 September 1978, and 18 June 1979, as well as in the speech made on their behalf on 25 September 1979 by the Irish Minister of Foreign Affairs at the thirty-fourth United Nations General Assembly.

4. On the bases thus set out, the time has come to promote the recognition and implementation of the two principles universally accepted by the international community: the right to existence and to security of all the States in the region, including Israel, and justice for all the peoples, which implies the recognition of the legitimate rights of the Palestinian people.

5. All of the countries in the area are entitled to live in peace within secure, recognized and guaranteed borders. The necessary guarantees for a peace settlement should be provided by the UN by a decision of the Security Council and, if necessary, on the basis of other mutually agreed procedures. The Nine declare that they are prepared to participate within the framework of a comprehensive settlement in a system of concrete and binding international guarantees, including (guarantees) on the ground.

6. A just solution must finally be found to the Palestinian problem, which is not simply one of refugees. The Palestinian people, who are conscious of existing as such, must be placed in a position, by an appropriate process defined within the framework of the comprehensive peace settlement, to exercise fully their right to self-determination.

7. The achievement of these objectives requires the involvement and support of all the parties concerned in the peace settlement which the Nine are endeavouring to promote in keeping with the principles formulated in the declaration referred to above. These principles apply to all the parties concerned, and thus the Palestinian people, and to the PLO, which will have to be associated with the negotiations.

8. The Nine recognize the special importance of the role played by the question of Jerusalem for all the parties concerned. The Nine stress that they will not accept any unilateral initiative designed to change the status of Jerusalem and that any agreement on the city's status should guarantee freedom of access for everyone to the Holy Places.

9. The Nine stress the need for Israel to put an end to the territorial occupation which it has maintained since the conflict of 1967, as it has done for part of Sinai. They are deeply convinced that the Israeli settlements constitute a serious obstacle to the peace process in the Middle East. The Nine consider that these settlements, as well as modifications in population and property in the occupied Arab territories, are illegal under international law.

10. Concerned as they are to put an end to violence, the Nine consider that only the renunciation of force or the threatened use of force by all the parties can create a climate of confidence in the area, and constitute a basic element for a comprehensive settlement of the conflict in the Middle East.

11. The Nine have decided to make the necessary contacts with all the parties concerned. The objective of these contacts would be to ascertain the position of the various parties with respect to the principles set out in this declaration and in the light of the results of this consultation process to determine the form which such an initiative on their part could take.

Most Arab countries and the PLO greeted most of the elements of the Venice Declaration as a step in the right direction, although for the PLO and its Arab supporters the Europeans' failure to recognize the PLO as the "sole legitimate representative of the Palestinian people" was a major disappointment. In its official response to the declaration, the Palestinian organization criticized this failure — the Europeans' adherence to Security Council resolution 242, and their unwillingness to reject Camp David — and the statement's perceived vagueness about Palestinian national rights and the nature of an Israeli withdrawal from the occupied territories. The PLO also stated that it welcomed the European move, but called upon Europe to "take more independent stances and to free themselves of the pressures and blackmail of US policy." Israel strongly condemned the declaration, categorizing it as a "Munich-like surrender, the second in our generation, to tyrannic extortion, and an encouragement to all the elements which are undermining the Camp David accords." Israeli Prime Minister Menachem Begin stated that the European powers were, because of their failure to save the Jewish population of Europe during World War II, unqualified to advise Israel on its policies. Begin also criticized the EC for seeking to "interfere with the status of Jerusalem, our eternal capital, which is not subject to any division, and our right to settle and live in Eretz Yisrael." For its part, the United States had in the months prior to the Venice Summit attempted to head off any European declaration that might tend to undermine its own Camp David peace process. It now cautiously welcomed the "sense of restraint" shown by the EC statement, and expressed the hope that Europe would support, rather than undermine, U.S.-sponsored peace efforts.[40]

After the Venice declaration, successive presidents of the Community's council of ministers traveled to the Middle East in an attempt to further the initiative: Gaston Thorn in 1980, Van der Klaauw and Lord Carrington in 1981, and Leo Tindemans in 1982. However, in the face of a mixed reception both in the Arab capitals and from the PLO, implacable hostility to the declaration on the part of Israel, and developments within the Middle East itself nothing was achieved. The United States was especially annoyed at Europe's attempt to involve itself in the Arab-Israeli dispute at a time when Washington was attempting to shore up its own faltering Camp David–inspired peace process. Considerable friction arose in 1981–82 between US Secretary of State Alexander Haig and British Foreign Secretary Lord Carrington over the latter's opposition to European participation in the multinational Sinai observer force which was to monitor compliance with the Egyptian-Israeli treaty. This tension became still more acute when, during a visit to Saudi Arabia, Carrington criticized the Camp David accords and praised the peace plan proposed by Saudi Arabian Crown Prince Fahd.[41]

Europe and Energy

A second major development in Western European–Middle Eastern relations during this period centered on the EC's attempts to reduce energy dependence on the Arab world. A variety of measures were employed, individually and collectively, in an attempt to achieve this objective. First, Europe sought to lessen its dependence on oil, the price of which was quadrupled by OPEC members between 1972 and 1974. In December 1974, the EC Council of Ministers approved a plan that proposed to reduce the Community's dependence on oil from 61.4 percent of European energy needs in 1973 to 41 percent in 1985 through corresponding increases in the utilization of natural gas and nuclear power.[42] Second, Europe sought to secure alternative, non-Arab oil supplies. The most important of these were to be found in Europe's own North Sea reserves. North Sea oil production, rendered economically feasible now by the increasing world price of oil, grew from a negligible amount in 1973 to 2.2 million barrels per day by 1980—enough to satisfy approximately one-sixth of Western European oil requirements. (The EC also showed a heightened interest in Latin American and South East Asian oil reserves.) Finally, Western Europe implemented various energy conservation measures after 1973–74. These measures, together with the high price of oil and an economic atmosphere of recession, contributed to a 2.5 percent reduction in EC energy consumption in 1976, and a stabilization of European oil consumption during the latter half of the 1970s at a level slightly below that of 1973.

European energy diversification policies proved moderately successful: the EC's dependence on Arab fuel products dropped from 62 percent in 1973 to 42 percent eight years later. At the same time, European energy policies made for a certain amount of diplomatic friction with other nations. The United States and Europe differed sharply over how best to deal with the economic problems and future dangers created by the energy crisis. The United States was particularly unhappy with the decision to construct a natural gas pipeline from the USSR to Western Europe, seeing it as a means by which the

Soviet Union could increase its political leverage in Europe. In a very different vein, tension also arose between OPEC and European oil producers outside the cartel. OPEC argued that British and Norwegian production and price-cutting was a serious threat to the stability and profitability of the world petroleum market.[43]

The importance of European attempts to reduce energy dependence on oil generally and on the Middle East specifically was highlighted in 1979–80, when the Iranian revolution and Iran-Iraq War caused world oil prices to increase still further. When the Gulf war broke out in 1980, the EC imported approximately 10 percent of its crude oil supplies from Iraq and 4 percent from Iran, while some 58 percent of European oil imports passed through the Arab Gulf and the Straits of Hormuz.[44] It soon became apparent, however, that more than adequate supplies could easily be secured from elsewhere in an increasingly oil-surplus world market.

OVERVIEW: EUROPOLICY AND THE MIDDLE EAST

The third phase of modern European–Middle East relations—that of "Europolicy"—lasted only for approximately one decade between 1970 and 1980. The impetus behind this approach was not only the oil crisis of 1973–74, but also the general growth of importance of the European Community and the desire on the part of many European states to pursue a coordinated, distinctly European foreign policy. Europolicy toward the Middle East was thus not only a European response to political and economic circumstances, but the test case for a new style of European diplomacy.

The Euro-Arab dialogue and the Venice declaration represented something of an apogee for this approach, and as the 1980s progressed the importance of multilateral interaction on a regional basis between Western Europe and the Middle East declined. A number of factors contributed to this situation. To begin with, formulating a common European approach to Middle East issues was always a difficult process, with differing perceptions of and interests in the region inhibiting the formation of any meaningful policy consensus. For some EC countries (Denmark, Luxembourg, the Netherlands), the Venice declaration was as far as they were willing to go; others (Britain, West Germany, Belgium) believed the declaration struck an appropriate balance between Palestinian rights and Israeli security; still others (France,

Italy, Ireland), finally, felt the declaration did not go far enough in upholding Palestinian rights. The entry of Greece into the EC in 1981 complicated matters still further, for the Greek government was strongly supportive of the PLO and the Palestinian cause.[45]

U.S. opposition to European initiatives on the Middle East also had a significant effect on European diplomacy toward the Middle East. The election of Margaret Thatcher in Britain in 1979 and of Ronald Reagan in the United States in 1980 served to strengthen U.S.-British political cooperation (although to a degree at the expense of a distinct European position). At the same time, the replacement of Giscard d'Estaing with Francois Mitterand in France saw that country abandon its earlier role as the driving force behind a common EC Middle East policy in favor of bilateral dealings.

The Camp David accords, the Iranian Revolution and ensuing Iran-Iraq War, the Israeli invasion of Lebanon, and the split in the PLO has diverted Arab attention inward, and fostered divisions which make Arab contacts with Europe on a regional basis difficult, while simultaneously changing the political context within which any settlement would take place. The growing value of the petrodollar-rich Middle East as a source of investment capital and as a market for European exports has fostered considerable competition among West European countries, making multilateral policy cooperation or coordination still more difficult. Finally, the drop in world oil prices and, more important, the increase in world supply since 1980 has reduced the salience of the Middle East in European eyes. According to figures released by the U.S. Department of Energy, North Sea production grew to approximately 3.5 million barrels per day in 1984, an amount sufficient to meet about one-quarter of Western Europe's oil requirements. In the 1980s Europe's major energy problem has become not that of supply, then, but rather of the high value of the U.S. dollar used in most petroleum transactions.

RELATIONS IN THE 1980s: THE NEW BILATERALISM

The decline of multilateral European initiatives in the Middle East has been manifest in a number of ways. The announcement by Britain, France, Ireland, and the Netherlands on 23 November 1981 that they would participate in the U.S.-sponsored Sinai Multinational Force and Observers (MFO), and their clarification two days later that such participation was not linked to the Venice declaration, provided clear evidence of the demise of the Euro-approach. Israel, still resentful of the Venice declaration, in fact made such a disavowal (and an acceptance of Camp David) prerequisites for European participation. Furthermore, the absence of any major developments in a coordinated European position since June 1980, statements by European foreign ministers regarding the unlikelihood of new initiatives in the near future, and the lack of coordination between the nations participating in the Beirut multinational force of 1982–84 are all indications of an emerging new bilateralism in European-Middle East relations.

For most countries in Western Europe, however, this new bilateralism is motivated primarily by economic and commercial interest. Faced with stagnant domestic economies, these countries have found that an active commercial policy aimed at the Middle East promises a lucrative payoff in exports and investment. Political statements and diplomatic activity, no longer prerequisites for a significant presence in the divided Arab world, are seen as threatening too much cost for too little benefit. The result is what might be called *mercantilist* foreign policies. France is the major exception to this approach, continuing to pursue an active independent Middle East policy in the Gaullist tradition despite the election of a non-Gaullist government under Francois Mitterand. Nevertheless, even in the case of France, economic motives still rank high, and coordinated Europolicy has been rejected in favor of bilateral diplomacy. Given this new bilateralism that characterizes West European–Middle East relations in the 1980s, we will now examine the contemporary nature of European policy toward the Middle East on a country-by-country basis.

France

As has already been shown, French policy in the Middle East since the late 1960s has done its best to cultivate friendly and close relations with the Arab countries. Under de Gaulle, Pompidou, and Giscard d'Estaing, France became a major trading partner and weapons supplier to the Arab countries—much to the dismay of Israel. Moreover, French policy sought to expand French involvement in the region. In addition to maintaining its ties with formerly French-administered territories (particularly Lebanon, Morocco, Tunisia, and Algeria), French policy placed considerable emphasis on the Arab Gulf states—notably Iraq and Saudi Arabia. With the former, France benefited from Soviet-Iraqi differences, and supplied fighter aircraft and other military equipment. The scope of cooperation between Saudi Arabia and France was clearly evident not only in terms of arms sales, but also in the assistance that French experts provided the Saudi Arabian forces who recaptured the Kabaa at Mecca from Islamic fundamentalists in 1979, and in the internal security cooperation agreement signed between the two countries the following year.

With the election of Francois Mitterand as president in May 1981, however, many observers predicted a major shift in France's approach to the Middle East. Certainly, Mitterand's Socialist Party, in addition to its traditional pro-Israeli sympathies, had been highly critical during the French election campaign of Giscard d'Estaing's support for the Arab cause, including his willingness to supply arms to the Arab countries. The extent to which a shift has and has not taken place in French diplomacy provides a good indication of the interests and constraints operating on French policy in the region.

In fact, however, despite the thrust of Mitterand's views before the election, French-Israeli relations have seen no improvement since 1981, nor has the new Socialist government proven any less cooperative with the Arab states. Israel's 6 June 1981 raid against Iraq's Osiraq nuclear reactor (which resulted in the death of one French technician) presented one obstacle to rapprochement early in Mitterand's term. France was naturally angered by the attack, while the Israeli government was far from happy with France's offer to supply Iraq with a second reactor (albeit with the imposition of more stringent safeguards on its use). Still, relations had improved significantly by the time French Foreign Minister Claude Cheysson traveled to Israel in December. During this visit Cheysson implicitly signaled the demise of the multilateral European approach to the Arab-Israeli conflict when he noted that no new European initiatives on the issue were to be expected. Cheysson's visit paved the way for Mitterand himself to visit Israel in March 1982—the first such visit of a French head of state to that country.

From this high point, France and Israel moved sharply apart with Israel's invasion of Lebanon in June. France, with extensive cultural and political ties to the Lebanese Republic, was outraged by the invasion, and Mitterand strongly condemned Israel's actions, likening them to the World War II Nazi massacre of French civilians at Oradour. Such criticism, combined with an upsurge of anti-Jewish incidents in France, led Israeli Prime Minister Begin to describe French statements and the French media as fostering antisemitism—a charge which served only to hasten further the deterioration of bilateral relations.

During the Israeli invasion of Lebanon and siege of Beirut, France (often in association with Egypt) was very active in seeking an end to the conflict. In June, a French-sponsored resolution calling for a ceasefire and disengagement of forces was vetoed in the United Nations Security Council by the United States. In August, France contributed a contingent to the multinational peacekeeping force that oversaw the departure of PLO and Syrian troops from Beirut, and French troops returned to Lebanon the following month in response to the massacre of Palestinian civilians at the Sabra and Shatila refugee camps. During their stay, the 2,100-strong French force was subjected to an increasing number of attacks from those Lebanese groups that opposed both France's apparent backing of Lebanese President Amin Gemayel and its support for Iraq in the Gulf War. The most serious of these attacks occured on 23 October 1983, when a truck-bomb destroyed a French military headquarters in Beirut, killing 56 French soldiers. France responded to this particular incident with retaliatory air raids against the fundamentalist Shi'ite group believed responsible.

The years 1982–84 also saw differences developing between France and the United States over the role of the multinational force and the best method of achieving a peace settlement: France was critical of U.S. attempts to negotiate a Lebanese-Israeli—rather than a more comprehensive—agreement, and further claimed that U.S. military assistance to the Lebanese government jeopardized the neutrality and security of its peacekeepers. French troops remained in Lebanon until March 1984.

In addition to the Beirut multinational force, France contributed forces to several other peacekeeping operations. Five French warships provided an escort to Greek ships evacuating pro-Arafat PLO forces from the Lebanese city of Tripoli in December 1983, and French ships were provided for multinational minesweeping operations in the Red Sea the following year. French troops also continued to serve with UNIFIL in southern Lebanon, and with the MFO in the Sinai.

Despite Israel's continued occupation of Lebanon, French-Israeli relations improved in 1984, particularly after Labour Party leader Shimon Peres became prime minister of an Israeli coalition government in September. Trade between the countries remained relatively stable at $569 million in 1984.[46] In December Peres visited France, and praised France's "important and constructive role in the search for peace." (For his part, Mitterand offered to supply Israel with nuclear reactors.) In the aftermath of Peres's Paris trip, the Israeli press noted the renewed warmth of French-Israeli ties, remarking that they represented "a return to normality rather than a revival of the love affair that characterized relations between France and Israel in the Fifties and Sixties."[47] Israeli actions in southern Lebanon remained a major irritant in bilateral relations into 1985, however.

Throughout his period in office it has been apparent that Mitterand has not allowed rapprochement with Israel to come at the expense of France's extensive economic and political interests in the Arab world, or of its diplomatic stance in support of Palestinian national rights. Thus, almost immediately upon assuming power, Mitterand launched a diplomatic offensive designed to reassure Arab countries of continued French friendship.[48] Particular emphasis was placed on strengthening friendly ties with Saudi Arabia, a country that supplied 55% of French oil imports and purchased $1.9 billion in French goods in 1981, and which had placed a lucrative order for $3.1 billion worth of naval vessels and helicopters with Mitterand's predecessor a year earlier. Mindful of Arab sensibilities, and in accordance with the French government's continued stance on the issue, Mitterand made a point during his March 1982 visit of urging Israel to recognize the legitimate rights of the Palestinian people by allowing the creation of a Palestinian state in the occupied territories. Mitterand's use of the term "state" in this context was particularly significant, since earlier French presidents (and the language of the Venice declaration of June 1980) had restricted their support to a Palestinian "homeland."

French efforts to retain and if possible expand ties to the Arab world while simultaneously improving relations with Israel appear to have been thus far successful. France enjoys very good political and economic relations with most Arab countries, and especially with the Arab Gulf states and with all of North Africa except Libya. In 1984 France imported goods (primarily oil) worth $10.1 billion from Arab countries, while exporting goods worth $11.4 billion in exchange. Algeria has continued to represent France's major trading partner in the Middle East, with French exports and imports to and from Algeria valued at $2.7 and $2.8 billion, respectively.[49] Overall, the Arab world accounts for about 11 percent of all French exports. At the same time, this figure (and the dollar amount of French exports, too) have shown no clear growth in recent years. This reflects the effect of stagnant or declining oil revenues on Arab oil producers, and has only served to sharpen commercial rivalry in the area.

One area in which France has had significant economic success is in arms sales. In addition to the 1980 Franco-Saudi arms deal noted above, it was revealed in January 1984 that France had secured a further Saudi order for $4.3 billion worth of air defense equipment —the largest foreign arms sale in French history. The Middle East has in fact become the largest regional market for French weapons, accounting for 76.6 percent of total French arms exports in 1984, or some $5.1 billion.[50]

Among all of the Arab countries, France's links to Iraq have acquired perhaps the greatest international significance in light of their impact on the continuing Iran-Iraq War. Since the outbreak of the war, France has continued to rank with the Soviet Union as one of Iraq's largest arms suppliers (despite Mitterand's pre-election criticism of such sales). Between 1980 and mid-1984, French arms sales to Iraq were valued at some $5 billion, constituting 40% of all French exports to the country in 1982. In 1983, the arms supplied included the loan of five Super Etendard naval attack aircraft equipped with Exocet missiles, a weapons system that enabled Iraq to strike at both Iranian shipping in the Arab Gulf and Iran's Kharg Island oil terminus, and which consequently raised Western fears that the "tanker war" between Iraq and Iran might escalate to a serious disruption of Gulf oil flows.

France's motives for supporting Iraq are varied. On the one hand, French support is part of a general policy of bolstering stability and French political influence in the strategically important Gulf region. Mitterand himself has noted that "Iraq cannot be allowed to collapse. The stability of the Near and Middle East depends on it."[51] In this sense, French backing of Iraq has not only stalemated what French decision-makers see as an expansionist, destabilizing Iran, but has also further increased France's popularity with Iraq and other Arab Gulf states, thus further strengthening the French position in the area. At the same time, this motive is complemented by a purely economic one. In addition to being a source of valuable arms orders, Iraq owes French creditors more than $1.2 billion in outstanding civilian loans —loans whose repayment would clearly be put at risk by an Iranian victory.[52] An even larger amount is owed in the form of deferred payments for French military and other equipment. Nevertheless, the continuation of the war does not harm (and may even further) French interest, since France—despite its support for Iraq—would not welcome a crushing and possibly destabilizing defeat of Iran.

French support for Iraq has not been without its costs, however. In addition to drawing attacks upon French members of the multinational force in Beirut in 1982–84, French backing of Iraq and the shelter it has extended to Iranian opponents of the Khomeini regime (notably former president Abol-Hassan Bani Sadr and Mujaheddin leader Ma'sud Rajavi), have led to periodic hijackings of French commercial aircraft by pro-Khomeini extremists.

An important but less successful area of French diplomacy centers on Libya and its activities in the former French territory of Chad. In 1981 France supported the successful efforts of President Oueddie of Chad and the Organization of African Unity to secure a withdrawal of those Libyan troops that had entered Chad at Oueddie's request the previous year. Oueddie was later overthrown by Hissene Habre, and when Libyan troops reentered the conflict in mid-1983 in support of Oueddie's forces, France sent troops and aircraft to support President Habre and deter further Libyan advance. On 17 September 1984, after a long stalemate between the two, France and Libya announced that they would simultaneously withdraw their forces from Chad. French forces began withdrawing nine days later, and by early November all 3,200 French troops had departed. It soon became apparent, however, that Libya had failed to hold up its side of the bargain, and on November 15 Mitterand met with Libya's Qaddafi on the island of Crete in an attempt to resolve the dilemma. As of the end of 1985, however, France had made little further progress toward a Libyan withdrawal (and had suffered considerable diplomatic embarrassment as a result of the affair). The incident led to the resignation of French Foreign Minister Claude Cheysson in December 1984.

Britain

Compared with France, Britain has shown far less diplomatic activity in the Middle East since 1980. British trade with the region was valued at $12.6 billion in 1984, Britain's major trading partners being Saudi Arabia, Iran, and the United Arab Emirates. Because North Sea oil production obviates the need for substantial Middle East oil liftings, the ratio of trade has been highly favorable to Britain, running better than two to one in Britain's favor ($8.7 billion in British exports compared to $3.9 billion in imports). Britain also benefits from large investments and petrodollar deposits by the Arab oil-producing states. As of June 1982, approximately $15 billion of identifiable OPEC assets were invested in the United Kingdom. A further

$55 billion was held in non-sterling U.K. bank deposits. Next to the United States, Britain is the largest Western recipient of such assets and investments.[53]

As the decade has progressed (and particularly since the resignation of Lord Carrington as Foreign Secretary in 1982), British policy vis-à-vis the Palestine question and the Arab-Israeli conflict appears to have undergone a subtle change in style and content. First, the British government—although it continues to expound the view that found formal expression in the Venice declaration on June 1980—has modified its political activity in the region. Britain did condemn the Israel invasion of Lebanon, and British arms sales to Israel have been embargoed since June 1982. Britain's commitment to the multinational force in Beirut, however, was a mere 100 personnel. This muffling of Britain's voice doubtless reflects a desire to concentrate on Britain's economic interests in the region.

At the same time, Britain has moved away from a Euro-approach to the conflict and closer to the stance of the Reagan Administration. Foreign secretary Francis Pym's October 1983 statement in Cairo that Britain viewed the so-called Reagan plan as so close to the Venice declaration that it had decided to lend its support to the former was indicative of this shift. It is also noteworthy that Britain, unlike a number of other European countries (including France, Italy, Spain, Greece, and Austria) but like the United States, has continued to refuse to meet with PLO representatives. In January 1983 Prime Minister Thatcher's refusal to meet with an Arab League delegation that included a PLO representative led Saudi Arabia and several other Gulf states to cancel a planned tour by Pym.

In September 1985, some indications of a gradual revitalization of British policy in the Middle East nevertheless became apparent. Prime Minister Thatcher announced Britain's support for joint Jordanian-PLO peace initiatives, and stated a willingness to meet with PLO representatives forming part of a joint Jordanian-Palestinian delegation. At the same time, Britain concluded major arms deals with both Jordan and Saudi Arabia—the value of the latter being estimated at more than $4.3 billion. Ultimately, however, U.S. and domestic opposition to possible British-PLO talks led the Thatcher government to once again refuse to meet with PLO representatives in October of that year.

Britain, like France, has found its relations with Libya to be problematic. Past Libyan support for the Irish Republican Army, and Libya's offer of support to striking British coal miners during their extended industrial dispute, did not endear Muammar Qaddafi to the British government, nor have the armed attacks that Libyan agents occasionally carry out against Libyan exiles living in Britain. Moreover, the Thatcher government clearly shares the Reagan administration's view that Qaddafi is a dangerous madman who threatens Western interests in the Middle East. At the same time, Libya employs a significant number of British technicians in its oilfields and in other operations.

All of these difficulties came to the fore when, on 17 April 1984, members of the Libyan "People's Bureau" in London opened fire on anti-Qaddafi demonstrators outside the embassy, killing a British policewoman and wounding 11 Libyan students. The British authorities immediately surrounded the building, and the Libyan government responded with a parallel siege of the British embassy in Tripoli. The standoff finally ended on April 27 when the diplomatic personnel of the two missions were simultaneously repatriated. As a result of the incident, though, Britain broke off diplomatic relations on April 22 and restricted its financial support for exports bound for Libya. In April 1986 London went a step further and allowed Washington to use American F-111 bombers based in Britain for its military strike against Libya.

Other Western European Countries

Like Britain, many other Western European countries—notably Belgium, the Netherlands, Denmark, and West Germany—have generally refrained from any active involvement in Middle East political issues while concentrating instead on pursuing their economic interests in the region. West Germany is clearly the most significant of these other nations, ranking as it does with France as the Middle East's major European trading partner. In 1983 West German two-way trade with the Middle East was worth some $25.7 billion, representing 9.5% of all German exports and 6.3% of its imports. Iran and Saudi Arabia represent by far the largest German export markets in the region at roughly $3 billion per year each.[54] Because of the importance of this trade, its close ties with the United States, and the particular nature and constraints of its relationship with Israel, West Germany has remained circumspect and muted on the Arab-Israeli conflict. No substantive change in Germany's position on the Palestine Question has occurred since the Venice declaration.

There has, however, been a change in West Germany's arms sales policy toward the region as Germany attempts to cash in on this lucrative export market. In April 1981, then Chancellor Schmidt suggested to Saudi Arabia that Germany might review its ban on arms exports to areas of tension. The policy was subsequently revised to allow German arms to be sold when such sales were in the national interest, and Saudi Arabian–German negotiations on possible sales were initiated in 1983 following Chancellor Helmut Kohl's October visit to Riyadh. This change in policy has provoked bitter criticism from Israel, and when Kohl visited Israel in January 1984 he was severely criticized for Germany's actions. The negotiations, however, continued.

West Germany's relations with Iran—relations primarily motivated by the value of the Iranian market—are also regionally significant. West Germany has perhaps the most cordial relations with the Islamic Republic of any major Western nation, and when in July 1984 German Foreign Minister Hans-Dietrich Genscher visited Tehran it marked the first visit of any EC foreign minister to Iran since the revolution. According to a 1984 article in *Arab-American Affairs*, West German policy toward Iran is guided by a desire to prevent the isolation of the regime (which might lead to its radicalization and/or to closer ties with the USSR), while at the same time maintaining a "bridgehead to the West" that might provide a basis for future improvement of relations.[55]

Unlike West Germany, and despite the fact that the Middle East provides a market for more than $13 billion in Italian exports every year, Italy's involvement in the Middle East in the 1980s has not been confined to economic matters. PLO leaders, including Yasser Arafat, have visited Rome on several occasions to meet with Italian officials. Italy contributed some 2,200 troops to the multinational peacekeeping force in Beirut—the single largest contingent. During the period that these forces were in Lebanon, Italy was even more critical than France of U.S. actions. In December 1983, Italian Prime Minister Giovanni Spandolini condemned US military support for the presidency of Amin Gemayel as "escalatory," while Italian President Sandro Pertini stated that U.S. policy seemed designed to help Israel rather than Lebanon. As a result of the United States' increased involvement in Lebanon's civil war, Italy announced the withdrawal of one half of its forces at this time. The entire Italian contingent was withdrawn in February 1984, twelve days after the withdrawal of US forces on February 8. Italy, together with France, Britain, the United

States and the USSR, assisted in the multinational minesweeping operations in the Red Sea in 1984. In October 1985, the closeness of Italian-PLO and Italian-Egyptian relations was clearly evident in Rome's strong condemnation of Israel's air raid on PLO headquarters in Tunis, and in PLO and Egyptian efforts to bring a peaceful end to the hijacking of the Italian cruise ship *Achille Lauro* by Palestinian radicals.

Spain has also been diplomatically active in the region. Because of its historical ties to the area, Spain has been energetic in trying to bring about a negotiated settlement to the dispute in what was once the Spanish Sahara. With regard to the Palestine question, the government of Adolfo Suarez (1977–82) continued to exhibit Spain's traditional support for the Arab cause. Spain usually voted with Arab delegations on Arab-Israel resolutions that came before the United Nations General Assembly, and consistently refused to establish diplomatic relations with Israel until such time as it recognized the legitimate national rights of the Palestinian people. After the 1982 election of the Socialist Party under Felipe Gonzalez, however, Spanish-Israeli economic interaction expanded, but diplomatic relations remained unestablished, despite the socialists' traditionally greater sympathy for Israel. One Spanish foreign minister, Fernando Morano, stated that the establishment of relations must come "through a true diplomatic process in which there would be counterconcessions," a position that appeared to indicate that Spain would continue to tie Spanish-Israeli normalization to progress on the Palestinian issue.[56]

Nevertheless, in January 1986 Spanish-Israeli diplomatic relations were established, despite little advancement in the peace process. In an attempt to offset the expected Arab dismay and concern at the Spanish move, Spain simultaneously issued a unilateral communique calling for PLO participation in Middle East peace talks.

The European Community

A final aspect of European–Middle East relations continues to be centered around the European Community. Although the importance of the EC as a mechanism for multilateral European policy statements and initiatives on the Middle East has progressively declined since 1980, it has not vanished: in addition to an unsuccessful initiative in 1980–81 designed to secure a Soviet withdrawal from

Afghanistan and repeated calls for an end to the Iran-Iraq War, the period since the Venice declaration has seen strong, univocal EC condemnation of Israel's annexation of the Golan Heights and its invasion and occupation of Lebanon. In the latter declaration the nine called for an immediate ceasefire, the withdrawal of both Israeli and PLO forces from Beirut, and the negotiation of a comprehensive settlement of the Arab-Israeli conflict in which the Palestinians would participate.[57] In March 1985 the EC, with urging from Italian Prime Minister Bettino Craxi, issued a declaration welcoming the conclusion of the "Amman Accords" between PLO Chairman Yasser Arafat and King Hussein of Jordan and recent peace initiatives by Egyptian President Hosni Mubarak earlier in the year.

The early 1980s also saw limited progress towards a resumption of the Euro-Arab dialogue. Following a preliminary planning meeting in Luxembourg in November 1980, the Fifth meeting of the Euro-Arab Dialogue General Committee was finally held in Athens in December 1983. The fact that, for the first time, the two sides were unable to agree on a final communique at the Athens meeting suggests that little progress in the dialogue is to be expected in the foreseeable future.

The most important development in EC–Middle East relations in the 1980s is likely to occur because of changes within the Community itself. On 1 January 1981 Greece — many of whose agricultural and other products compete for the European market with Israel and Maghreb countries — became the tenth member of the EC. This immediately created pressure from within the Community for a revision of its Mediterranean trade policies. The planned entrance of Spain and Portugal into the Community in 1986 had a similar effect. Because EC markets are so important for the affected Middle East countries — constituting 30–60% of the export market for Israel, Morocco, Algeria, and Tunisia, for instance — any such revision of EC import regulations could have a severe impact on local economies. These countries have been engaged in intensive lobbying of the EC in an attempt to mitigate the effect of Spanish and Portuguese admission, and in March 1985 the EC Commission recognized the validity of their concerns in a statement that noted the "disastrous social and political consequences" of closing "necessary and irreplaceable [European] markets" to southern Mediterranean goods.[58] Although northern EC nations are prepared to allow these goods continued access to the Community, Greece, France and Italy (as well as Spain and Portugal) have demanded that their local agricultural producers receive EC subsidies in the event such a policy is adopted. Even as Spain and Portugal joined the Community in January 1986 the issue remained unresolved.

Conclusion

Contemporary relations between Western Europe and the Middle East are characterized by extensive interaction, primarily of an economic and technical nature. This interaction is conducted bilaterally between the countries (and corporations) of the two regions, rather than on an interregional basis mediated by such regional organizations as the European Community and the League of Arab States. The circumstances conditioning this relationship can be found on both sides of the Mediterranean. In Europe, diverging national policy views have inhibited Europolicy formation while economic needs and commercial competition arising from the attractions of Arab petrodollar wealth have encouraged bilateralism. In the Middle East, the fragmentation of the Arab world has both undermined the Euro-Arab dialogue and prevented Arab countries from demanding clear statements of European policy on important Arab issues. The apparent decline of the importance of the Palestine question that was once central to Arab foreign policies has both hastened and been hastened by inter-Arab divisions. So too the Iran-Iraq War has seriously damaged Arab unity, attempts by Iraq and its allies to bill the issue as an "Arab" one notwithstanding. The current oil glut has also had an important effect, weakening Arab leverage over Europe and hence weakening the ability of Arab countries to focus European eyes on Arab concerns.

Within the general context of bilateral Western European-Middle East relations in the 1980s, the foreign policy of France deserves particular attention—not only because it departs from the general pattern insofar as it retains substantial political content, but also because (excepting the Chad-Libyan problem) it has been so successful. France is clearly the most significant and influential European actor in the Middle East—a status belatedly recognized even by Iran, which in 1984–85 made some attempts to improve relations with Paris in the apparent hope of weakening French support for Iraq thereby.

Upon examination, it seems clear that much of France's diplomatic success in the Middle East is attributable to the unique role among major powers that France performs in the region. Of France's potential rivals, the United States is able to supply the Arab countries with the manufactured goods, technical assistance, and military equipment they require; yet close U.S.-Arab relations are still inhibited by U.S. support for Israel and U.S. insensitivity to many Arab concerns. Both of these limitations are evident in the continued unwillingness of the American government to provide certain weapons systems to even its closest Arab friends. The Soviet Union, on the other hand, has supported the Palestinian cause and the Arab countries politically and materially. The USSR, however, is largely unable to supply technical and military assistance of the quality available from the West. Furthermore, the conservative regimes of the Arab world remain staunchly anticommunist, thus creating a further obstacle to the expansion of Soviet influence in the Arabian peninsula and elsewhere.

Other major external powers have either scaled down their current political involvement in the region (China, much of Western Europe) or have refrained from substantial political involvement altogether (Japan). Thus, in many ways, France has the field to itself in the Middle East as the only major external power able to satisfy Arab needs while simultaneously espousing an active political position acceptable to the Arab countries. It follows from this that France's political and economic position in the Middle East is likely to endure until such time as a rival appears to pursue a similar diplomatic strategy. (Increased British diplomatic activity in the region in the autumn of 1985 would appear to indicate a recognition of this on the part of London, and an effort to approximate more closely the style—and success—of French policy. If the Thatcher-PLO episode of October 1985 is any guide, however, the British government lacks the determination to shrug off potential domestic and U.S. criticism and chart a truly independent and assertive course in the region. British support for U.S. military action against Libya only confirms this analysis.)

The broader question of whether the current pattern of relations between Western Europe and the Middle East will continue hinges on the degree to which the factors conditioning that relationship—Arab oil wealth without oil power, European commercial competition, Arab disunity, and the reduced salience of the Palestine question (and the absence of any similarly uniting issue)—remain unchanged. Should Middle East oil revenues fall dramatically, prompting fewer Arab imports from Europe, an initial period of intensified competition would likely give way to an overall lower level of European concern with the area. Conversely, should the oil crisis of the mid-1970s return in the mid-1980s or 1990s; or should a strong regional leader or increased Arab unity emerge; or should Arab-Israeli tensions heat up throughout the Middle East, pressure for greater European diplomatic concern with Middle East issues would soon build up. In the near future, however, none of these developments appears likely. The era of the "new bilateralism" in Western European–Middle East relations and the mercantilist nature of most contemporary European foreign policy toward the region seem likely to continue.

NOTES

1. Harry Howard, "Historical Backgrounds," in Tareq Y. Ismael, ed., *The Middle East in World Politics* (Syracuse: Syracuse University Press, 1974). See also L. Carl Brown, *International Politics and the Middle East: Old Rules, Dangerous Games* (Princeton, NJ.: Princeton University Press, 1984) for an insightful analysis of the Eastern Question which has considerably influenced the present authors' interpretation.

2. P. Edward Haley, "Britain and the Middle East," in *Middle East*, p. 32.

3. Quoted in Alistair Horne, *A Savage War of Peace: Algeria 1954–1962* (London: Macmillan, 1977), p. 30.

4. In 1904 Britain recognized French influence in Morocco, while in 1906 the Algeciras Conference saw general European recognition of France's and Spain's particular interests there. France (and Spain) did not acquire formal protectorates in Morocco until 1912.

5. For details see George Antonius, *The Arab Awakening* (New York, London: H. Hamilton, 1938), and T. E. Lawrence, *Revolt in the Desert* (New York, Doran, 1927). The latter work tends to exaggerate Lawrence's role in the revolt.

6. For details of the Hussein-McMahon correspondence and the postwar dispute over its interpretation, see Great Britain, *Report of a Committee Set Up to Consider Certain Correspondence between Sir Henry McMahon and the Sherif of Mecca in 1915 and 1916,* Cmd. 5974 (1939), and Elie Khedourie, *In the Anglo-Arab Labyrinth: the McMahon Correspondence and its Interpretations 1914–1939* (Cambridge: Cambridge University Press, 1976).

7. The text of the Balfour Declaration can be found in John Norton Moore, ed., *The Arab-Israeli Conflict* vol. 3: Documents (Princeton, N.J.: Princeton University Press, 1974), p. 32.

8. For an overview of the secret treaties concluded by the Entente powers 1914–18 see George Lenczowski, *The Middle East in World Affairs*, 4th ed. (Ithaca, N.Y.: Cornell University Press, 1980), pp. 75–79, and J. C. Hurewitz, ed., *The Middle East and North Africa in World Politics: A Documentary Record* (New Haven: Yale University Press, 1979).

9. Walid Khalidi, ed., *Conquest to Haven: Readings in Zionism and the Palestine Problem until 1948* (Beirut: Institute of Palestine Studies, 1971), pp. 846–849.

10. *Palestine Royal Commission Report*, Cmd. 5479 (1937).

11. League of Nations, *Mandate for Palestine, Together with a Note by the Secretary-General Relating to its Application to the Territories Known as Trans-Jordan,* Cmd. 1785 (1922).

12. Great Britain, *Parliamentary Papers 1931,* Treaty Series 15, Cd. 3797.

13. Hurewitz, *Middle East,* vol. 2, pp. 298–301.

14. League of Nations, *Treaty Series* vol. 173, Nos. 4031–4032.

15. Claudio G. Segre, *The Fourth Shore: the Italian Colonization of Libya* (Chicago: University of Chicago Press, 1974), p. 161.

16. Stephen Hemsley Longrigg, *Oil in the Middle East: Its Discovery and Development* (London: Oxford University Press, 1954), p. 277. See also Haley, "Britain and the Middle East," pp. 31–32, 44–47.

17. Haj Amin Husseini, the exiled mufti of Jerusalem and leader of the Palestinian nationalist movement in the 1930s, did offer his services to the Axis in WWII and even helped form a Muslim SS unit in the Balkans. Similarly, some Zionist terrorist groups, including the Irgun and especially the "Stern Gang," attacked British targets during the war, and some of the most extreme elements of these groups even approached Nazi Germany for assistance. In both cases, hatred for Britain was the primary motivating factor.

18. Habib Bourguiba, *La Tunisie et La France: vingt-cing ans de lutte pour une cooperation libre* (Paris: Julliard, 1954), pp. 200–205.

19. Speech to the National Assembly, quoted in Horne, *Savage War,* p. 98.

20. Guy Mollet, quoted in *ibid.,* p. 162.

21. The British-officered Arab Legion of Transjordan did take part in the fighting on the Arab side. Alone among the Arab armies, it proved to be an effective fighting force. For details, see John Bagot Glubb, *A Soldier with the Arabs* (New York: Harper, 1957).

22. These members included Iraq, Syria, Lebanon, Jordan, Saudi Arabia, Yemen, Egypt, and Libya.

23. Anthony Eden, *Full Circle* (Boston: Houghton Mifflin, 1960), pp. 393–394.

24. *Ibid.,* p. 478. In 1955 alone, almost 15,000 ships transited the Suez Canal. Of these, two-thirds carried oil and one-third belonged to Britain. See Wilfred Knapp, *A History of War and Peace 1939–1965* (London: Oxford University Press, 1967), p. 404.

25. Eden, *Full Circle,* pp. 430–432.

26. From its outbreak in 1954 until its end in 1962, the war in Algeria cost the FLN some 141,000 dead and the French Army 14,500. Some 2,800 European civilians and 16,400 Algerians also died. 500,000 French troops were deployed in Algeria at the height of the war. Following Algerian independence, the European population of Algeria dropped from 910,000 to approximately 100,000. See Edgar O'Ballance, *The Algerian Insurrection 1954–62* (Hamden, Conn.: Archon Bocks, 1967), pp. 200–201, and Richard M. Bruce, *Morocco, Algeria, Tunisia* (Englewood Cliffs, N.J.: Prentice-Hall, 1964), p. 5.

27. *Official Statements* 207 (10 January 1968).

28. Naseer H. Aruri and Natalie K. Hevener, "France and the Middle East," in T. Y. Ismael, *Middle East,* pp. 78, 83.

29. See Tony Hodges, *Western Sahara: The Roots of a Desert War* (Westport, Conn.: Lawrence Hill & Co., 1983).

30. Harold Lubell, *Middle East Oil and Western Europe's Energy Supplies* (Baltimore: Johns Hopkins Press/RAND, 1963), p. 13.

31. Ibrahim Sus, "Western Europe and the October War," *Journal of Palestine Studies* 3, No. 4 (Winter 1974): 66.

32. Text in *International Documents on Palestine 1973* (Beirut: Institute for Palestine Studies, annual), pp. 348–349.

33. Bulletin of the European Communities, 6, No. 12 (1973): 11.

34. For details, see Alan R. Taylor, "The Euro-Arab Dialogue: Quest for an Interregional Partnership," *Middle East Journal* 32, No. 4 (Autumn 1978): 429–443.

35. Ahmad Sidqi al-Dajani, "The PLO and the Euro-Arab Dialogue," *Journal of Palestine Studies* 35 (Spring 1980): 81–98.

36. Saleh al-Mani', *The Euro-Arab Dialogue: A Study in Associative Diplomacy* (London: Frances Pinter, 1983), p. 29. See also Mitsue Osada, "Basic Data on the Arab World," in Ali E. Hillal Dessouki, ed., *International Relations in the Arab World 1973–1982*, Joint Research Program Series No. 39, (Tokyo: Institute of Developing Economies, 1983), p. 216.

37. al-Mani', *Euro-Arab Dialogue*, p. 28. Note that these figures include deposits in Swiss, Swedish, and Austrian banks as well as those of the EC.

38. Text in *Bulletin of the European Communities* 10, No. 6 (1977): 62

39. *Bulletin of the European Communities* 13, No. 6 (1980): 10–11.

40. For the PLO, Syrian, Jordanian, and Saudi responses to the Venice Declaration see *International Documents on Palestine 1980*, pp. 183–185, 189–190; for the Israeli response, see ibid., p. 185, and *New York Times*, 16 June 1980, pp. 1, 9. For the American response, see *New York Times*, 14 June 1980, pp. 1, 3.

41. As a result of Carrington's criticisms of and opposition to elements of US Middle East policy, Haig reportedly told his staff that the British Foreign Secretary was a "duplicitous bastard." See Harvey Sicherman, "Europe's Role in the Middle East: Illusions and Reality," *Orbis* 28, No. 4 (Winter 1985).

42. Werner J. Feld, "Western European Foreign Policies: The Impact of the Oil Crisis," *Orbis* 22 (Spring 1978): 66.

43. al-Mani', *Euro-Arab Dialogue*, p. 28. On differences between the United States and Europe on energy, see Joan Garratt, "Euro-American Energy in the Middle East 1970–1980: The Pervasive Crisis," in Steven L. Speigel, ed., *The Middle East and the Western Alliance* (London: George Allen & Unwin, 1982), pp. 82–103.

44. *Bulletin of the European Communities* 13, No. 9 (1980): 8.

45. On the difficulties of European policy-making in this area, see David Allen and Michael Smith, "Europe, The United States, and the Middle East: A Case Study in Comparative Policy Making," *Journal of Common Market Studies* 22, No. 2 (December 1983).

46. *Middle East Economic Digest*, 8 February 1984, p. 42.

47. Jerusalem Post (International Edition) 22 December 1984.

48. Thomas Carothers, "Mitterand and the Middle East," *The World Today* 38, No. 10 (October 1982): 382. See also Dominique Moisi, "La France de Mitterand

et le conflit du Proche-Orient: comment concilier emotion et politique?" *Politique Etrangère* 2 (1982).

49. *Middle East Economic Digest,* 8 February 1985, p. 42.

50. Ibid., 3 May 1985.

51. Shahram Chubin, "La France et le Golfe: opportunisme ou continuité?" *Politique Etrangère* 4 (1983): 885.

52. *Middle East Economic Digest,* 29 March 1985, pp. 19–20.

53. *Middle East Economic Digest,* 8 March 1985, p. 39. See also Alan Stoga, "The Foreign Investments of OPEC and Arab Oil Producers," *Arab-American Affairs* 3 (Winter 1982/83): 61–62.

54. *West Germany: Middle East Economic Digest Special Report* (March 1984), p. 62.

55. Udo Steinbach, "Germany's Attitude Toward the Middle East," *Arab-American Affairs* 10 (Fall 1984): 40.

56. *Christian Science Monitor,* 8 April 1985, p. 13.

57. Text in *Bulletin of the European Communities,* 15, No. 6 (1982): 16.

58. *Middle East Economic Digest,* 29 March 1985, p. 25.

The United States and the Middle East

AMERICAN INTERESTS

THE UNITED STATES has a broad range of national interests, which it pursues both internally and in the world. In the international arena, these are perceived in terms of needs and challenges as they appear in distinct geographical regions—including the Middle East.

A somewhat loosely defined area, the Middle East is generally understood to extend across the entire width of northern Africa into the lands of western Asia as far as the Indian subcontinent. As such, it is the connecting link between Africa, Asia, and Europe. Within it, lie some of the major international waterways: the Turkish Straits, the Red Sea, the Suez Canal, and the Persian Gulf. It also produces a substantial amount of the world's crude oil, the key source of energy for human consumption. This combination of unique strategic location and rich petroleum reserves has made the Middle East one of the most critical regions of the modern world.

It is, however, also an extremely unstable area politically—a fact that intensifies and complicates the rivalry of the superpowers and lesser countries that seek to gain various advantages there. American interests in the Middle East are therefore not only related to maintaining access to its strategic position and petroleum resources, but also to preserving peace and stability in the area. The ways in

This chapter was written by Alan R. Taylor, Professor of International Relations at the School of International Service, The American University, Washington D.C.

which the United States has perceived these interests and sought to protect them have varied at different points in American history, but there has been an intense awareness of their importance during the past forty years.

Early U.S. Relationship to the Area

Before World War II, American involvement in the Middle East was limited to commercial ventures, missionary and educational activities, and the adoption and enforcement of measures designed to protect U.S. citizens and shipping interests. American trade with the Middle East dates back to 1767, and in 1801–1805 U.S. marines had military encounters with Tripoli coast pirates who had been menacing U.S. merchant vessels.[1] American Protestant missionary work began in the 1820s, with a particularly important center being established in Beirut. The missionaries had very limited success in religious conversion, but they made remarkable strides in modernizing education, setting an example in their own schools and colleges. The founding of the Syrian Protestant College (later the American University of Beirut) in 1866 was their crowning achievement. These educational activities were deeply appreciated by the indigenous populations and contributed enormously to the favorable image the United States enjoyed throughout the Middle East prior to 1945.

The United States concluded a number of treaties with Middle East governments in the late eighteenth and nineteenth centuries. A treaty recognizing Morocco's independence was signed in 1792, and a series of pacts promoting trade and guaranteeing freedom of passage through the Straits in peacetime was concluded with the Ottoman Empire in 1830, 1862, and 1871.[2] Friendship and commerce accords with Muscat and Persia were ratified in 1835 and 1857, respectively. These instruments were notably dissimilar from the many agreements that were reached between the Middle East states and the European powers in the nineteenth century, in that the United States was not an imperialist power with a record of exploiting Middle Eastern countries or treating them as political inferiors. Indeed, American shipbuilders had played a major role in reconstructing the Ottoman fleet destroyed by European powers at the battle of Navarino in 1827.[3]

U.S. prestige in the Middle East was further enhanced by President Woodrow Wilson's declaration of principles, submitted as the basis of a more equitable world order following World War I. The en-

dorsement of self-determination of nations was especially well received, as it expressed unequivocal support for the right of peoples
to decide their own political destiny. The Middle East at this time
was being transformed into a system of post-Ottoman nation-states,
and Wilson's position implicitly opposed the Anglo-French attempt
to extend colonial rule. The president also sent the King-Crane Commission to Greater Syria and the Harbord Commission to Armenia
after the war in an effort to ascertain the aspirations of the inhabitants of these areas. Though neither of these commissions was able
to influence the course of events, they demonstrated a genuine sympathy for the welfare of the emerging national movements of the Middle East. It is interesting to note that the King-Crane report reiterated
the resolution of the Syrian General Congress of 1919 calling for the
establishment of an American mandate in that region if it were deemed
necessary to have some kind of League of Nations trusteeship.

On the eve of World War II, the United States was the Western
nation most trusted in the Middle East. It had a reputation of fair play
and respect for other nations, and its history of philanthropic under-
takings and commitment to principle gave it a very lofty image—
especially in comparison with the European powers. Most important
to the peoples of the Middle East, perhaps, the United States was
widely regarded as anti-imperialist in its political philosophy and its
policies.

Unfortunately, however, this extremely favorable picture of
America in the eyes of Middle Easterners did not last long beyond the
end of the Second World War. The year 1945 marked the beginning
of an American involvement in the Middle East that would eventually become very intense, and which would reveal the great power as
less interested in the aspirations of the indigenous peoples than in
securing advantages for itself in an increasingly more complex international competition.

The Shift to Political Involvement

The United States began to develop a political presence in the
Middle East during World War II. Even before the American entry into
the war, President Roosevelt expressed his concern over the protection of Turkish territorial integrity from possible German encroachment. Later, U.S. troops took part in the occupation of Iran and in
the North Africa campaign. But though Roosevelt acknowledged the

importance of the Middle East to American and Allied security interests, it was not until the end of the war that the area came to assume any real significance in U.S. foreign policy.

There was a marked change in the international role of the United States beginning in 1945. Its rivalry with the Soviet Union suddenly dominated the global arena. Two superpowers with very divergent ideologies found themselves involved in an intense struggle for ideological supremacy in various parts of the world, as opposed to their earlier concentration on internal affairs. This created a concern in Washington over the intercontinental strategic viability of the United States.

Though all areas were strategically important, the Middle East was particularly so because of its location astride three continents, its crucially situated waterways and ports, and its proximity to both the Soviet Union and the Mediterranean. The latter circumstance shaped the political character of this primary American interest in the area. The Western European allies were beginning a process of evacuation from this admittedly major strategic zone just as the Soviet Union was trying to extend its influence to the south. A new version of the power vacuum situation that had been the focus of rivalries in the Middle East in the nineteenth century was thus recreated.

When the old Eastern Question came to an end after World War I, the West was firmly entrenched in most of the area, while the Soviet successor to the Russian Empire exercised relatively limited influence. However, the Soviet Union assumed an intrusive posture after the defeat of Germany in 1945. Given the earlier success of the Czarist Empire in occupying the Caucasus and Turkestan in the nineteenth century, this gave the impression that the traditional Russian drive to the south had been revived. The American reaction was one of alarm, and the protection of strategic assets quickly became the overriding U.S. interest in the Middle East.

As time elapsed, a corollary was added to this goal. The greatly expanded power of the Soviet Union and the character of the Soviet-American confrontation forced the United States to recognize that the Middle East could become an international battleground. This required a degree of restraint in dealing with Soviet moves, though such caution was not adequately exercised until the 1967 Arab-Israeli war and was not always taken into consideration after that. Nevertheless, U.S. attempts to contain Soviet maneuvers in the Middle East have been generally predicated on the premise that they must fall short of precipitating open hostility with the USSR.

Closely tied to the American interest in preserving access to Middle East waterways, ports, and other facilities is Washington's protective attitude toward the vast petroleum resources of the area. As of the end of 1983, 54.5% of the world's oil resources were in the Middle East, and the region's production of crude was approximately 21.4% of the international total.[4] The Soviet Union is self-sufficient in petroleum, but the West is dependent on Middle East supplies. For Europe, these supplies are indispensable, but they are also vital to fill the gap between production and demand in the United States.

Particularly since the temporary oil embargo imposed after the 1973 war, the U.S. has considered the preservation of the oil supply line from the Middle East to the West one of its most important national interests. President Carter posited as a basic principle of American foreign policy that the United States would go to war with any unfriendly external power that actively sought to gain control of the oil-rich Persian Gulf region. And in particular, Washington is extremely sensitive to any Soviet maneuvers in the Middle East that seem to threaten the established pattern of petroleum supply to the West. This is an issue of the highest possible priority.

The United States has carefully constructed a system of relationships with the oil producers to insure to the fullest extent possible the security of Middle East petroleum and its availability to Western markets. These relationships are essentially symbiotic, in that they protect the vulnerable Gulf states from external aggression while guaranteeing the unimpeded flow of oil. There has sometimes been conflict over pricing, but that has been resolved by the fact that the producers invest in Western economies and because they have agreed to keep production high enough to stabilize petroleum costs. The change of government in Iran was a loss, but one which has been adequately compensated by the continuing close relationship with the Arab Gulf states, especially Saudi Arabia.

Another primary American interest has been the establishment of a "strategic consensus" with certain Middle East states. More comprehensive than the arrangements with the oil producers—in fact, often close to an alliance system—this type of accord is largely political and usually directed against the Soviet Union. The United States has made numerous attempts to form such alignments since 1945, but with varying degrees of success. The underlying premise is that a number of the states in the area have common interests with the U.S. and share the same political orientation in international affairs. The major problem as far as the durability of these agreements is concerned is that Washington does not seem to fully recognize that its partners in the Middle East have other interests and cannot always conduct foreign policy strictly according to American requirements.

The United States has also opened itself to criticism for supporting Middle East regimes simply because they are willing to adopt foreign policy objectives based largely on American guidelines. The popularity of such regimes at home or the political methods they use to stay in power or to minimize opposition are often overlooked for the sake of strategic consensus. This creates the impression that the United States is so preoccupied with furthering its own interests that it is insensitive to the needs and aspirations of broad population segments in the Middle East. This lack of regard for popular opinion is potentially counterproductive to U.S. interests in that it promotes anti-American attitudes that can destabilize or even topple governments aligned with Washington.

In this connection, an important but not always clearly recognized American interest in the Middle East is the preservation of U.S. credibility. The United States sees itself as a bastion of democracy and justice, and regards its role in the world as one of defending its own political principles and protecting the rights of others to freedom and self-determination. Though it may be demonstrably true that the United States has actually pursued such goals at various times and in various places throughout the Middle East, the converse has been the case in a number of instances, as mentioned above. The problem, therefore, is one of inconsistency. And credibility remains a major American interest, for as people in the Middle East lose faith in the integrity of the United States, they tend to set in motion trends and movements that actively seek to obstruct the achievement of American aims. Credibility, on the other hand, engenders confidence, and confidence promotes good will and cooperation.

Finally, there is the question of Israel as an American interest. Beginning with the presidency of Harry Truman, all U.S. administrations have regarded the existence of the Jewish state as a major priority and have emphasized the importance of the "special relationship" between the United States and Israel. A number of recent books and articles have also taken the position that Israel is indeed one of America's primary interests in the Middle East. Yet in 1968 the former U.S. Ambassador to Egypt, John Badeau, declared that "In the context of American foreign policy, Israel . . . needs to be viewed as a problem, rather than as an interest."[5] Since this opinion is shared by virtually all Arab states as well as by many Third World countries, it is important to consider the question of Israel in full—that is, as both an asset and a liability of the United States.

The American understanding of Israel as an asset closely parallels the British attitude toward the prospective creation of a Jewish state in Palestine after World War I. The policy of Lloyd George and Arthur Balfour, first formally expressed in the Balfour Declaration of November 2, 1917, was based on the idea that a British-sponsored Jewish state would provide a valuable link in the imperial lifeline.[6] The subsequent U.S. support for the creation and security of Israel was premised on the conviction that the new state would serve both as a stabilizing force and a watchdog for American interests in the Middle East. Indeed, the major reason for the pro-Israeli stance of the U.S. Congress and of successive administrations is their firm belief that Israel is a reliable and dependable democracy capable of dealing effectively with those developments in the area that may threaten or compromise American interests.

Whether this perception is accurate or not, the way the United States deals with Israeli policy is in some respects counterproductive to American interests. Much of the Arab world's alienation from the United States stems directly from its predictably negative response to American favoritism for Israel. There is a particularly low tolerance for the seeming inability of Washington to exercise any political leverage on Israel, even when it violates principles that the United States has specifically formulated and upheld. Most Arabs find it incomprehensible that extensive aid to Israel continues unabated, despite such violations. Some explain it as evidence of a tacit U.S.-Israeli alliance that has little regard for Arab interests.

Without trying to assess either Israeli actions or U.S. policy in reaction to them, it is possible to recognize that in categorizing Israel as a "special" interest, the United States has helped to polarize the Arab world and to incite radicalism. Moreover, it has placed the moderate Arab states in a predicament, forcing them to diversify their foreign policies. The degree to which Israel can be considered a genuine American interest therefore depends on Washington's ability to establish a balance in its approach to both sides in the Arab-Israeli conflict. The U.S. can support the security and welfare of Israel without necessarily alienating the Arab world or weakening the viability of the relatively moderate Arab states, which comprise an equally valid American interest.

THE SEARCH FOR AN AMERICAN POLICY:
THE EXPERIMENTAL PHASE

Initial Policy Guidelines: Theory and Practice

The United States began its political involvement in the Middle East after World War II without a clearly defined policy toward the area. Rather, it had a set of guidelines with regard to basic concerns and somewhat vaguely conceived principles deemed to be "in the American interest." The approach to the region was therefore often reactive, lacking in long-range planning formulated in terms of comprehensive objectives.

The first of these guidelines reflected the major preoccupation of the United States at the outset of the Cold War. It was that the United States must employ any means at its disposal to prevent the Soviet Union from filling the power vacuum in the Middle East created by the incipient withdrawal of the old colonial powers. The undisguised Soviet attempts to establish footholds in the area at this time intensified American apprehensions and made containment the highest priority in U.S. Middle East policy.

Another clearly related guideline was that the United States had to maintain access to the resources and facilities of the Middle East. Awareness of the region's abundance of oil became increasingly acute as the decades passed, and eventually it came to be considered vital to Western interests. The West had also traditionally enjoyed a privileged status with regard to use of the area's waterways and ports, especially in the Red Sea and the Gulf. Because of their marked strategic importance, the United States felt a special concern with insuring the continued use and availability of these facilities.

A third guideline related to the area's political climate. It was generally assumed that peace and stability and the preservation of the territorial status quo in the Middle East were in the best interests of the United States. This was largely because the Middle East had been largely under Western control prior to 1945, and a continuation of this would seem to be the natural result of keeping the existing order intact. Conversely, destabilization and revision would be to the advantage of the Soviet Union, which was on the outside trying to establish footholds within.

The fourth guideline dealt with the question of alignments. It was obvious that the United States, which had been relatively uninvolved politically in the Middle East, would have to establish a system of cooperative relationships in the area. The early understanding of this was that something on the order of a regional alliance directed against Soviet intrusion should be set up. Also, it was reasoned that various kinds of friendship and cooperation accords should be concluded, and that in general the United States should make the most of its favorable reputation in the region. At the same time, there was a very negative attitude in Washington toward expressions of neutralism in the Cold War context, as this was considered to reflect either sympathy for the Soviet Union or a dangerous naivete.

The fifth and last guideline related to the emerging Jewish state. The Zionist issue became an international topic immediately after the war, when the Jewish community in Palestine inaugurated a policy of noncooperation with the British mandate authorities. The United Nations Special Committee on Palestine (UNSCOP) recommended partition of the country in 1947—a proposal that won the support of the Zionist Organization, which had established its headquarters in the United States during the war. The Zionists had succeeded in gaining sympathy for their cause in the American press and in certain political circles, and the United States took a strong position in favor of the partition resolution. It was passed by just over two-thirds of the General Assembly on November 29, 1947. It was at this point that Washington began to consider the Jewish state as a major American interest. This premise was increasingly emphasized in succeeding years, and virtually all foreign policy decisions touching on the Middle East took it into special consideration.

These theoretical guidelines for the formulation of U.S. Middle East policy were not always consistently utilized. Though the preoccupation with containment and the preservation of access to resources and facilities remained constant, the practical methodology varied and some projects were either aborted or gradually allowed to lapse. There was seldom evidence of a precise, comprehensive plan designed to deal effectively with Soviet intrusion into the area. Similarly, the principle of promoting peace and stability and upholding the territorial status quo was implemented in an irregular fashion. At times the United States did indeed act as a stabilizing force, but at other times its policies served to increase tensions in the region. And despite American commitment to the territorial status quo, the United States did not intervene to prevent change in some instances.

On the question of "strategic consensus," the United States did form a number of close relationships and alignments in the Middle East after the war; however, many of these were either tempo-

rary or ultimately unsuccessful. Endeavors in this field were usually fluid, and there were numerous examples of poor judgment. The
pattern of shifting accords with various states reflected in part the
instability of the area, but also the lack of forethought and planning
in Washington.

The most constant predisposition throughout was the special
relationship with Israel. Though the United States was occasionally
irritated by Israeli policy and was aware of some of the drawbacks in
terms of negative impact in the Arab world, it was clear that American policy-makers felt more comfortable with Israel than with any
of the other states in the region.

Managing the Cold War

From 1945 through 1960, U.S. Middle East policy was developed in the context of the Cold War: that is, the overriding concern
was to devise strategy capable of checking any Soviet intrusion into
the area. And the USSR was exerting pressure all along the northern
tier, from Greece to Iran. During the second half of 1945 and throughout 1946, they tried to force Turkey to revise the Montreux Conven-
tion so that the Straits would come under the control of the Black
Sea powers—a change that the Ankara government staunchly resisted.
The USSR also posed a threat to Greece by demanding a base in the
Dodecanese Islands, and by encouraging and assisting the guerrillas
in the northern part of the country. In Iran, the Soviets assisted local
communists in establishing an autonomous government in Azerbaijan and an independent Kurdish republic at the end of 1945. Early the
following year, the USSR refused to evacuate its troops from Iran, in
violation of an agreement made in 1942 to the effect that all occupying forces would be withdrawn within six months of the end of the war.

On August 15, 1946, President Truman informed the Turkish
government that the United States would assist its efforts to resist
Soviet demands with regard to the Straits. Then, on March 12, 1947,
he asked Congress to endorse a program of aid to Greece and Turkey
to protect them from Russian pressure.[7] This proposal, which would
become famous as the Truman Doctrine, formed the basis of postwar
American strategy in the Middle East. Congress subsequently authorized an expenditure of $400 million to Greece and Turkey, and
agreements extending financial assistance were concluded on June 20
and July 12, 1947, respectively.

Meanwhile, the Iranian crisis was also satisfactorily resolved, in part through American and British insistence that the USSR withdraw from Azerbaijan and Kurdistan. The Iranian government handled the affair adroitly, making certain tenuous concessions to the Soviets with regard to oil exploitation in the north of the country and offering to include three communists in the cabinet. Though these promises were never kept, Soviet forces left Iran on May 9, 1946.[8] Subsequent interpretation has suggested that Moscow agreed to evacuate its troops in order to preserve a favorable image in the Third World. Though this was undoubtedly true, the developing American policy of containment was certainly partly responsible for the decision.

At the time the Truman Doctrine was being implemented, the United States was drawn into the confrontation between Arabs and Jews in Palestine. On May 11, 1942, a special Zionist conference had adopted the Biltmore Program, which called for the establishment of a Jewish commonwealth in Palestine. This was followed by an intense public relations campaign designed to win broad support for the statehood project throughout the American political system. After the end of World War II, particular pressure was brought to bear on the White House. President Truman was personally sympathetic with Zionist aspirations although he seems not to have been aware of the international repercussions that would inevitably attend the creation of a Jewish state. He was also somewhat annoyed by the tactics Zionist leaders employed in trying to influence him, but he continued to cooperate with their endeavors.[9]

When the plan to partition Palestine was brought before the U.N. General Assembly in the autumn of 1947, the President ordered the U.S. delegation to back the proposal.[10] After weeks of intense Zionist lobbying, both in Washington and at the United Nations itself, the Partition Resolution was endorsed by just over two-thirds of the General Assembly. In the early spring of 1948, some of Truman's close advisors, concerned about the approaching war in Palestine, prevailed on him to submit the idea of a temporary U.N. trusteeship in the region. This never materialized as a substantial proposal, however, and when the State of Israel was proclaimed on May 15, 1948, the United States gave it immediate recognition. This was the beginning of what was to become the "special relationship" that would take priority over all other American considerations vis-à-vis U.S. Middle East policy.

The destabilization of the Middle East that followed the onset of the Arab-Israeli conflict and the changing political structure of the area prompted the United States to join Great Britain and France in issuing the Tripartite Declaration of May 25, 1950. This joint statement of policy sought to keep the military capabilities of Israel and the Arab states at reasonable levels, to promote peace and stability generally, and to prevent any violation of the established frontiers in the region.[11] It was the first of a series of Western attempts to guarantee the territorial status quo in the Middle East, attempts aimed at limiting the extension of Soviet influence and avoiding dislocations that would have adverse repercussions for the Western alliance. But though well-intentioned, these objectives were never consistently upheld.

American attempts to establish a strategic consensus in the Middle East also began under the Truman presidency. The basic goal here was to establish a link between the NATO alliance in the West and a related network of alignments in the Middle East—one that would specifically include the Arab countries. Egypt was to be the linchpin of the system, and in 1951 proposals were made to that country to consider membership in a Middle East command, or defense organization. Cairo, however, preferred to adopt a neutral position in the Cold War, and along with the other Arab countries refused to participate.

Attempts to extend the Western alliance into the Middle East continued under the presidency of Dwight D. Eisenhower. Secretary of State John Foster Dulles was intent on creating an interlocking defense system along the peripheries of the Soviet Union to bolster the containment policy with a more determined posture. Since the Middle East Command project had failed, he turned to the northern tier countries, which had already shown a willingness to cooperate with the West. On February 24, 1955, Turkey and Iraq concluded a five-year defense agreement at Baghdad. Great Britain, Pakistan, and Iran (where the United States had restored the Shah's power in 1953) adhered to this Pact of Mutual Cooperation later in the year, bringing into existence what was to become commonly known as the Baghdad Pact.[12] Though the United States was not officially a member, it served on some of the committees and was clearly the major architect of the alliance. Iraq abandoned the pact after the revolution of 1958, and it was reconstructed as the Central Treaty Organization (CENTO) in 1959—a network of bilateral accords between the United States and Turkey, Iran, and Pakistan. Nevertheless, the significance of the alignment diminished with the passage of time.

It was also during the Eisenhower administration that the

United States became directly involved as a mediator in the Suez crisis. The nationalization of the Canal, which was the principal issue at stake, had been a direct Egyptian response to U.S. anger at Nasser's neutralism and opposition to the Baghdad Pact, and the consequent withdrawal of the American offer to finance the Aswan dam project. The Anglo-French-Israeli attack on Egypt in October 1956 was sharply condemned, with both the president and Secretary Dulles taking an unequivocal position against the use of force to settle disputes. They insisted that aggressive action should not be rewarded, and demanded the withdrawal of Israeli troops from Gaza and Sinai. By early 1957, the territorial status quo was reinstated as a result of the U.S. intervention. American prestige in the Middle East was considerably enhanced by Eisenhower's staunch commitment to principle. "If we agree that armed attack can properly achieve the purposes of the assailant," he said on February 20, 1957, "then I fear we will have turned back the clock of international order. We will, in effect, have countenanced the use of force as a means of settling international differences."[13] The issue of the Canal had been essentially resolved before the attack, and it was clear that the real aim of Great Britain, France, and Israel was to topple Egyptian president Gamal Abd al-Nasser. By contrast, the United States seemed to have behaved in a relatively fair and even-handed manner in its reaction to the crisis.

Far less successful was the broader U.S. Middle East policy developed at this time. On January 5, 1957, the president asked Congress to authorize economic and military assistance to any country in the area that requested it, and to approve the use of U.S. troops to protect the states there "against overt armed aggression from any nation controlled by International Communism."[14] Congress passed legislation to this effect on March 9, 1957, formalizing what became known as the Eisenhower Doctrine. It was subsequently invoked in 1958 to assist Jordan and Lebanon. In the latter case, some 14,000 U.S. marines were landed to help settle what turned out to be an internal political destabilization.

The main shortcoming of the Eisenhower Doctrine was that it was focused almost exclusively on the American preoccupation with the Cold War. It demonstrated little interest in the concerns and aspirations of the Arab countries. Some of the latter had already received substantial aid from the Soviet Union, and in any case they found Israel far more threatening than communism. The Eisenhower Doctrine also encouraged precipitous and often ill-advised intervention, which became evident in the action taken in Lebanon. In many respects, it eradicated the advantages gained in the circumspect handling of the Suez crisis.

Shifting Policies of the 1960s

During the Kennedy and Johnson administrations, U.S. Middle East policy remained inconsistent and loosely defined. President Kennedy wanted to create a new American image, one which embodied sympathy for and encouragement of the aspirations of Third World peoples. The Peace Corps was one manifestation of this policy. With respect to the Middle East, Kennedy reassured Saudi Arabia and Jordan of continuing support, and he tempered the traditional U.S. commitment to Israel by placing it within a broader policy of building good relations with a wide range of Middle East states. He also emphazised the U.S. dedication to the search for peace and security throughout the region, and reaffirmed American opposition to the use of force as a means of changing the territorial status quo.[15] This amounted to a reaffirmation of the Tripartite Declaration of 1950 and of the principles invoked by Eisenhower in the Suez crisis. In appointing John Badeau, former president of the American University in Cairo, as ambassador to Egypt, Kennedy demonstrated a sincere desire for the establishment of better relations with the Arab nationalist and progressive countries. At the same time, however, U.S. opposed Nasser's involvement in the Yemen civil war and his hostility toward Saudi Arabia and Jordan. It was also during the Kennedy administration that the United States began to build up its Sixth Fleet in the Mediterranean, and to extend military aid exclusively to Israel.

President Johnson's initial Middle East policy was to maintain as good a relationship as possible with the progressive as well as the conservative Arab states while continuing to assist Israel. He reiterated U.S. support "for the territorial integrity and political independence of all countries in the Near East," and its opposition "to aggression and the use of force or threat of force against any country."[16] By early 1966, however, this policy had yielded to one of noncooperation with Egypt, reflecting U.S. impatience with Nasser's involvement in the Yemen dispute as well as with his neutralist stance in international politics.[17] The practice of selling surplus food to Egypt for local currency under Public Law 480 was discontinued, and the U.S. refused requests for assistance in locating funds for development projects. Also, a planned visit to Cairo by Secretary of State Rusk was indefinitely postponed, and pleas that Washington mediate the Yemen controversy were ignored. The shift in Middle East policy-making from the State Department to the President's national security advisors, who were generally less sympathetic with the interests of the Arab world than with those of Israel, had a major bearing on this change.

The most significant development of this period was an understanding reached with Israel before the 1967 war. With some reservations and a degree of ambiguity, the United States tacitly agreed to an Israeli military assault on Egypt as a way of dealing with Nasser's announced blockade of the Strait of Tiran.[18] The Johnson administration saw a number of advantages in an Israeli victory over Egypt—in particular the discrediting of Nasser and the embarrassment of the patron role that had been played by the Soviet Union.[19] But it was considered essential that the operation be swift and completely successful. Therefore, on May 23, 1967, President Johnson authorized an air shipment of military equipment and ammunition to Israel to facilitate the invasion.[20] According to an as yet unsubstantiated report by Stephen Green, the U.S. may have become even more directly involved in the affair by sending a special air reconnaissance squadron to photograph all activities in the battle area after the invasion had begun. These films were allegedly turned over to the Israelis to be analyzed and interpreted.[21]

The bizarre episode of the Israeli attack on the U.S.S. *Liberty*, a sophisticated American intelligence ship operating off the Israeli-Egyptian coastal areas at this time, throws further light on the new dimension that was emerging in the relationship between the United States and Israel.[22] The *Liberty* had been ordered to proceed to the eastern Mediterranean to monitor the military situation. By the time she reached her destination on June 7, the war had spread to three fronts, and Israeli forces were in the process of occupying not only the Sinai Peninsula, but also the West Bank and the Golan Heights. This extended operation had never been agreed to by Washington, and it seems certain that Israel wanted to conceal its broader intentions at this point. Hence, on June 8, Israeli aircraft and torpedo boats attacked the ship and came close to sinking her. Thirty-four of the crew were killed, and all attempts of the *Liberty* to get assistance from the Sixth Fleet ended in failure.

Though the *Liberty* was clearly marked and was flying a large American flag during the daylight hours when the attack took place, Israel claimed that the whole incident had been a matter of mistaken identity and submitted profuse apologies. What is most significant, however, is the fact that the United States readily accepted these apologies and, in effect, tried to cover up the affair and prevent an extensive public hearing. The failure of American naval forces to send aid to the *Liberty* in distress is best explained by the reluctance of Washington to permit a U.S.-Israeli adversary encounter, while the attempt to conceal and minimize the details seems to suggest a kind of collusion between the two countries. In many respects, then, a de facto alliance had been established.

When the war was over, President Johnson formally reaffirmed the traditional U.S. policy with regard to territorial integrity, though in reality he had already abandoned the U.S. commitment to the Tripartite Declaration of 1950. On June 19, 1967, he laid down the principles for resolving the Arab-Israeli conflict that were later embodied in U.N. Security Council Resolution 242 of November 22, 1967.[23] Though this resolution won the support of many countries, it sought to establish the return of conquered territories as a basis for peace negotiations and failed to specify adequate measures for enforcing the implementation of its own recommendations. Unlike President Eisenhower's position in 1956, the Johnson Administration did not use political leverage to restore the territorial status quo. The irreconcilable positions of the respective sides in the conflict notwithstanding, the United States had in effect established a policy in the Middle East based on the perceived pragmatic advantages of cooperation with Israel without regard to earlier commitments. The discrepancy between principle and actual behavior alienated the Arab states, and many of them suspended diplomatic relations with Washington.

THE SEARCH FOR AN AMERICAN POLICY: THE FORMATIVE PHASE

The Quest for a Viable Formula

After the election of Richard Nixon in November 1968, the president-elect dispatched the former governor of Pennsylvania, William Scranton, to the Middle East to investigate the situation in the area and to make recommendations regarding future U.S. policy there. In an obvious reference to the recent pro-Israeli tilt of the Johnson administration, Scranton advised a more "even-handed" approach on the part of Washington. This set the tone of the early phase of the Nixon presidency, but it was not to last more than two years.

During late 1968 and early 1969, the mounting tension between Egypt and Israel in the Suez Canal region had precipitated what came to be known as the War of Attrition. In an attempt to deescalate the sporadic hostilities, the United States and the Soviet Union initiated the so-called Two-Power Talks on April 3, 1969—a series of discussions occasionally joined by Great Britain and France as well. Ultimately, however, these negotiations ended in failure, primarily because the U.S. endorsed the bargaining position of Israel while the Soviet Union backed the Egyptian stand on the resolution of the conflict.

This led to the unilateral American peace initiative commonly referred to as the Rogers Plan. In a speech delivered in Washington on December 9, 1969, Secretary of State William Rogers outlined the conceptual framework of a balanced approach to peace in the Middle East. The statement reflected a change of attitude in that it was notably non-partisan, and took a strong position on Israeli withdrawal from the occupied territories. "Any changes in the pre-existing [boundary] lines," Rogers said, "should not reflect the weight of conquest and should be confined to insubstantial alterations required for mutual security."[24] The Rogers Plan proved to be no more than a transitory shift of emphasis in Washington, and never became a major element in U.S. Middle East policy. Its only tangible accomplishment was its role in bringing the War of Attrition to an end on August 7, 1970.

By 1971, the Nixon administration had decided that the safest course for the United States was to enhance Israel's military capability to the point that the Arab states would be forced to accept a settlement on Israeli terms. In that year, American aid to Israel was radically increased to nearly five times the largest amount and close to fifty times the smallest amount given in any previous year.[25] The total amount loaned was $600.8 million, of which $545 million was in the form of military assistance.

This policy of massive military support for Israel was adopted at a time when the use of surrogates, especially Iran, had become an established tactic under the Nixon Doctrine. But the United States was not yet aware that the new Egyptian leader, Anwar Sadat, would be much more moderate that his predecessor. Sadat demonstrated a willingness to cooperate with the February 1971 peace initiative of the U.N. mediator, Ambassador Gunnar Jarring, and in July 1972 he evicted most of the large contingent of Soviet advisors and technicians from Egypt. Still, the Nixon administration's only response to Sadat's move was a proposal by the President on February 9, 1972 that the Suez Canal be reopened as a first step toward a broader settlement.[26] In this way, the U.S. was inadvertently forcing Sadat to seriously consider the war option to break the no war/no peace impasse that had evolved from the American-Israeli working relationship.

By the early months of 1973 it had become clear that Israel intended to maintain control of at least significant portions of the occupied territories, while continuing to establish Jewish settlements in them. This prompted Sadat to call for a Security Council discussion of the Middle East situation in the spring of that year. The debate continued for several months, and a resolution designed to increase pressure on Israel to withdraw from the occupied territories was introduced on July 24, 1973, by seven members of the Council.[27] Despite its endorsement by Great Britain, France, and all other Security Council members except China (which abstained), the United States vetoed the resolution on July 26 on the grounds that it was unbalanced.[28] This undoubtedly played a major role in encouraging Egypt, Syria, and Saudi Arabia to complete their plans for an attack on Israel's positions in the Sinai Peninsula and the Golan Heights. The so-called October War that was the result of these preparations caught Israel and the world in general off guard, and opened a new era in U.S. Middle East policy-making.

Peace Initiatives and New Allies

The fourth Arab-Israeli war and the brief oil embargo that followed produced a change in the American perception of the increasingly complex Middle East crisis. The Arab ability to plan, coordinate, and execute a successful military attack and to profoundly disturb the status quo had now been clearly demonstrated. The issue of international dependency on Middle East petroleum resources also became a matter of concern in the West, especially among the European allies of the United States. There was, furthermore, a sharpened awareness worldwide of the degree to which local conflicts in the area could bring the superpowers dangerously close to confrontation.

With these considerations in mind, the Nixon administration moved swiftly to alter its relationship with the Arab states and to play a still highly active but less partisan role in promoting a settlement of the Arab-Israeli dispute. The Secretary of State, Henry Kissinger, became the first architect of this new American policy. Kissinger initially worked with the Soviets to stop the fighting, after which he concentrated on convening at Geneva a conference of all parties to the conflict, direct and indirect. This meeting finally took place on December 21, 1973.[29] Representatives of Israel, Egypt, Jordan, and the two superpowers were in attendance, but Syria and the PLO were conspicuously absent. Following considerable bickering and a mainly ceremonial beginning the conference was adjourned, never to be reopened. But Kissinger had laid the foundations of a more successful peace initiative—the establishment of a cordial working relationship with Anwar Sadat, and the assumption of a mediating role between Egypt and Israel.

Between early 1974 and late March 1975, the American Secretary of State became involved in a series of intense negotiations with the Egyptian and Israeli governments that came to be known as "step-by-step" or "shuttle" diplomacy. The main stumbling block in these endeavors was Israel's unwillingness to seriously pursue any settlement with Egypt. In an interview published in *Haaretz* on December 3, 1974, Prime Minister Rabin succinctly expressed the Israeli attitude when he said that "the central aim of Israel should be to gain time," so that Israel would not have to conclude a comprehensive agreement with Egypt until the United States had become less dependent on Arab oil, and would no longer try to pressure Israel into accepting conditions it found incompatible with its own interests.[30] However, Kissinger, for his part, realized that the peace initiative would collapse if the momentum were lost.

The new President, Gerald Ford, was annoyed by Israel's failure to cooperate. "I am disappointed to learn that Israel has not moved as far as it might," he wrote Rabin on March 21, 1975.[31] The following day, Kissinger held his final meeting with the Israeli leaders, after which he terminated this phase of his shuttle diplomacy. At this point, he initiated a "reassessment" of American Middle East policy designed to pressure Israel into a more conciliatory bargaining position.[32] This tactic ultimately succeeded, and on September 1, 1975, Israel and Egypt concluded an interim agreement (Sinai II) that included a significant pull-back of Israeli forces in the Sinai Peninsula.[33] But in exchange for its cooperation, Israel was able to exact from Kissinger a secret commitment that the United States would supply the Jewish state with sophisticated weaponry and that it would "not recognize or negotiate with the Palestine Liberation Organization so long as the Palestine Liberation Organization does not recognize Israel's right to exist and does not accept Security Council Resolutions 242 and 338."[34]

Though Sinai II marked some progress toward an Egyptian-Israeli settlement, the Jerusalem government interpreted its own com-

pliance as a concession that would have the long-range effect of de-
laying a comprehensive agreement with Egypt. The American news
magazine, *Time*, quoted an unnamed senior Israeli official as saying
that Sinai II had the advantage of putting off a future Geneva conference or any other development that would force Israel to go back
to the 1967 borders. "The interim agreement," the anonymous official
reportedly said, "has delayed Geneva, while at the same time assur-
ing us arms, money, a coordinated policy with Washington and quiet
in Sinai. Relatively speaking, we have given up a little for a lot."[35]

The American response to this attitude was to discard the step-
by-step diplomatic approach and make it clear that the reassessment
was a continuing process. On November 12, 1975, then Deputy Assis-
tant Secretary of State for Near Eastern and South Asian Affairs Harold
Saunders made a prepared statement before the House of Representatives International Affairs Subcommittee on the Middle East in
which he emphasized the importance of the Palestinian issue in the
search for a solution to the Middle East crisis:

> In many ways the Palestinian dimension of the Arab-Israeli conflict
> is the heart of that conflict. Final resolution of the problems arising
> from the partition of Palestine, the establishment of the State of Israel,
> and Arab opposition to those events will not be possible until agree-
> ment is reached defining a just and permanent status for the people
> who consider themselves Palestinians. . . . The issue is not whether
> Palestinian interests should be expressed in a final settlement, but
> how. There will be no peace until an answer is found.[36]

In January 1976, the Ford administration cut the proposed
military aid package for Israel from one and a half billion to one billion
dollars, and in other ways made it clear to Rabin that the U.S. was
determined to maintain the momentum of the peace initiative. It was
in this context that the President appointed William Scranton to be
his ambassador to the United Nations in March 1976. Because of Scranton's earlier statement about the need for even-handedness in U.S.
Middle East policy, the very appointment itself represented a form
of pressure on Israel.

In his first speech at the Security Council on March 23, Scranton referred to the occupation of territories in the 1967 war as "an ab-
normal state of affairs that would be brought to an end as part of a
peaceful settlement," and also criticized Israel for its alterations in

the status of Jerusalem and the establishment of Jewish settlements in the West Bank, Golan Heights, and the Sinai Peninsula. "The future of Jerusalem," he continued, "will be determined only through the instruments and processes of negotiation, agreement, and accommodation." On the question of Jewish settlements, he asserted that this practice was illegal under international law, and pointed out that "the presence of settlements is seen by my Government as an obstacle to the success of the negotiations for a just and final peace between Israel and its neighbors."[37]

Two days after this speech, Ambassador Scranton was instructed by Washington to veto a Security Council resolution censuring Israel for the very transgressions he had cited in his own address. The reason given was that the resolution was "unbalanced," but the closeness of its wording to Scranton's statement and the fact that such countries as Great Britain and Sweden voted for the resolution suggest that the Ford administration was concerned about the domestic political consequences that might ensue in a presidential election year from an affirmative vote or even an abstention. Nevertheless, the policy of reassessment was not abandoned, and near the end of Ford's presidency the United States voted in favor of a more carefully worded Security Council resolution censuring Israel for its practice of establishing Jewish settlements in the occupied territories, and rejecting Israel's annexation of East Jerusalem.

President Jimmy Carter's Middle East policy followed the general guidelines established by his predecessor. In answer to a question posed at a town meeting in Clinton, Massachusetts, on March 16, 1977, the President said that while the first prerequisite for a lasting peace was the recognition by Israel's neighbors of its right to exist, he also believed that "There has to be a homeland provided for the Palestinian refugees who have suffered for many, many years."[38] To assuage any Israeli concern with this statement, he made it clear on May 12 that the United States still had a special relationship with Israel that included a commitment to Israel's right to exist.[39] But at another press conference, on May 26, Carter reaffirmed his position that Israel must withdraw from occupied Arab territories as part of an overall peace agreement, and that the Palestinians had the right to a homeland and to compensation for the losses they had suffered.[40] On July 12, however, he qualified his position on the Palestinian homeland by saying at a press conference that his own preference "was that the Palestinian entity, whatever form it might take and whatever area it might occupy, should be tied in with Jordan and not be independent. But I don't

have the authority nor the inclination to try to impose that preference on the parties that will negotiate."[41]

With the formation of a new Israeli government by Menachem
Begin in June 1977, relations between Washington and Jerusalem became strained. In a press conference on August 23, Carter said that
Israel's practice of establishing Jewish settlements in the occupied territories "creates an unnecessary obstacle to peace."[42] Referring indi-
rectly to Israel three days later, he concluded: "I think any nation in
the Middle East that proved to be intransigent or an obstacle to progress [toward peace] would suffer at least to some degree the condemnation of the rest of the world."[43] Then, on September 29, he asserted
at a press conference that if the PLO accepted Resolution 242 and the
right of Israel to exist, he would go along with the PLO's contention
that Resolution 242 did not adequately address the Palestinian issue
because it refers only to refugees.[44] Two days later, on October 1, the
United States and the Soviet Union issued a Joint Communiqué which
called for the withdrawal of Israeli forces from territories occupied
in the 1967 conflict, the resolution of the Palestinian question in a
way that insured the legitimate rights of the Palestinian people, and
the establishment of normal peaceful relations on the basis of mutual recognition of sovereign and territorial independence.[45] On October 4, President Carter reiterated the U.S. commitment to these
principles in a speech before the United Nations.

Though President Carter clearly wanted to establish a balanced
policy that took the Palestinian issue into serious consideration, his
position was never fully consistent. On December 28, 1977, for example, he reiterated his preference that the new Palestinian entity
be not independent, but tied in some way to Jordan or Israel.[46] Yet Anwar Sadat, with whom the United States had become increasingly cordial since late 1973, had advocated Palestinian statehood before the
Israeli Knesset the previous month.[47] This divergence in policy was
offset, however, when Carter made a public statement to Sadat in
Aswan on January 4, 1978, which asserted that Israel must withdraw
from territories occupied in 1967 and that there must be a recognition
of the legitimate rights of the Palestinian people, enabling "the Palestinians to participate in the determination of their own future."[48]

During the first half of 1978, Sadat's peace effort failed to
achieve a meeting of minds between the governments of Egypt and
Israel, and there were several acrimonious exchanges between the two
leaders. President Carter also expressed annoyance at Begin's intran-

sigence, particularly with regard to the Jewish settlements issue. To break the deadlock, Carter proposed that Sadat and Begin meet with him at the presidential retreat to try and resolve the differences between Egypt and Israel. The meetings convened at Camp David on September 5 and concluded on September 17, 1978, with an agreement on the framework for peace between Egypt and Israel and the establishment of autonomy in the West Bank and Gaza.[49]

Though the Camp David accords led to a peace treaty between Egypt and Israel on March 26, 1979, they left the issue of Palestinian self-determination very loosely defined and shrouded in ambiguity. As Ezer Weizman put it, "Whereas the Egyptians saw the Sinai agreement as a model for similar understandings with Jordan and Syria over the West Bank and the Golan Heights, Begin saw it as . . . the end of the story."[50] In terms of U.S. policy, George Lenczowski has pointed out that the agreements represented "substantial retreat from the earlier position of President Carter regarding Israel's withdrawal, a homeland for the Palestinians, and the need to take the PLO into account in the peacemaking process. . . . President Carter did not obtain from Begin any formal commitment to desist from further expansion of Jewish settlements in the West Bank and the Gaza Strip and did not insist on the return of Arab sovereignty over these areas."[51] These shortcomings in the American stand on basic issues were partly responsible for the inadequate linkage between the Egyptian-Israeli agreement and the other dimensions of the overall conflict. They therefore contributed to the isolation of Egypt from many of its former regional allies and to a polarization of inter-Arab politics.

There were also some shifts in the structure of U.S. alignments in the Middle East during the Carter administration. Egypt, which had begun to develop its cordial relationship with Washington in late 1973, had become by 1979 a virtual American client. That very year, however, the new Islamic revolutionary regime in Iran reversed the essentially pro-American policy of the former shah, demonstrating an increasing hostility toward the United States that culminated in the hostage crisis of November 1979–January 1981. Still another disquieting development was the Soviet invasion of Afghanistan in December 1979. President Carter's response to the situation was to clarify the importance of the Persian Gulf to American interests. He did this in his State of the Union address on January 23, 1980:

> Let our position be absolutely clear: An attempt by any outside force to gain control of the Persian Gulf region will be regarded

as an assault on the vital interests of the United States of America, and such an assault will be repelled by any means necessary, including military force.[52]

This statement become known as the Carter Doctrine, and established a new dimension of U.S. Middle East policy.

The reorganization of U.S. alignments in the Middle East continued to be based on the concept of "strategic consensus," now complemented by a strengthened US military presence in the region that was most apparent in the form of the newly created regional "Rapid Deployment Force." The major change was the replacement of Iran with Egypt as a tacit ally, while Israel and Saudi Arabia remained the other two principal components of the American defense system. The United States tried to extend this circle of friends to include other countries in the area. The agreements with Turkey, though modified, remained intact, partly because the United States had not acted to prevent the Turkish invasion and partition of Cyprus in the summer of 1974. Oman and Morocco, which were for the most part supportive of Egyptian policy, allowed the United States to use various military base facilities. Also, reasonably cordial relations were maintained with Jordan, Tunisia, Algeria, North Yemen, and the Gulf sheikhdoms. But the policies of the United States and Jordan diverged over King Hussein's disinclination to participate in the American peace initiatives of the late 1970s and early 1980s.

During the first year and a half of his administration, President Ronald Reagan neither developed a clear-cut Middle East policy nor made any concerted effort to pursue the peace initiatives launched by Presidents Ford and Carter. However, the Israeli attack on Iraqi nuclear facilities in June 1981, the assassination of Anwar Sadat the following October, the continuing Iraq-Iran hostilities, and Israel's invasion of Lebanon on June 6, 1982, so destabilized the Middle East that the United States was forced to adopt some position to protect its imperilled interests in the area. The first attempt to fill this need was the Reagan proposal of September 1, 1982, embodied in a television address to the nation. Reaffirming the U.S. role as mediator and reactivating the Camp David framework and other aspects of Carter's policy, President Reagan called for a freeze on further Jewish settlements in the occupied territories and the establishment of full Palestinian autonomy in the West Bank and Gaza in association with Jordan. He specifically ruled out an independent state as a solution to the Palestinian problem, but held to the principle that negotiations be based on "an exchange of territory for peace."[53]

Though the Reagan proposal was rejected by Israel, it evoked a positive response in many Arab countries and indeed throughout much of the world. Its major shortcomings were that it did not go beyond the general guidelines of a framework for a broader peace in the Middle East, and that it established the precondition that Palestinian statehood was an unacceptable component of any overall settlement. It was, nevertheless, productive in that it reiterated earlier U.S. opposition to the establishment of Jewish settlements in the occupied territories, and implied that the solution to Palestinian autonomy in the West Bank and Gaza could not be achieved through the auspices of Israel.

The Reagan proposal never gathered sufficient momentum to make it an effective peace initiative. Secretary of State George Shultz attempted to preserve the image of the United States as an impartial mediator committed to a just resolution of the Palestinian problem in his answer to a question posed after an address delivered in Atlanta, Georgia, on February 24, 1983. "It must be true," he said" that one of the principal reasons why we have so much difficulty with peace in the Middle East is that we haven't been able to find the answer to the legitimate rights and aspirations of the Palestinian people. . . . I don't think you can pass off the Palestinian issue with a statement about the Palestinians and Jordan. The problem is bigger and deeper than that."[54]

During the following months, however, the civil strife in Lebanon became so intense that the United States concentrated its attention on this more immediate crisis. U.S. marines had been stationed in Lebanon from late August to mid-September, 1982, as part of the multinational force set up to preside over the evacuation of the Palestinian guerrillas. But American troops returned after the massacre of Palestinian civilians at the Sabra and Shatila refugee camps in what was described as an attempt to restore Lebanese sovereignty in the country. Ultimately, however, this military presence led to a direct U.S. involvement in the sectarian conflict in Lebanon.

By the spring of 1983, the United States had embarked on a policy of supporting President Gemayel and the Maronites in an attempt to harness the Syrian-backed Muslim-Druze opposition.[55] This included the promotion of the Lebanese-Israeli accord of May 17, 1983—an agreement vehemently rejected by the Muslim-Druze faction, which sought to prevent Christian supremacy and the establishment of a dominant Israeli (rather than Syrian) presence in Lebanon. The sharp disparity of sectarian positions on these issues led to escalating hostilities between the warring sides throughout the summer of 1983. The United States was gradually drawn into the conflict on behalf of the Christian militias, and on September 19, 1983, American warships bombarded Druze positions in the mountain village of Suq al-Gharb. Attacks upon the U.S. embassy on April 18, 1983, the marine compound on October 23, 1983, and the embassy annex on September 20, 1984, reflect the hostile response to the Reagan administration's policy of taking sides in a struggle that was poorly understood in terms of the incredibly complex issues involved.

By the end of November 1983, Reagan's advisors had decided on a reorientation of U.S. Middle East policy designed to emphasize Washington's close working relationship with Israel.[56] On November 29, the President and Israeli Prime Minister Yitzhak Shamir announced after a meeting in Washington that they had greatly expanded the U.S.-Israeli partnership for political and strategic cooperation, including the establishment of a joint military committee to work together in planning, maneuvers, and the stockpiling of U.S. equipment in Israel.[57] Commenting on the accord, King Hussein of Jordan said on December 1 that the Reagan administration's decision to establish close political and military ties with Israel without exacting some concessions would have a "negative effect" on U.S. credibility in the Arab world.[58] Certainly, the move generated considerable pessimism among the moderate Arab states that had traditionally shown a willingness to cooperate with the United States. But it was a recapitulation of the tendency of American administrations to strengthen the relationship with Israel when the political drift in the Arab world seemed hostile and unmanageable.

During the 1982 presidential election campaign, Reagan and Walter Mondale tried to outdo each other in pledging their support for Israel. Both candidates were extravagant in their commitments, although Reagan refused to condone the idea of moving the U.S. embassy in Israel to Jerusalem—a step which would alienate the entire Muslim world. Mondale favored the change. The reelection of Reagan left the future course of U.S. Middle East policy uncertain, since his policy was never fully defined in the first term.

In the early months of 1985, however, the administration was beginning to reactivate the Reagan initiative of September 1, 1982. While Saudi Arabia's King Fahd was on a state visit to Washington in February, Arafat and King Hussein of Jordan concluded a "framework for common action." American receptivity to the implied coordination of Jordanian and Palestinian bargaining positions in future negotiations stimulated a renewed Arab interest in the peace process.

President Mubarak of Egypt proposed direct talks between Israel and a joint Jordanian-Palestinian delegation, a suggestion that evoked a favorable response from Prime Minister Shimon Peres. On an official visit to Washington in March, the Egyptian leader urged President Reagan to act on these developments and revive the quest for peace.

Despite the improved political atmosphere, however, the likelihood of a substantive change in the Arab-Israeli impasse was minimized by the negative attitude toward a compromise settlement on both sides. The Likud members of Israel's coalition government and the radical members of the PLO (backed by Syria) openly opposed the proposed negotiations. The ability of the Reagan administration to transform the positive elements of the equation into a constructive movement toward peace will depend on the degree to which it can act with sufficient authority to overcome confining political pressures, both at home and abroad.

The Reagan administration's record on influencing Middle East events in a positive direction, however, is not very encouraging. In his recent book, *The Blood of Abraham*, former President Jimmy Carter accuses Reagan of having obstructed the peace process because "he has tended to prefer the threat or use of American military force instead of negotiation."[59] Taking issue with the way the administration handled the situation in Lebanon, Carter recounts his own attempts to stop the Israeli invasion in June 1982. At the outset of the campaign, he recalls, he appealed to Israeli leaders but their reply was simply: "We have a green light from Washington."[60]

The administration's involvement in the Lebanese conflict during the summer of 1983 was another manifestation of ill-advised decision-making, as was the overall failure to enlarge on Reagan's 1982 peace initiative. The diplomatic activities of early 1985 provided an opportunity to develop a more constructive policy. But Mubarak's visit to Washington in March evoked a less than enthusiastic official response, and at the end of his stay the Egyptian president was openly critical of U.S. disinclination to play a more active role.

The handling of a series of violent episodes during the latter part of 1985 further undermined the credibility of the United States as an effective mediator in the Middle East peace process. On October 1, Israel launched a devastating air attack on the PLO headquarters just outside Tunis. The Jerusalem government said the action was in retaliation for the shooting on September 25 of three Israelis at Larnaca, Cyprus, by Palestinians presumed to be members of the PLO security unit, Force 17. Torn between its approval of the raid as what appeared to be a bold strike against terrorism and its desire to maintain good relations with Tunisia and other moderate Arab states, the Reagan administration's response to the event was equivocal and inept. By describing the blatant breach of Tunisia's sovereignty as "legitimate" and "understandable" on the one hand, and as "cannot be condoned" on the other, it created a vivid impression of itself as indecisive and inconsistent. Though the U.S. refrained from vetoing the subsequent U.N. Security Council resolution condemning Israel, its abstention only underlined the lack of a clear Middle East policy in Washington.

A week following the Tunis raid, the bizarre episode of the Achille Lauro affair began to unfold. Four Palestinians aboard the ship, on a mission to attack a military installation in Israel, panicked when their arms were discovered at an Egyptian port and hijacked the Italian cruise liner. As they were members of the Tunis-based Palestine Liberation Front, a non-Fatah faction still loyal to Arafat, their action was interpreted by the United States as a reprisal for the Israeli attack on October 1. The hijacking itself and the subsequent murder of an elderly Jewish-American passenger were condemned by Arafat, who promised to bring the four Palestinians to justice after they surrendered to the Egyptian authorities. But when Mubarak put them on an Egyptian 737 to be tried in Tunis, American F-14s intercepted the aircraft and forced it to land at a U.S. air base in Sicily, where Italian police arrested the four for eventual indictment and trial.

Though the precipitous intervention by the Reagan administration may have been an understandable response, considering the series of attacks on American citizens and installations in recent years, it was nevertheless counterproductive in terms of the peace process. It not only strained U.S.-Egyptian relations, but impeded Mubarak's attempts to play a constructive role by furthering the moderate Arab position. It also effectively ruled out Arafat as a negotiating partner by denying him the right to try the hijackers and thereby improve the image of the PLO. Yet a peaceful resolution of the Arab-Israeli conflict seems unlikely without PLO participation in any future negotiations.

Finally, on December 27, terrorists associated with the Libyan-based maverick Palestinian, Abu Nidal, launched vicious attacks on El Al passengers at the Rome and Vienna airports. The Reagan administration singled out Muammar Qaddafi as the major accomplice, though the subsequent Italian and Austrian investigations showed no direct Libyan connection. As U.S. naval activities in the Mediterranean suggested a possible strike against Libya, which eventually materialized in the April 15, 1986, raids on Tripoli and Benghazi, even the most moderate Arab states indicated a strong disapproval of any military intervention. Reagan's appeal to America's European allies to impose economic sanctions on Libya also met with a negative response. The net effect of U.S. policy in this instance also was to give virtually all the Arab states the impression that Washington was so preoccupied with the problem of terrorism that it could not make any serious headway in promoting the peace process. By applying the terrorist label to all Palestinian groups without much consideration of their varying positions, the United States appeared to be intent on barring the PLO from negotiations aimed at resolving the conflict. At the same time, its interest in promoting a genuine settlement was open to question, given the continuing disinclination of the administration and the Congress to provide effective support and encouragement for the major Arab advocates of a peace conference — Egypt and Jordan.

PROBLEMS AND PROSPECTS OF AMERICAN POLICY

The greatest weakness of U.S. Middle East policy over the past forty years was succinctly summarized by the British analyst, Peter Mansfield, in a BBC radio broadcast in the summer of 1983. Instead of examining the situation on the ground and acting in terms of actual options and constraints, he pointed out, successive administrations have usually based their positions on what they think the public or the media or the lobbies would prefer and consider reasonable. The result has been a decision-making process that has had difficulty in dealing with the real world because of an inordinate preoccupation with popularity.

Another aspect of the problem has been the underlying insecurity in Washington as to how to deal with the fluid and sometimes unpredictable course of events in the Middle East. This has led most administrations to assign the highest priority to maintaining Israel as the principal partner of the United States in the area. The overall effect of this policy, however, is that it tends to obscure the real dimensions of the broader political developments and dislocations in the Middle East. Yet these very alterations in the regional system are what determine its character and direction.

The Middle East is passing through a transitional period in its history, one in which all the foundations of traditional sociopolitical orientation are undergoing rapid and profound change. This has given rise to numerous incidents of tension and conflict. The most important trend in this context is the increasingly low tolerance of ever larger numbers of people for the vestiges of colonialism manifest in the superpower rivalry. There is also the disenchantment of many with ruling elites that try to mask their monopolization of power with paternalistic handouts and empty promises. The more sensitive issues have found their way to the street, unleashing volatile reactions that all too often take anti-Americanism as a major theme.

It is not possible to deal effectively with mass alienation and the Islamic resurgence movements that arise from it without understanding in depth the sociopolitical dynamics involved. But the strong inclination of American administrations to reinforce the "special relationship" with Israel, while dismissing or misinterpreting developments on the ground in the Middle East is the most formidable obstacle to the emergence of a mature and considered U.S. policy. Furthermore, the perception of many people in the area that the United States engages in a pronounced favoritism for Israel is in itself perhaps the major source of their anti-American sentiments.

The search for useful alignments and agreements on "strategic consensus" in the Middle East has also presented certain problems for the United States. Often the concern with developing such relationships overlooks the bearing they may have on political unrest in the area, and on the quest for a peaceful resolution of the Arab-Israeli conflict. The policy of supporting the shah in Iran certainly played some role in stimulating the popular uprising that unseated him in 1979, and in bringing to power a staunchly anti-American regime. Similarly, the strong U.S. backing of Anwar Sadat and the failure to insure that the Egyptian-Israeli peace treaty included adequate linkage to the other unresolved issues of the Arab-Israeli conflict were instrumental in isolating Egypt from most of the Arab states and in polarizing inter-Arab politics. Even moderate regimes have found it difficult or impossible to cooperate as closely with Washington as they had in the past.

The special relationship with Israel may have been a reassuring element in the American defense system in the Middle East, but it was also detrimental to the various U.S. peace initiatives. In accommodating Israeli policy, the United States has often undermined its own credibility among the Arabs and its ability to draw them into the negotiating process. There has seldom been a clear recognition in Washington that when the United States fails to maintain a balanced policy, it relinquishes its role as an effective mediator. Every time the special relationship with Israel is allowed to exclude other considerations, the quest for peace is obstructed.

Another counterproductive aspect of U.S. Middle East policy has been its inconsistency. On many occasions, the United States has taken positions that have been equitable and even-handed, including numerous criticisms of Israeli as well as Arab behavior. But most attempts to keep Israel in line with American policy have not been consistently pursued. Even those presidents who seemed determined to maintain a balance in their approach to the Middle East, such as Ford and Carter, occasionally reversed their positions, creating uncertainty as to their real intentions and commitments.

The establishment of a constructive and effective U.S. Middle East policy depends on clarity of purpose and on a consistent adherence to announced principles in all fields. This requires not only a nonpartisan role in mediating the Arab-Israeli dispute, but also an unequivocal position on upholding the territorial sovereignty and independence of all states in the area, and a genuine commitment to the right of peoples to self-determination. It also requires a doctrine with regard to alignments that takes into consideration the political principles to which the United States itself adheres, and avoids the practice of taking sides in regional conflicts. It is unrealistic to expect that the United States can deal effectively with such a volatile area and prevent dislocations from occuring if a mature policy is not defined and implemented.

Finally, there is the question of whether it is possible to reach a lasting settlement of the major issues at stake in the Middle East without the participation of the Soviet Union. Though the United States is suspicious of Soviet motives, the fact remains that ultimately it will be difficult to exclude Moscow from the process of conflict resolution. This is because the USSR itself has major interests in the area, and can influence the course of events through its proximity, its power, and its connections with the regional states.

NOTES

1. Harry N. Howard, "The United States and the Middle East," in Tareq Ismael, ed. *The Middle East in World Politics* (Syracuse, N.Y.: Syracuse University Press, 1974), p. 117.

2. *Ibid.*, pp. 117–118.

3. *Ibid.*, p. 118.

4. *British Petroleum Statistical Review of World Energy,* June 1984, pp. 2–4. Middle East oil production is slightly higher than production in North America and slightly lower than production in the Soviet Union.

5. John Badeau, *The American Approach to the Arab World* (New York: Harper and Row, 1968), p. 27.

6. See Doreen Ingrams, *Palestine Papers, 1917–1922* (New York: George Braziller, 1973), pp. 140, 146.

7. George Lenczowski, *The Middle East in World Affairs* (Ithaca, N.Y.: Cornell University Press, 1980), p. 136.

8. *Ibid.*, p. 183.

9. Harry S. Truman, *Memoirs* (Garden City, N.Y.: Doubleday, 1956), vol. II, *Years of Trial and Hope,* p. 158.

10. *Ibid.*, p. 155.

11. J. C. Hurewitz, ed., *Diplomacy in the Near and Middle East: A Documentary Record* (Princeton, N.J.: Van Nostrand, 1956), vol. II, pp. 308–309.

12. *Ibid.*, pp. 390–91.

13. John Norton Moore, ed., *The Arab-Israeli Conflict: Readings and Documents* (Princeton, N.J.: Princeton University Press, 1977), p. 1017.

14. J. C. Hurewitz, ed., *Soviet-American Rivalry in the Middle East* (New York: Praeger, 1969), p. 11.

15. Dept. of State, *American Foreign Policy: Current Documents, 1963* (Washington, D.C.: U.S. Government Printing Office, 1967), p. 581.

16. Howard, "United States and Middle East, p. 127.

17. See Fred Khouri, *The Arab-Israeli Dilemma* (Syracuse, N.Y.: Syracuse University Press, 1976), p. 245; Nadav Safran, *From War to War: The Arab-Israeli Confrontation, 1948–1967* (New York: Pegasus, 1969), pp. 129, 132–37; and Hisham Sharabi, *Palestine and Israel: The Lethal Dilemma* (New York: Pegasus, 1969), pp. 77–78.

18. William Quandt, *Decade of Decisions: American Policy toward the Arab-Israeli Conflict, 1967–1976* (Berkeley and Los Angeles, Cal.: University of California Press, 1977), pp. 57–59.

19. Stephen Green, *Taking Sides: America's Secret Relations with a Militant Israel* (New York: William Morrow, 1984), p. 199.

20. *Ibid.*, p. 201.

21. *Ibid.*, pp. 204–11.

22. *Ibid.*, pp. 212–42. See also James M. Ennes, Jr., *Assault on the Liberty: The True Story of an Israeli Attack on an American Intelligence Ship* (New York: Random House, 1979).

23. Department of State, *The Quest for Peace: Principal United States Public Statements and Related Documents on the Arab-Israeli Peace Process, 1967–1983* (Washington, D.C.: U.S. Government Printing Office, 1984), pp. 1–4, 17–18.

24. *Ibid.*, pp. 23–29.

25. Agency for International Development, *U.S. Overseas Loans and Grants*

and Assistance from International Organizations: Obligations and Loan Authorizations, July 1, 1945–June 30, 1974 (Washington, D.C.: U.S. Government Printing Office, 1975), p. 17.

26. Dept. of State, *Quest for Peace*, pp. 34–37.

27. U.N. Security Council, *Guinea, India, Indonesia, Panama, Peru, Sudan, Yugoslavia: Draft Resolution, S/10974*, 24 July 1973.

28. U.S. Mission to the United Nations, *Press Release USUN-68 (73)*, July 26, 1973.

29. Edward Sheehan, *The Arabs, Israelis, and Kissinger: A Secret History of American Diplomacy in the Middle East* (New York: Reader's Digest Press, 1976), pp. 106–8.

30. *Ibid.*, p. 155.

31. *Ibid.*, p. 159.

32. *Ibid.*, p. 165.

33. See text in *ibid.*, pp. 245–50.

34. *Ibid.*, pp. 190–91.

35. *Time*, September 22, 1975, p. 34.

36. Yehuda Lukacs, ed., *Documents on the Israeli-Palestinian Conflict, 1967–1983* (Cambridge: Cambridge University Press, 1984), pp. 24–28.

37. *Ibid.*, pp. 30–32.

38. Dept. of State, *Quest for Peace*, pp. 66–67.

39. *Public Papers of the Presidents of the United States: Jimmy Carter, Book I: January 20 to June 24, 1977* (Washington, D.C.: U.S. Government Printing Office, 1977), p. 861.

40. *Public Papers of President Carter, January 20–June 24, 1977*, p. 1019.

41. Dept. of State, *Quest for Peace*, pp. 68–69.

42. *Public Papers of President Carter, Book II: June 25–December 31, 1977* (Washington, D.C.: U.S. Government Printing Office, 1978), p. 1489.

43. *Ibid.*, p. 1515.

44. *Ibid.*, p. 1687.

45. Dept. of State, *Quest for Peace*, pp. 70–71.

46. *Public Papers of President Carter, June 25–December 31, 1977*, p. 2190.

47. Lukacs, *Documents*, p. 52.

48. Dept. of State, *Quest for Peace*, pp. 72–73.

49. *Ibid.*, pp. 76–81.

50. Seth Tillman, *The United States in the Middle East: Interests and Obstacles* (Bloomington, Ind.: Indiana University Press, 1982), p. 27.

51. Lenczowski, *Middle East in World Affairs*, pp. 809–10.

52. *Public Papers of President Carter, Book I: January 1–May 23, 1980* (Washington, D.C.: U.S. Government Printing Office, 1981), p. 197.

53. Dept. of State, *Quest for Peace*, pp. 108–14.

54. Dept. of State, *Press Release No. 62A*, February 28, 1983.

55. See Thomas L. Friedman, "America's Failure in Lebanon," *New York Times Magazine*, April 8, 1984.

56. See John M. Goshko, "U.S. Pursues Israeli Connection Anew as Key to Mideast Peace," *Washington Post*, November 23, 1983.

57. Goshko, "U.S. and Israelis Expand Strategic and Political Ties," *Washington Post*, November 30, 1983.

58. Edward Walsh, "Israel Accord Hurts U.S., Hussein Says," *Washington Post*, December 2, 1983.

59. Jimmy Carter, *The Blood of Abraham* (Boston: Houghton Mifflin, 1985), pp. 201–02.

60. *Ibid.*, p. 98.

The Soviet Union and the Middle East

THE ROLE OF THE SOVIET UNION in the Middle East has interested
Western political scientists, historians, strategists, and policy-makers
since the Revolution of 1917, when the West's concern over traditional
Russian interests in the area was compounded by the fear of the new
Bolshevism. The onset of a cold war between West and East in the
late 1940s; the revolutionary transformation of the Middle East beginning in the 1950s; superpower concern over and/or involvement in the
1956 Suez Crisis, the "war of attrition" of 1969–70, and the 1967 and
1973 Arab-Israeli wars; the rise of the Palestinian movement as a force
in Middle East politics and international relations; the growing value
of petroleum resources, and the recognition of their strategic and economic importance after the Arab oil embargo of 1973–74; the decline
of detente; the 1979 Iranian revolution and Soviet invasion of Afghanistan; the Israeli invasion of Lebanon in 1982; and the apparent onset
of a new cold war in the 1980s — all these events have served to heighten
the interest of Western analysts both in the region generally and in
Soviet involvement there specifically.

The purpose of this chapter on Soviet relations with the Middle East is to examine recent developments in the light of earlier trends,
and then to analyze the significance of these events in terms of their
impact upon this critical region of the developing world. The 1917–
1945 period of Soviet involvement in the region is not examined here
because of its relatively minor impact on the international relations
of the area. The years from the end of World War II to 1973 are examined chiefly in terms of the trends they reveal, and for the infor-

167

mation they furnish on Soviet views and objectives. Finally, the period after the 1973 Arab-Israeli war is analyzed in an attempt to derive an understanding of the current status—and future potentialities—of Soviet policy in the Middle East.

THE POSTWAR SETTING, 1945–56

While observing the growth of Soviet relations with the Middle East, we may find it helpful to keep in mind that three sets of factors have influenced the development of the foreign policies of the major powers in their relations with the Third World—and, indeed, with each other. First, the foreign activities of a state are shaped in the context of domestic politics and decision-making structures. Thus, in periods when the USSR was involved in domestic crises—as in 1917–21, 1936–39, and 1953–56, for example—the scope and nature of its involvement in foreign affairs have undergone change. Furthermore, Soviet policy has usually borne the stamp of the rigid and conservative bureaucratic and executive process from which it has arisen. Second, the foreign policies of a state and its rivals are not independent of each other, but rather interact to create a situation that neither may have intended. Finally, in relations with the Third World, the countries that are the objects of foreign policy initiatives are not simply malleable puppets, to be changed and directed at will; rather, these countries have a range of choice, which makes the matter of their receptivity an important variable. It is the interaction of these factor sets, rather than any one of them acting alone, that determines the effect and direction of the foreign policy thrust of both East and West.

In particular, a coincidence of factors culminating in the 1945–55 period interacted to introduce the Soviet Union as a potential actor in Middle East international politics. The nationalist movements seeking independence in the area had gathered strength during the war, while the colonial powers had been weakened. At the same time, a reaction against Western imperialism and the political and moral bankruptcy of the regimes in power, together with growing support for social reform, contributed to the growth of pro-Soviet and pro-Communist sympathies. The Communist parties of Egypt, Syria, Iraq, and Iran (which were small and illegal in all cases) gained strength, particularly among the intelligentsia. The Soviet Union, isolated from any direct contact with the Arab world before the war, was able to establish diplomatic relations with most of the Arab countries as a result of the Soviet WW II alliance with Britain and the United States. Thus, the Soviet Union was in a favorable position to establish friendly relations with the emerging governments and peoples of the Middle East at the very time that the influence of the Western powers was weak and imperilled.

Following the war, however, Soviet relations with Middle Eastern governments hardly flourished. A long-smoldering dispute with Turkey over the Turkish Straits and the east Anatolian border areas surfaced in early 1945, threatening to seethe into open hostilities. It was abated, although not resolved, in 1947 with President Truman's enunciation of the Truman Doctrine. Iran's common border with the USSR, like that of Turkey, gave the Soviets special interest in the political, military, and economic affairs of that country. Unlike the dispute with Turkey, however, the Soviet Union attempted overt intervention in Iran to resolve certain outstanding Iranian-Soviet issues, including the questions of oil concessions and commercial and strategic relationships. Soviet troops had occupied Iran during the war, both to guarantee its status as a valuable source of oil and to maintain it as a transit route between the Allies and the USSR. According to the Tripartite Treaty of 1942, however, the troops were to withdraw within six months of the termination of the war. Not only did the troops remain, but they assisted in the secession of two provinces, Azerbaijan and Mahabad, which became autonomous republics under the Soviet tutelage.

Iran protested to the United Nations, but to no significant avail. The Iranian premier, Qauvam es-Saltaneh, through bilateral negotiations with Moscow, secured the withdrawal of Soviet troops from Iran on May 9, 1946, but at the expense of far-reaching concessions to Moscow on oil exploitation, the status of Azerbaijan, and communist participation in the Iranian government. The agreement was short-lived, in any case, for with the Soviet troops departed, the Iranian government was able to crush the Azerbaijan rebellion, suppress the Tudeh (Iranian Communist) Party, and withhold the ratification of the Irano-Soviet oil agreement. Thus, the Soviet Union's policies in Turkey and Iran achieved only the alienation of large segments of Turkish and Iranian society, not to mention the enduring distrust of their governments. The subsequent participation of Turkey and Iran in Western alliance systems is, consequently, hardly surprising.

While practical considerations of security may have motivated Soviet policies in bordering Turkey and Iran, it was ideological conceptions that shaped Soviet relations throughout the remainder of the area. National liberation movements, it was believed in Moscow, could never suceed in moving the Arab states out of the orbit of imperialism. The fate of the newly independent countries seemed to confirm this tenet, since all were governed by conservative pro-Western elites. The possibility of a neutral posture was not considered feasible in the regional environment, either among states or by the various national liberation movements. Thus, neither the Syrian military coups between 1949 and 1954 nor the 1952 Egyptian revolution were viewed as examples of potential progressive forces opposing the regional imperialist order. Indeed, in the latter case, Gamal Abd al-Nasser and the Egyptian "Free Officers" were initially viewed by the Soviet Union as a "reactionary officers group linked with the USA" which, after seizing power, had set in motion the "savage repression of the workers' movement".[1]

Surprisingly enough, the feudal monarchies of Jordan (except during King Abdullah's reign) and Saudi Arabia, as well as the Zionist movement (previously under consistent attack) and Israel, largely escaped Soviet attention during most of this period. As to the latter, the Soviet government reversed its long-standing opposition to Zionism to support the creation of Israel in the United Nations. This shift in policy was at least partially motivated by the Soviet desire to see Britain expelled from Palestine, and by the hope that the Zionist state would adopt a post-independence leftist orientation in contrast to the pro-Western, anti-Soviet Arab regimes of the region. The Soviet Union followed through with the sale of arms and aircraft to Israel (through the agency of Czechoslovakia) in 1948, and with an affirmative vote for Israel's admission to the United Nations in March 1949.

Although events of the postwar decade revealed a continuing Soviet interest in the Middle East, the USSR was faced with Western resistance and with a lack of rapport with the leaders of the independent countries of the area. However, Western influence, especially that of France and Britain, was rapidly diminishing, and a series of developments created a fertile environment for the flowering of Soviet influence in the 1953–56 period.

First, out of its perception of "Russian expansionism," the United States had initiated the formation of a series of organizations and alliances designed to contain the Soviet Union within its formal boundaries. After the Truman Doctrine was enunciated in 1948 (and massive aid granted to Greece and Turkey as a consequence), this policy was vigorously prosecuted, as witness the formation of NATO in

1949, and the provision of its military forces in 1950; a series of bilateral American treaties with Turkey, Iran, and Pakistan for coordination of defense policy in the Middle East; the abortive attempt to form a Middle East Defense Organization; and the formation of the Baghdad Pact in February 1955. This organization of the area into a network of alliances was strenuously opposed by Egypt, precipitating the beginning of the deterioration of American-Egyptian relations. Egyptian policy thus came to coincide with Soviet policy, which, not unnaturally, opposed the creation of military alliances on its southern borders.

By the time of the Bandung Conference in April 1955, Egyptian-Western relations were seriously strained. A degree of rapport had earlier been established between Egypt and the USSR, but it was at this conference—where the Soviet Union strongly supported and encouraged Nasser's neutralism—that close Soviet-Egyptian ties were initiated. Ironically, it was the issue of the Baghdad Pact, the instrument through which the West intended to combat the threat of communism in the Middle East, that precipitated closer ties between the Arab national liberation movement, led by Nasser, and the socialist bloc.

An additional factor was the more flexible and lenient Soviet foreign policy that had emerged after Stalin's death in 1953. Throughout 1955, Soviet policy tended to be more conciliatory, not only in the Middle East, but also in Europe—Austria, Yugoslavia, Finland—and in the United Nations. This relaxation of tensions was later to lead to the development of the line of "peaceful coexistence." (The elements of the policy were there in 1954, even though the enunciation of it was still to come.) It should also be noted that this policy was the subject (and the product) of the contest for power in the Kremlin subsequent to Stalin's death.

As a result of this change in Soviet outlook, some Arab regimes were reappraised as constituting progressive forces, and a national-front policy was adopted. This ideological shift was paralleled by a moderating trend in the Soviet Union's diplomatic and political stance. The Kremlin was now willing, as Walter Laqueur stated in *The Struggle for the Middle East*, "to cooperate with kings and sheiks as well as ultra-revolutionaries. The fact that some of these leaders were militantly anti-communist was no obstacle."[2] Egypt's President Nasser remarked on the Soviet approach while opening a Soviet-funded spinning mill at Damietta: "In spite of the clouds that have, at times, loomed over our relations, the economic agreement [of January 1958] was never affected. At no time did the Soviet Union utter one single word threatening to boycott us economically and on no occasion did the Soviets reproachfully remind us of the economic aid they extended to us or the loans they provided for our industrialization schemes."[3] Similarly, Khrushchev, while denouncing Nasser's suppression of Egyptian communists in an address to the Twenty-First Congress of the Communist Party of the Soviet Union (CPSU) in 1959, was careful to stress that "differences in ideological views must not interfere with the development of friendly relations [between the USSR and Egypt] and the business of a joint struggle against imperialism."[4]

Arab anti-imperialism—particularly as enunciated by the emerging nationalist regimes in Egypt, Syria and later Iraq—provided an appropriate ideological and political basis for improved Arab-Soviet relations in the 1950s. While Turkey and Iran were border states sensitive to threats of Russian domination, none of the nations of the Arab world had ever had a hostile experience with the Soviet Union. All had, however, experienced the inequities of Western colonialism. Moreover, the Arab world linked "the United States and the West with the evils of the past and the present and [placed] on them the burden of reform".[5] And although the Arabs condemned Soviet support of the founding of the state of Israel, this was seen as a relatively minor affront in the face of continuing American and British support of an expansionist Zionist state.

There was also suspicion among the Arabs that the West did not wish to further (but perhaps wished to retard) their development, and that U.S. refusal to supply certain kinds and quantities of arms to Arab states, together with the involvement of some Middle Eastern countries in U.S. defense alliances, were designed not merely to allow Israel to survive, but to extend her borders. The publication, *al-Ahram*, a semi-official organ of the Egyptian government, reflected this view when it commented in a 1955 editorial that "America has chosen Israel and will never arm the Arab states because Israel doesn't want that."[6] Nasser, seeing the Baghdad Pact as a manifestation of the West's policy toward Israel geared to contain Nasser's leadership of the pan-Arab struggle, noted in the same issue of *al-Ahram*: "As long as Egypt is the shield of Arabism in its fight with Zionism, complete victory for the Western policies requires, first of all, the isolation of Egypt from her Arab sisters."[7]

The formation of the Baghdad Pact coincided with a major Israeli raid on the Gaza Strip. This attack lent new urgency to Egyptian demands for arms, demands that were still denied by the United

States and its allies. In the autumn of 1955, therefore, Egypt was able to conclude an agreement with the Soviet Union for the purchase of arms from Czechoslovakia for Egyptian cotton.

As early as 1953 Egypt had been seeking an arms deal with the Soviet Union. However, contrary to the prevailing Western view that the Soviet Union was waiting impatiently to seize any opportunity to supply arms to Egypt (or to any disaffected government in the Middle East), the Soviet Union was actually reluctant to escalate the arms traffic in the area.[8] According to Murad Ghalab, who served as Ambassador to Moscow under Nasser and later as Minister of Foreign Affairs under Sadat, and who was the architect of Egypt's relations with the Soviet Union during the Nasser era:

> When the revolution occurred, it immediately directed its effort toward the liberation of the country and its people from imperialist domination and British bases. . . . From its inception, the revolution realized that to face imperialism we must turn to the Soviet Union. This direction crystallized early. Precisely in 1953 (and I don't say this as an inference of analysis; rather, I am speaking from the facts), the mission [our government] expected from us [diplomats] prior to my departure for Moscow in 1953 to assume my post [Second Secretary of the Egyptian Embassy in Moscow] was to discuss with the Soviet Union the issue of arms. . . . These were the instructions our ambassador in Moscow had received from Cairo. The instructions delineated first and foremost the question of arms and the issue of supplying us with oil in the case of a clash between the revolution and British imperialism. . . . In regard to oil, the Soviet Union responded positively immediately; but on the question of arms, the Soviet response was that they needed time to consider it. The subject continued under discussion from 1953 to the signing of the arms agreement in 1955.[9]

General Muhammad Hafidh Ismail, who served as an ambassador and national security advisor under Anwar Sadat, negotiated the arms deal with Czechoslovakia in August 1955. Commenting on the terms of the agreement, he noted:

> I can state firsthand that the deals of 1955 and 1956 were much cheaper than the prices Egypt paid for arms brought from Western countries. In fact, the prices cannot be compared with Western prices.[10]

Some of the causal relationships underlying the events that followed are unclear to this day, but in May 1956 Nasser's government recognized the People's Republic of China—at that time still on the closest terms with the Soviet Union. Although recognition had previously been extended by America's ally, Britain, Egypt was the first Arab state to take this step. At this point, the American line, as enunciated by Secretary of State John Foster Dulles, was that Egypt was anti-Western and not to be trusted. In July 1956, therefore, the United States withdrew its offer of $56 million for the financing of the first stage of the High Dam at Aswan, and the contingent loans from the World Bank and Great Britain—totaling $214 million—were also withdrawn. In heated reaction, Nasser nationalized the International Maritime Suez Canal Company. The resultant crisis was capped by the Israeli invasion of the Sinai on October 29, 1956, followed by British and French attacks on the Canal Zone in early November. The Soviet Union (which until the Bandung Conference of 1955 had maintained friendly relations with Israel) seized on the occasion to demonstrate its solidarity with the Arab cause. However, it was the strong opposition of the United States to the invasion that made the United Nations cease-fire agreements and peacekeeping operation successful. Whatever goodwill the United States might have generated over its posture in the Suez crisis, though, was soon dissipated by the enunciation of the Eisenhower Doctrine in January 1957. The Arabs were unwilling to accept the implication in the Eisenhower Doctrine that the Soviet Union, as an enemy of the West, was thereby an enemy of the Arab people.

DEVELOPMENT OF THE SOVIET POSITION, 1956–67

The record of Soviet–Middle East relations in the decade following the Suez crisis certainly seems to justify the judgment of one scholar, O. M. Slomansky, that "Soviet gains have more often than not resulted from Western blunders or from the West's inability to resolve conflicting interests and commitments in the area."[11] Indeed, Soviet economic and cultural relations with some Arab countries gathered momentum in the second half of the fifties, largely as a result of Soviet support for the doctrines of Third World liberation, independence, and positive neutralism. According to Soviet Premier Nikita Krushchev:

The Soviet Union places a great importance on the struggle of the nations of Africa and the Middle East and its policy on this is to participate in supporting the political and economic independence of the independent states until their freedom is secure, and we will support all who struggle for their freedom until they achieve complete independence.[12]

Parallel to the growth of Soviet relations with the Arab Middle East, another Soviet initiative with its neighbors in the south was being shaped. Soviet-Iranian relations, while marred by a history of Russian imperialism, were never characterized by the same degree of hostility apparent in Soviet-Turkish interaction. The dispute of 1946 relative to Soviet troop placements, the Azerbaijan dispute, the fall of the government of Mohammed Mossadegh, and the suppression of the Tudeh Party in 1953–54—all of these proved to be but temporary setbacks for Soviet relations with Iran. In the post-Stalin era, the Soviet Union adopted a new foreign policy based on peaceful coexistence with countries committed to different political, social, and economic systems. Consequently, the Soviet government adopted the position that it would achieve its foreign policy aims and protect its vital interests in Iran without establishing a position of dominance, and thus without having to take the risks necessary to such a venture.

This new development dovetailed with the U.S.-supported Iranian domestic policy aimed at widening its base of support by seeking rapport with the USSR in an attempt to appease the local anti-Western forces. Consequently, in 1956, Shah Mohammed Reza Pahlevi visited Moscow and came away with a three-year commercial agreement that resulted, in the following year, in the Soviet Union providing the market for 27 percent of Iran's exports.

This rapprochement appeared threatened when Iran rejected a Soviet nonaggression treaty proposal while concluding a bilateral defense treaty with the United States in 1959; however, this incipient crisis was defused in August 1960. The Soviet Union laid aside its concerns when, in 1962, Iran decided not to permit the stationing of nuclear missiles on its territory. In succeeding years a number of economic and technical agreements were signed, culminating in the arms agreements concluded in 1967–68 and materialized by a steel mill constructed at Isfahan and the trans-Iranian gasline.

The strain in Soviet-Turkish relations, too, began to relax in 1961, when Ismet Inonu became prime minister of Turkey. A temporary setback occurred when the conservative, pro-Western Justice Party came to power in 1965, but after Premier Alexei Kosygin paid a visit to Ankara in December 1966 relations once again began to improve. The Soviet shift in policy with regard to Cyprus, combined with Premier Suleyman Demirel's visit to Moscow in 1967, "eliminated the last traces of hostility from Soviet-Turkish relations."[13] Trade relations between Turkey and the USSR, supplemented by Turkish trade with several Eastern European countries, helped to further promote the rapprochement.

While the Soviet Union was implementing a good neighbor policy with respect to Turkey and Iran, the United States—while removing its Jupiter missile bases from Turkey in 1962—informed the Turkish government "that it could not count on automatic American support if by its actions [with regard to Cyprus] it provoked Moscow to intervene."[14] Moreover, at a time when the Soviet Union was acting as if the Turkish communists did not exist, condoning the suppression of the Tudeh Party in Iran, and building trade bridges with both Turkey and Iran, the United States cancelled its aid mission to Tehran (in 1967) and cut back economic aid to Turkey the following year.

The Soviet foreign policy-makers aimed their policy at the less-developed countries (LDCs) based on their conviction that economic aid to as well as smooth economic relations with these countries would certainly promote the gradual elimination of Western predominance while at the same time widening the opportunity for more Soviet influence. For this reason, trade with the LDCs grew sixfold between 1955 and 1966 in comparison with total Soviet trade, which increased only about two and one-half times. The proportion of LDC trade to the total increased both in exports (from 4.0 to 13.0 percent) and imports (from 6.0 to 11.0 percent). Trade with the nations of the Middle East amounted in 1966 to about one-third (exports) and one-fourth (imports) of total Soviet-LDC trade. More than half of this trade was with Egypt.[15] Egyptian exports to the Soviet Union grew from a mere $15 million in 1955, to $163 million in 1965, to a peak of $621 million in 1975. Soviet exports to Egypt also increased, from $11 million in 1955 to $363 million by 1975. Between 1970 and 1975, some 37 percent of Egypt's exports went to the USSR. In Iraq, exports to the Soviet Union grew from nil in 1956 to 7,424 Iraqi dinars (0.05% of Iraqi exports) in 1958, to ID 387,779 (4.86%) in 1960, to ID 2,029,669 (12.13%) in 1963. Iraqi imports from the USSR similarly increased: ID 13,900 (0.01% of Iraqi imports) in 1956 to ID 2,625,031 (1.88%) in 1960, to ID 9,346, 253 (8.20%) in 1963.[16]

IMPACT OF THE JUNE WAR

By 1967 the United States had alienated about half of the Arab governments and much of Arab public opinion through its affronts to President Nasser and other Arab nationalists. This situation was aggravated
by the anti-Nasser tone of U.S. utterances, based as they were on the
belief that Nasser's prestige in the Middle East constituted a threat
to American policies. The June War, which confirmed Arab convic-
tions that the United States was wholly committed to Israel, further
alienated the Arabs from America. Many believed the United States
had furnished military support for the Israeli attack on Egypt. On
June 6, the U.A.R., Syria, and Algeria broke diplomatic relations with
the U.S., and on June 7, Iraq and Sudan followed suit. According to
President Nasser in his resignation speech on June 9, 1967:

> All the evidence indicates the existence of imperialist collusion . . .
> they learned from the open collusion of 1956 to cover up this time.
> . . . It's proven that there were American and British carriers on the
> enemy's coast supporting his military efforts . . . in addition to a
> number of American reconnaissance planes that flew over some of
> our positions.[17]

In contrast, the Soviet Union by 1967 had created much goodwill throughout the Middle East through its diplomatic and political
support for Arab independence and Palestinian rights, and through
generous aid programs provided" with no strings attached." Aziz Sidqi,
Egyptian Minister of Industries from 1956 to 1965, and again from
1967 until he became Prime Minister in 1972, was the architect of
Egypt's industrialization policies. He commented on the reasons why
Egypt sought economic and industrial development relations with the
USSR:

> The conditions of dealing with Western states require either imme-
> diate payment in full or 25 percent down and the remainder in five
> annual payments with an interest rate of six percent. As for the So-
> viet conditions, their payment begins a year after completion of the
> factory, so payment can be made from the production of the factory.
> Payment is spread over twelve years, with interest not exceeding 2½
> percent a year.[18]

During the June 1967 war, the USSR condemned Israel's aggression, supplied both Egypt and Syria with military hardware, and supported the United Nations Security Council's repeated calls for a ceasefire. An emergency meeting of communist parties and governments was held in Moscow on June 9 to discuss the eruption of the war. A statement issued at the conclusion of the conference condemned Israel and promised the continuing support of the socialist states to the Arab countries.[19] According to General Muhammad Fawzi, Egyptian Chief of Staff at the time of the war, the Soviet Union committed military aid to Egypt on June 9:

> The first month of the defeat witnessed 544 air transport deliveries to Egypt and 15 cargo ships carrying 48,000 tons of arms and ammunition to substitute for the losses of the June war. The Soviet Union did not ask for payment for these arms and ammunition.[20]

On June 10, the Soviet Union broke diplomatic relations with Israel. It was soon followed by all the socialist states with the exception of Romania. President Hourai Boumedienne of Algeria traveled to Moscow on June 11 for a two-day visit with Premier Kosygin and President Podgorny. Although the nature of Boumedienne's mission to Moscow was not revealed, on June 12 *Pravda* declared Moscow's complete support for the Arabs and pledged to provide "the necessary material support to repel the aggression . . . and to defend the territorial integrity of the Arab land." Subsequently, on June 21, President Podgorny headed a powerful Soviet delegation that included the Chief of Staff and the Deputy Foreign Minister. The delegation went to Cairo, Damascus, and Baghdad. After three days in Cairo, it issued a communique emphasizing cooperation between Egypt and the Soviet Union "to eradicate the consequences of Israeli aggression."[21] According to Mahmoud Riad, Egypt's Foreign Minister at the time (1964–1971), President Nasser spoke as follows to the Podgorny delegation:

> We in Egypt have been the victims of aggression both in 1956 and 1967 because the US and the West considered us in both instances as aligned to the Soviet bloc, inasmuch as we rejected colonialist stances and policies. Our policies were, in fact, based on our national interest and the principles of non-alignment which allow for friendship with the Soviet Union. Now we have seen Israel attack us and occupy our territories, with the consent of the United States. With

the growing US support to Israel we feel it is not logical to maintain neutrality between those who strike us and those who help us. We wish to deepen and strengthen Egyptian-Soviet relations with the aim of eliminating the consequences of Israeli aggression.

There are two alternatives before us: either to submit to the United States which would then help us in the same way it helps some of the Asian countries, imposing the condition that we submit to its colonial hegemony. The other is to struggle and fight for our freedom. Since the struggle to free our territories will depend on the deployment of armed force, we have to conclude an agreement with the Soviet Union. We are ready to extend facilities to your fleet in the Mediterranean. Naturally we will hear people in this country say "you drove the British from the door to let in the Soviets through the window". Yet we can take such talk in our stride for the sake of liberating our land, and as long as this is pursued by a serious and effective military support from your side. I know that our people are resilient and understanding enough to accept it.

The building of our armed forces should come within the framework of a joint effort, a Soviet-Egyptian venture, which would offer our officers and soldiers the experience and training of your cadres ... if we cannot drive the Israelis from Sinai peacefully we shall resort to war, yet this is not your responsibility, it is exclusively ours. We would, however, ask you to help in the air defence of Egyptian territory. Israel may attempt to cross the Suez Canal and penetrate deep into Egypt. Confronting such an attack should be the responsibility of our joint defence systems. For if an attack of this nature happens it will be at the behest of the United States and primarily because we would have concluded an agreement with you and opened our ports to your fleet.[22]

While the Soviet Union refused to commit troops, it did commit full support to the strengthening of the Egyptian military.[23] Throughout the summer of 1967, the interaction between Soviet and Arab governments dramatically increased along with the evidence of tangible Soviet diplomatic, military, and economic support to the Arabs. In his speech of 24 July 1967 commemorating the Egyptian revolution, President Nasser assessed the international situation for the Arab world:

Our enemies are Israel and her supporters. We must define our enemy. Who supported Israel and who helped Israel? ... America and Britain supported Israel. The Soviet Union stood up with us and supported us politically, helped us economically, worked to strengthen our armed forces. The President of the Soviet Union, Nicolai Podgorny came to Egypt and clearly conveyed that the Soviet Union would stand by us . . . in the West, there is a campaign against Russia claiming that the Arabs are angry because the Soviet Union did not send Soviet troops. I don't think that we ever expected Soviet troops to fight on our behalf.[24]

Thus, in the core region of the Arab world, the Soviet image improved still further after 1967. Even relations with Jordan, unfriendly as late as June 1967, improved somewhat after the war when the Soviet Union offered to supply arms to Jordan to replace losses sustained in the conflict. True, Jordan rejected the offer, but King Hussein visited Moscow for the first time in October 1967. The Jordanians took the view that events had shown the USSR to be a friend of the Arabs, and as such it should be treated cordially unless and until it attempted to interfere in the internal affairs of Jordan. Nevertheless, Jordan remained firmly in the Western camp, and King Hussein benefitted from U.S. gestures of support when his regime was threatened by Palestinian and Syrian forces in the civil war of 1970–71.

Among all Arab countries, the extent of Soviet economic and military aid to the United Arab Republic, the most influential Arab country in the Middle East, was particularly significant. Reequipping the army of a state in complete defeat, including the dispatch of a number of training missions (mainly to Egypt), carried the Soviets into the heart of the U.A.R. military establishment—which is the basis of political power in many Arab countries. Between 1967 and 1973, the Soviet Union supplied some $2.96 billion in arms to Middle East countries, of which $1.77 billion went to Egypt.[25] In return, "The Soviet Mediterranean fleet was given storage and repair facilities, or the equivalent of naval base rights, at Alexandria and Port Sa'id; and Soviet pilots were allowed to fly Soviet-made planes with Egyptian markings on Soviet missions in the Mediterranean, representing the equivalent in Egypt of air-base rights."[26] On 27 May 1971, a fifteen-year Treaty of Friendship and Cooperation between the United Arab Republic and the USSR was signed in Cairo.[27]

Soviet-Egyptian relations were complicated, however, by diverging views over the use of force in the Arab-Israeli conflict. At first, because of the United Arab Republic's general weakness, there was a tendency on the part of the Egyptians not to distinguish between defensive and offensive weaponry. As late as 1970, Egyptian strategy was limited to the prevention of deep penetration raids by Israeli aircraft. (These were eventually curtailed by the installation of SAM-2 and SAM-3 shields around Cairo and Alexandria.) Egypt's growing self-defense capability was matched by a corresponding desire for offensively oriented weapons—MIG-23's, and the latest Soviet tanks. The USSR, however, released only a small number of new aircraft to Egyptian control, the remainder being operated by Soviet technical and military personnel. These Soviet qualifications of and limitations on the offensive strength of the Egyptian armed forces caused Sadat to lose much credibility in 1971—his uneventful though highly touted "year of decision." This led Sadat to send a long letter to Brezhnev in the fall of 1971 complaining of the restrictions and conditions placed on Soviet military aid, and precipitated the eviction of Soviet advisors en masse in July 1972.[28] According to Mohamed Heikal, the 1972 expulsion led the USSR to step up its arms shipments to Egypt in 1972–73, in the fear that a refusal to do so would lead to further deterioration in the Soviet position, both in Egypt and in the Middle East generally.[29]

This Soviet policy of technical aid coupled with military restraint was received more favorably in Iraq. In April 1972, a Soviet-Iraqi Treaty of Friendship and Cooperation that placed heavy emphasis on economic and technical, rather than on military, assistance was concluded. The treaty was attacked in some Arab newspapers (and by the Libyan government) as a revival of imperialism in the tradition of the Baghdad Pact. On April 13, 1972, Libya announced it was withdrawing its ambassador from Iraq, and requested that Iraq recall its ambassador from Libya.

It is important to note that, in all these instances, the Soviet Union—while declaring and demonstrating its support for the Arab countries—continued to support Israel's "right to exist" within its pre-1967 boundaries. Indeed, most Western observers of the period failed to note the degree to which the Soviet Union's acceptance of the State of Israel had remained unchanged despite its close ties with the Arab world. Although condemning Israeli occupation of the West Bank, Gaza, Sinai, and Golan, the USSR continued to uphold Israeli sovereignty and independence, and generally to oppose the use of force in the Arab-Israeli conflict. Furthermore, Moscow repeatedly urged moderation and compromise on Arab leaders and local communist parties.[30] This general attitude was clearly manifest in the United Nations Security Council debate on the principles for a just and lasting peace in the Middle East that followed the 1967 war. A Soviet draft resolution (S/8253) stressed that "the seizure of territories as a result of war is inadmissible," and called for an Israeli withdrawal from occupied territories and a "just settlement of the question of the Palestine refugees." At the same time, the Soviet draft also recognized the right of all states, including Israel, to "exist as an independent national state and live in peace and security."[31] The British-sponsored resolution 242 that was eventually adopted by the Council was broadly similar in content and was supported by the USSR.

Meanwhile, the content of Soviet support for Arab nations was conditioned by the Soviet aim of stabilizing the region in order to consolidate the influence it had thus far managed to obtain, and by the Soviet Union's desire to avoid superpower confrontation with the United States. Soviet support for the Arab cause (and the strengths and limitations of the regional foreign policy of which it formed a part) came into sharp focus with the outbreak of another Arab-Israeli war in October 1973.

Further from the core of the region and the Arab-Israeli issue, Soviet policy was considerably less successful. In the Arab Gulf, the exaggerated Western fear that the USSR would be able to exploit Britain's withdrawal from the area to establish a significant presence in the region whereby it could threaten Gulf oil flow proved largely baseless, as did predictions in the late 1960s and early 1970s that a Soviet Union increasingly short of oil would attempt to secure influence over Middle East energy for its own use. The Kingdom of Saudi Arabia seemed unwilling to forego either its military or its economic relationship with the West, in spite of its expressed disapproval of U.S. support for Israel and U.S. insensitivity toward the Palestinians. Similarly, Kuwait, concerned with its own wealth and security, showed no enthusiasm for departing from its established policy of neutrality vis-à-vis both the Soviet-American and the Arab conservative-revolutionary issues. In the rest of the Arabian peninsula, only Yemen and South Yemen maintained friendly relations with the Soviet Union, and its record there after 1967 was cautiously anti-imperialist. After providing moral and diplomatic support for the conservative monarchy of Yemen's Imam Yahya against the British for years, the Soviets quickly recognized (and moved to support) the revolutionary republican regime of Abdullah Sallal against that of Imam Badr. Later, the USSR was careful to avoid involvement in local disputes while trying to develop friendly relations with both Yemen and South Yemen.

THE 1973 WAR AND AFTER

At first glance, the October 1973 Arab-Israeli War would seem to have provided all of the elements necessary for the further expansion of Soviet influence in the Middle East. Much more so than in 1967, the USSR had proven itself this time a staunch supporter of the Arab cause. Upon the outbreak of the war on October 6, the USSR accused Israel of bearing full responsibility for the conflict, condemned Israel's "constant provocations," "obstructionist position," and "expansionist policy," and stressed that the Soviet Union was a "reliable friend of the Arab states."[32] The Soviet Union also began a massive air- and sea-lift of military equipment to Egypt and Syria: Between October 10 and mid-November, some 30 freighters and one thousand air flights transferred approximately 100,000 tons of war materiel to the Arab states.[33] Later, when it became obvious in the second week of the war that the Arab military position was deteriorating, the USSR placed some of its airborne forces on alert while pressing for a ceasefire both in public statements and at the United Nations. On October 24, the USSR reacted to Israel's refusal to obey United Nations Security Council ceasefire resolutions by warning U.S. President Nixon that if the United States did not act jointly with the USSR in bringing the fighting to an end, the latter would "consider the question of taking appropriate steps unilaterally."[34] For its part, the United States' firm support for Israel was even more apparent during the war: the United States lent massive diplomatic and material support to Israel, and responded to the Soviet warning on October 24 by placing both conventional and nuclear forces on alert so as to deter Soviet intervention. Because of its continued backing of Israel, the United States (along with Portugal and the Netherlands) was made a primary target of the Arab oil embargo of 1973–74.

Yet, despite these developments, the Soviet Union's position in the Middle East declined sharply after 1973—particularly in Egypt, which had, despite differences in the early 1970s, remained the cornerstone of Soviet policy in the region. A number of factors, corresponding to the three sets of factors identified in the introduction to this chapter, can be seen as having led to this deterioration.

First and perhaps most important, the Soviet Union was unable to affect the policies of its erstwhile Egyptian ally—policies that moved post-Nasser Egypt increasingly into a Western orbit as the 1970s progressed. Before the war, relations between Egyptian President Anwar al-Sadat and the USSR were damaged by the former's perception of Soviet support for his domestic opponents (notably Ali Sabri); by Soviet support of the unsuccessful 1971 coup in the Sudan; and by Soviet restrictions on arms transfers. The expulsion of Soviet technicians from Egypt in 1972 provided stark evidence of the deteriorated state of USSR-Egyptian relations.

After the 1973 war, Sadat initiated a diplomatic strategy predicated on the assumption that only the United States could exert sufficient leverage over Israel to secure Israeli withdrawal from occupied Egyptian territory and a negotiated settlement—a belief, in other words, that the road to the Sinai (if not to Palestine) lay through Washington. According to Muhammad Ibrahim Kamil, who served as Egyptian Foreign Minister from December 1977 until September 1978, "[Sadat] was a true believer that his [peace] initiative could not fail, and that the theory of the two superpowers was a false one as there is only one superpower, and that is the USA. It alone would be able and could guarantee to carry his initiative toward its goal of achieving a just and lasting peace in the Middle East."[35] In order to achieve his objective, however, Egyptian-American relations would have to be improved, and Sadat felt this could be done through reducing and finally eliminating Soviet-Egyptian ties and actively opposing Soviet influence in the region. In Kamil's words, "Sadat was under the impression that the more he attacked the Soviets, the more America would support him."[36]

For the duration of the decade, Egypt's progress toward a separate peace treaty with Israel occurred simultaneously with (and as a result of) Egypt's realignment with the West. Sadat's announcement that he would seek arms from the West, and his promulgation of an "open door" economic policy to attract foreign investment (1974); his abrogation of the Egyptian-Soviet Treaty of Friendship and Cooperation (1976); the cessation of Egyptian cotton exports to the USSR, and the suspension of Egypt's servicing of its Soviet debt (1977); and, finally, Sadat's increasingly harsh anti-Soviet rhetoric and acceptance of growing amounts of U.S. aid provided a suitable context within which the U.S.-sponsored Sinai I (January 1974) and Sinai II (September 1975) disengagement agreements, the Camp David accords (September 1978), and the Egyptian-Israeli Peace Treaty (March 1979) could be negotiated. Sadat's realignment from the Soviet Union to the West was capped by the expulsion from Egypt of all remaining Soviet technicians, as well as Soviet diplomats, in September 1981.

As noted earlier, the interaction of foreign policies has an important impact on their outcome, and during this period U.S. diplomacy played an important role in the weakening of the Soviet Union's position in the Middle East. From 1970 to 1973, Egypt's realignment had been blocked by the United States' refusal to reciprocate. When, in early 1971, Sadat informed Washington through the American Interests section of the Spanish embassy in Cairo that he was prepared to expel the Soviets from Egypt if disengagement and a reopening of the Suez Canal could be achieved, bureaucratic struggles within the U.S. administration and the refusal of Nixon and Kissinger to see Egypt as anything more than a Soviet client inhibited an appropriate U.S. response.[37] After 1973, however, the United States was more receptive, actively encouraging Egypt's shift away from the USSR. While Sadat was attempting to secure U.S. assistance and direct U.S. pressure on Israel, Henry Kissinger's "step by step" diplomacy and later President Carter's Camp David peace process succeeded in driving wedges not only between Egypt and the Soviet Union but also between Egypt and most of the rest of the Arab world. As relations between Cairo and Moscow deteriorated, the United States was careful to step in to fill the resultant breaches in trade and economic, technical, and even military aid—thus bolstering the stability of Sadat's regime while further exacerbating the deterioration in USSR-Egyptian relations. An eminent student of Soviet-Arab relations, Ali Dessouki, made the following observations:

> Economic aid agreements [with the USSR] declined from $1 billion in 1955–1964 to $440 million in 1965–1975, and then to zero in 1975–1979. Trade relations also declined after the cotton embargo and Egypt's refusal to maintain the large trade surplus used to service its debt. The Soviet share of Egyptian exports fell from 50% in 1970–1975 to less than 15% in 1975. Egyptian imports from the Soviet Union also dropped from about 25% of Egypt's total imports to around 10%. . . . By 1979 a few Soviet technicians and a limited volume of trade were the remnants of a once flourishing relationship.[38]

In contrast, U.S. aid increased dramatically: "between 1946 and 1980 U.S. economic aid totalled $7.2 billion, most of which ($6.8 billion or 94%) was given in the late 1970s".[39] American arms sales to Egypt (many of which were financed with U.S. military credits) rose from $68.4 million in 1976 to $937.3 million three years later.[40]

The conservative states of the Arab world also played a role in limiting the effectiveness of Soviet policy during this period. Staunchly antisocialist, anti-Soviet Saudi Arabia, its regional and international influence bolstered by the demise of Nasserism and the crisis of Arab nationalism (and by increased oil revenues and global recognition of the strategic and economic value of petroleum resources in the wake of the 1973–74 Arab oil embargo), was particularly important in this regard. Although ostensibly opposed to the negotiation of a separate peace treaty with Israel, the Saudis supported Sadat's shift from the USSR to the United States. They also poured considerable funds into North Yemen, subsidized Syria, and funded much of the Iraqi war effort against Iran in order to (among other things) offset Soviet influence. American efforts to encourage Egypt's move away from the USSR and to generally limit the Soviet Union's presence in the Middle East found further support from most Western countries and from China.

The final set of factors to limit the success of Soviet foreign policy in the region in general and towards Egypt in particular could be found within the Soviet foreign policy process itself. According to Mohamed Heikal—who, as editor of *al-Ahram*, was close to the center of Egyptian decision-making from 1952 to the mid-1970s (and who had intimate contact with numerous Soviet leaders)—the staid Soviet foreign policy apparatus often showed "astonishing insensitivity" to Third World representatives; proved "inept" at public relations; was often unable to "understand the realities of power in other parts of the world"; and was characterized, from its weighty and ponderous bureaucracy up to the top leadership in the Politburo, by rigidity and immobility.[41] Heikal added that middle-class Third World leaders often found communication with their counterparts in the West much easier—political disagreements notwithstanding. In a similar vein, Lt. General Saad al-Shazly, Egyptian Chief of Staff from 1971 to 1973, has described Soviet advisors to the Egyptian army as often "brusque, harsh, frequently arrogant and usually unwilling to believe that anyone has anything to teach them."[42] As will be discussed later, Soviet relations with Arab countries have tended to be conducted almost exclusively on an official, political level, with little social penetration—and are hence easily broken by executive fiat. Finally, Soviet leader Leonid Brezhnev grew increasingly infirm as the 1970s progressed, which led to the cancellation of several official meetings and doubtless reduced still further the already severely limited dynamism of Soviet foreign policy.

Soviet-Egyptian political and economic relations improved somewhat after Sadat's death in 1981; under Egyptian President Hosni Mubarak, a limited number of Soviet technicians have been invited back to the country. In addition, in 1983 and again in 1984, significant Soviet-Egyptian trade and cooperation agreements were signed, while 1984 saw the resumption of normal diplomatic relations. Nevertheless, as of the mid-1980s Egypt still remained firmly in the Western camp.

AFTER EGYPT: THE SEARCH FOR ALTERNATIVES

The growing estrangement between the USSR and Egypt in the 1970s led the Soviet Union to seek strengthening of its ties with other Arab countries. Libya, despite its past criticism of the Soviet Union and its strong anticommunism, was made receptive to Soviet overtures by increasing U.S. hostility. Motivated by its animus for Sadat's Egypt (and for the United States due to its support of Israel), and by the fear of U.S. intervention, while attracted by Soviet support of Arab and Palestinian rights and the technical aid and military equipment that the USSR was willing to supply, Libya's Qaddafi and Moscow forged close ties after the 1973 war. The first Libyan-Soviet trade agreement was signed in 1974, and trade between the two grew steadily thereafter. Two-way trade increased ninefold from 1977 to 1982, with Libya becoming the USSR's largest Arab trading partner in the latter half of this period.[43] Military equipment, including SCUD surface-to-surface missiles and the latest Mig 25 aircraft and T-72 tanks, has accounted for a considerable portion of Soviet sales to Libya. In the decade following the 1973 war, Libya received nearly 3,000 tanks, nearly 2,000 other armored fighting vehicles, and nearly 400 combat aircraft from the Soviet Union.[44]

The USSR also improved its relations with the Palestinian nationalist movement. Up until the late 1960s, the USSR tended to reject the Palestinian resistance as reckless and ineffectual. Toward the end of 1969, however, the first official Soviet references to the Palestinian "people" or "nation" began to appear—a significant shift from the earlier references to "Palestinian Arabs" and "refugees".[45] In February 1970, the first Palestine Liberation Organization (PLO) delegation visited Moscow, and in 1972 the PLO received its first shipments of Soviet arms.

However, it was not until after the 1973 Arab-Israeli war that Moscow began to substantially expand ties with the Palestinian movement. In 1974, following policy decisions by the PLO National Council that suggested PLO acceptance of a Palestinian "mini-state;" Arab recognition of the PLO as the "sole legitimate representative of the Palestinian people" at the Rabat Arab summit conference; and Yasser Arafat's appearance before the United Nations, the USSR began to lend its official support to the concept of Palestinian statehood on the West Bank and the Gaza strip. Also in 1974 the Soviets promised the PLO that it could open an office in Moscow—a promise that was fulfilled two years later. By 1978 the Soviet Union had officially recognized the PLO as the "sole legitimate representative of the Palestinian people," and in 1981 the PLO office in Moscow was upgraded to embassy status.

At the same time that new allies were being found to offset the deterioration of relations with Egypt, the Soviet Union was seeking to consolidate relations with those Arab countries with whom ties had remained friendly. One of these was the People's Democratic Republic of (South) Yemen (PDRY), which continued to pursue pro-Soviet policies—particularly after the execution of President Salem Rubai Ali in the summer of 1978 put an end to South Yemen's cautious attempts to improve diplomatic relations with Saudi Arabia. In the summer of 1979, South Yemen became the first Arab state to gain observer status within the Council of Mutual Economic Assistance, and in October of that year it signed a twenty-year treaty of friendship and cooperation. In January 1980 the PDRY voted against a UN resolution condemning the Soviet invasion of Afghanistan. In August 1981 an alliance between Soviet-supported South Yemen, Ethiopia, and Libya was concluded in Aden. Seen by many at the time as a major consolidation of Soviet influence in the Red Sea/Indian Ocean area, the "Aden Pact" has in fact proven to have little real substance.[46]

Since the late 1960s, the Soviet Union has extended considerable economic and technical aid to the PDRY, particularly in the areas of irrigation, mineral exploration, and fish processing and transportation facilities. The USSR also supplies the South Yemeni armed forces, and there are an estimated 1,500 Soviet military advisors in the country. Furthermore, the Soviet Union has access to docking facilities at Socotra, and to docking and airfield facilities at Aden.

In Iraq, the close relations formalized by the 1972 treaty of friendship and cooperation continued, and in 1976–77 further trade agreements were concluded with the USSR, Czechoslovakia, and the German Democratic Republic. The USSR and its East European allies supplied and trained the Iraqi armed forces, and provided significant technical assistance to Iraq's oil industry. Soviet arms shipments to Iraq between 1975 and 1979 were worth some $4.9 billion dollars.[47]

Nevertheless, a number of issues contributed to rising tensions between Iraq and the Soviet Union as the decade progressed, peaking in 1978. George Lenczowski has enumerated these issues as sevenfold: (1) Soviet-Iraqi differences over the Palestine question and Arab-Israeli dispute; (2) Iraqi opposition to Soviet support of Ethiopia against Somalia and Eritrea; (3) Ba'athist suppression and execution of Iraqi communists; (4) Iraq's refusal to condemn Eurocommunism, China, and other ideological opponents of the CPSU; (5) a similar refusal to grant the Soviet Union automatic support for Soviet actions elsewhere in the world; (6) Iraqi communist support for the Kurdish nationalist movement; and (7) Iraq's growing wealth, which gave it a greater measure of independence.[48] It might be added that Iraq "shook the rope tying it to the Soviets"[49] so as to dispel Western and Gulf perceptions of Iraq as a Soviet proxy while simultaneously putting Moscow on notice that Baghdad would act to protect its domestic and regional interests, and should not be taken for granted. At the same time, Iraqi officials were careful to stress that there would be no severance of relations or abrogation of the 1972 Treaty, since the Iraqi government viewed its alliance with the USSR as a "strategic" one. Relations improved in late 1978 and early 1979, only to deteriorate again after the Iranian revolution and particularly with the Soviet invasion of Afghanistan: Iraqi President Saddam Hussein not only condemned the Soviet Union's actions but Iraq voted against Moscow on the issue in the United Nations General Assembly in January 1980.

The Iranian Revolution and especially the outbreak of the Iran-Iraq war in September 1980 posed a serious foreign policy dilemma for Soviet decision-makers. Should the USSR fulfill the letter and spirit of its 1972 Treaty and support Iraq? Or should it transfer its backing to the Islamic revolution in Iran, which seemed to have successfully challenged U.S. interests in the region? In practice, the Soviet Union has oscillated between both of these positions, while consistently calling for an end to the conflict. For the first year of the war, the Soviet Union—although not severing ties with Iraq—tilted toward Iran, offering to supply the Islamic Republic with technical assistance and military equipment. Its overtures rebuffed,[50] the Soviet Union assumed a more neutral position after mid-1982. By early 1984, the USSR had clearly shifted its support to Iraq, supplying massive quantities of war materiel and several hundred advisors, extending a $2 billion loan on very generous terms, and undertaking a number of development and petroleum projects, including the construction of a dam across the Tigris in northern Iraq.[51] A year later, however, there were indications that Iraq's continued ties to conservative Arab regimes, its resumption of diplomatic relations with the United States (in November 1984), and renewed Iranian flexibility vis-à-vis the Soviet Union were causing the latter to move somewhat closer to a neutral position once again. Iranian Deputy Foreign Minister Hossain Kozempour Ardebili visited Moscow in early 1985, and major Soviet-Iranian trade talks were slated for the summer of that year.

With the rupture of Soviet-Egyptian relations, however, it was Syria that became the Soviet Union's most important ally in the Middle East—a status formalized in October 1980 with the signing of a twenty-five year treaty of friendship and cooperation between the two countries. The Soviet Union supplied Damascus with large quantities of arms during and immediately after the 1973 war, and a further $3.6 billion in arms between 1975 and 1979. In 1982 it provided an immediate $500 million in military equipment to make good Syrian losses in Lebanon, and made several other gestures of support. These included the supply of conventionally armed SS-21 surface-to-surface missiles and the deployment of Soviet-manned SA-5 surface-to-air missiles. Approximately 7,000 Soviet military advisors still served in the country as of 1984.[52]

Outside the military realm, Soviet economic and technical assistance tripled between 1971 and 1980, and Syrian-Soviet trade increased sevenfold between 1977 and 1982. Under a bilateral agreement signed in 1981, the two sides hope to increase this level of trade by 10% per year over its 1981 level of $186 million. Syrian-Soviet trade represented 13% of all Soviet-Arab trade in 1982.[53]

The scale of Soviet support for Syria has not brought a corresponding Soviet influence over Syrian policy, however. In 1976, for example, the Soviet Union was singularly unsuccessful in forestalling Syrian intervention against the National Movement and PLO in Lebanon, despite open criticism by Moscow of Syrian actions and a reported punitive slowdown of Soviet arms shipments.[54] More recently, the USSR has proven unable to bring about an improvement in relations between Syria and Iraq, or between Syrian President Hafez al-Assad and PLO Chairman Yasser Arafat. Indeed, Syria's status as the Soviet Union's last major ally in the Middle East (and the lesson of Egypt) appear to give Damascus considerable leverage over Moscow, rather than vice versa. After the outbreak of a 1983 rebellion within al-Fatah, Yasser Arafat's Palestinian guerrilla organization, and the growth of a Syrian-supported challenge to Arafat's leadership of the PLO, for example, the Soviet Union—although still strongly favoring Arafat—refused to back him openly, to provide military equipment, or to assist in the evacuation of his forces from Tripoli, for fear of angering Syria.[55]

Although Syria, Iraq, South Yemen, Libya, and the PLO (and, on the periphery, Afghanistan and Ethiopia) represent the foundations and focus of Soviet policy in the Middle East after the mid-1970s, the USSR's cordial relations with other countries in the area are also important. In Algeria, the Soviet Union has continued to be the major supplier and trainer of the Algerian armed forces. The Soviets have also maintained friendly relations in North Yemen, and have supplied considerable amounts of (low-cost) military equipment—although any presence Moscow may have been able to achieve in Sanaa has been more than counterbalanced by the force of Saudi money and influence. Despite the Morocco's pro-Western orientation, the Soviet Union has forged relatively extensive economic links with that country. Soviet-Kuwaiti ties are significant, since Kuwait was until recently the only member of the Gulf Cooperation Council to have diplomatic relations with the USSR. Moreover, in pursuance of its policy of neutralism, Kuwait has purchased weapons from the Soviet Union as well as from the West. In the winter of 1985, perceptions of Soviet moderation led both Oman and the United Arab Emirates to follow Kuwait's lead and establish formal relations of their own with Moscow.

Like all of its closest friends and allies, the USSR has shared a common opposition to the U.S.-sponsored Camp David peace process and the expansion of Western (especially American) influence in the region. Other issues, however, have divided the USSR's friends in the Arab world, and hence undermined Soviet policy to a degree. Differences between Soviet and Arab interests and actions have had a similar effect. The intense rivalry between the rival Ba'athist regimes in Damascus and Baghdad has been one such obstacle; divergence between the position on the Arab-Israeli conflict held by Moscow and that held by Arab countries (particularly staunchly rejectionist Iraq and Libya) has been another source of difficulty. So too was the Lebanese Civil War, which in 1976 pitted Syria against the PLO (supported by Iraq). As noted above, the Iranian Revolution and the subsequent Iran-Iraq war raised for the Soviet Union the dilemma of whether it should maintain its alliance with Iraq (backed by the conservative pro-Western Gulf states, Saudi Arabia, and Egypt) or transfer its support to the Islamic Republic of Iran (backed by Syria and Libya). Finally, the Israeli invasion of Lebanon found the USSR supporting Syria and the PLO against Israel, while the subsequent split in the ranks of the PLO has found the Soviet Union weakly supporting Yasser Arafat against Syria and his Palestinian opponents.

CONCLUSION

Contemporary Soviet policy in the Middle East can hardly be described as assertive, expansionist, or even very successful, despite the tendency of some observers to represent it as such. Rather, the Soviet tendency toward a reactive, conservative policy that responds to events as they arise (rather than actively attempting to create them) has, in the Middle East, largely rendered the USSR Union a prisoner of developments in the regional and global systems. In the 1950s and 1960s, the USSR benefitted from rising levels of Arab anti-imperialism, and from the recognition by Nasser and other nonaligned nationalist leaders that the Soviet Union provided a useful counter to Western hegemony. The Arab-Israeli conflict and its associated challenges made the Soviet Union an even more appropriate ally in Arab eyes by creating Arab demands for the economic and military wherewithall to confront Israel while simultaneously discrediting the United States. Even so, the USSR's involvement in the issue and in the region as a whole is often characterized by seeming reluctance, as the history of the 1955 Egyptian-Czech arms deal clearly shows.

Given such an approach on the part of the Soviet Union, it is not surprising to find that much of the Soviet presence in the Middle East was dependent on the perceptions, interests, and hence political goodwill of Middle East states, and it followed that, when these factors changed, the Soviet position would be rendered vulnerable. This of course is precisely what happened after 1973—particularly in Egypt, but also elsewhere in the region. Sadat's realignment of Egyptian foreign policy removed the foundations from beneath Soviet Middle East policy, while the declining salience of the Palestine question and the profusion of other regional disputes weakened what had been the political focal point of the Soviet position. Finally, Europe's post-1973 shift to a diplomatic position more sympathetic to Palestinian rights (a shift we examined in chapter 4) removed a major barrier to Euro-Arab interaction, and hence brought—at least from the Soviet perspective—a new rival for Arab attentions.

Above and beyond this, the vulnerability of Soviet policy to local developments in the Middle East has been exacerbated by a further weakness of Soviet policy in the Third World, namely, the shallowness with which the Soviets have penetrated noncommunist regimes. Diplomatically, political agreements and treaties concluded at an official level have proven as easy to break as to make—a situation clearly illustrated in the case of Egypt. Moreover, as Heikal has noted, there is often a communication gap between Third World and Soviet leaders, a gap that does not yawn quite so wide between the Third World and the West. George Lenczowski, among others, has pointed to the importance of the "basically pro-Western orientation of the Middle East intelligentsia" who are so influential over state policy.[56] Arab communists have only rarely won or been allowed any access to real political power in Arab countries. More often, any apparent participation in government has been little more than a public relations exercise, with precarious positions in ineffectual cabinets being assigned to them in order to maintain a facade of national unity (or perhaps to send diplomatic signals to this or that international actor).

Militarily, Soviet supply and training of Arab armed forces has generally failed to create any considerable pro-Soviet sympathy within military ranks; indeed, as in Egypt, the reverse may be the case. Nor has Soviet military assistance served to create an unbreakable bond of dependence on the USSR for technical support and the supply of spare parts. Many states with Soviet-equipped armed forces (notably China) are willing to supply the required parts, while—as a quick glance through any Western defense industry magazine will quickly demonstrate—a profusion of Western firms also stands ready to step in and maintain or refurbish Soviet-bloc equipment. Soviet military aid and assistance, a major aspect of Soviet foreign policy, has thus had only a limited effect in the long-term.

Culturally, Soviet policy tends to have a minimal impact on the populations of Arab countries. Because of this, little popular support or sympathy for ties with the Soviet Union is created. Pro-Soviet communist parties are usually ruthlessly suppressed, even by those regimes with whom Moscow enjoys good relations. Soviet Marxist-Leninist ideology appears very alien to the Arab world (thus further inhibiting the formation of cultural and ideological ties), while Soviet atheism alienates some segments of the population to the point that it can trigger an anti-Soviet backlash from religious (and especially fundamentalist) elements. (The Muslim Brotherhood, for example, has

maintained a staunch anti-Soviet position in Egypt and elsewhere.)
Even in those countries that enjoy good relations with the USSR,
Western tourism usually exceeds that from the East, while as many
and probably more Arab students study abroad in the West as in the
Soviet Union or Eastern Europe.[57]

Finally, and perhaps most important, the economic impact
of the USSR on the Middle East remains limited. Certainly, Soviet
aid has played an important role in the economic development of
several Arab countries, while trade has grown at a substantial rate.
A report by the General Association of Chambers of Commerce, Industry, and Agriculture in the Arab Countries makes this clear:

> The volume of trade between the Arab countries and the Soviet Union
> rose from about $50 million in [1956] to $4.488 billion in 1981, that
> is, about 89 times more than in 1956. Calculations show that while
> the volume of trade [increased] about threefold in the 1960s (from
> $237 million in 1960 to $775.5 million in 1970), it increased in the
> 1970s at a faster rate, rising from 1970 to 1981 by a factor of 8.5.[58]

At the same time, Soviet trade with the Arab world is negligible in
global terms, accounting for only about 2% of total Arab trade and
3% of Soviet trade. Total Soviet two-way trade with Arab countries
in 1981, for example, represented less than one fifth of the value of
French-Arab, West German-Arab, Italian-Arab, or U.S.-Arab trade, and
total Soviet and East European trade with the Middle East pales in
comparison to that of the West.[59] The value of Soviet aid and trade
credits is also relatively small. Furthermore, Western trade and aid
tend to create or bolster those elements of the local Arab bourgeoisie
who profit from them, often creating or strengthening a politically
influential class whose self-interest recommends continued friendly
relations with the West. This was particularly evident in Egypt, where
Sadat's realignment of Egyptian foreign policy and his *infitah* (open-
door) economic policy encouraging Western trade and investment had
a significant impact on Egypt's social structure. There was a dramatic
growth in the size of the wealthy stratum of Egyptian society, and this
wealthy and politically powerful class lent strong support to Sadat's
pro-Western policies.[60] In contrast, Soviet economic interaction—less
pronounced, and often conducted at a more official level—has had no
such socioeconomic effect. The Marxist-Leninist observation that capitalism marches behind an army of cheap goods would appear to have

been confirmed by this Soviet foreign policy experience, much to its dismay and disadvantage.

Whether these weaknesses are endemic in the Soviet foreign policy process, or whether the dynamism and style of Soviet policy might undergo considerable change as the result of external or internal developments, are considerations beyond the scope of this study. One thing is clear, however: until such time as the Soviet approach to the Middle East does change, its presence there will continue to be less the product of superpower initiative than of factors and circumstances at the regional and national levels.

NOTES

1. *Bol'shaya Sovetskaya Ensiklopediya*, vol. 15, p. 460, cited in *Mizan Newsletter* 2, No. 11 (December 1960): 2.

2. Walter Lacquer, *The Struggle for the Middle East* (London: Macmillan, 1969), p. 181.

3. *President Gamal Abdel Nasser's Speeches and Press Interviews*, 1960 (April–June) (Cairo: UAR Information Department, 1961), p. 98.

4. Khrushchev's statement on the Middle East to the 21st Congress of the CPSU is translated and excerpted in *Mizan Newsletter* 1, No. 2 (February 1959), appendix A.

5. Charles D. Cremeans, *The Arabs and the World: Nasser's Arab Nationalist Policy* (New York: Praeger, 1963), p. 286.

6. al-Ahram (Cairo) 9 March 1955.

7. Ibid.

8. For a presentation of this commonly held Western view see Cremeans, *Arabs and the World*, p. 280.

9. Interview conducted in November 1974 with Dr. Murad Ghalib. Cited in Filib Galab, ed., *Qisat al-Soviet ma' Misr* [The Story of the Soviets with Egypt] (Cairo: Dar al-Thaqafah al-Jadidah, 1983), pp. 123–124.

10. Interview with General Muhammad Hafidh Ismail, November 1974, cited in *ibid.*, p. 99.

11. O. M. Smolansky, "Moscow and the Persian Gulf: An Analysis of Soviet Ambition and Potential," *Orbis* 14, No. 1 (Spring 1970): 106–107.

12. *al-Ahram* (Cairo), November 22, 1957.

13. Lacquer, *The Struggle for the Middle East*, p. 23.

14. *Ibid.*, pp. 16–17.

15. Franklyn D. Holzman, "Soviet Trade and Aid Policies," in J. C. Hurewitz, ed., *Soviet-American Rivalry in the Middle East* (New York: Praeger, 1969), pp. 21–22.

16. Karen Dawisha, *Soviet Foreign Policy Towards Egypt* (London: Macmillan Press, 1979), p. 175. See also Abd al-Munaf Shukr Jasim, *al-'alaqat al-Iraquiah al-Sovietiyah 1944–8 February 1963* [Iraqi-Soviet Relations 1944–8 February 1963] (Baghdad: Jamil Press, 1980), p. 194.

17. *al-Ahram* (Cairo), June 10, 1967.

18. Interview with Aziz Sidqi, November, 1974. Galab, *Qisat al-Soviet ma' Misr*, p. 51.

19. *Pravda* (Moscow), June 10, 1967.

20. Muhammad Fawzi, *Harb al-Thalath Sanawaat 1967–1970* [The Three Years War] (Cairo: Dar al-Mustaqbal al-Arabi, 1984), p. 194.

21. *al-Ahram* (Cairo), June 25, 1967.

22. Mahmoud Riad, *The Struggle for Peace in the Middle East* (London: Quartet Books, 1981), pp. 42–43.

23. *Ibid.*, p. 43.

24. *al-Ahram* (Cairo), July 24, 1967.

25. This figure represented more than 96% of Egyptian arms imports during this period. See Dawisha, *Soviet Foreign Policy*, p. 180.

26. J.C. Hurewitz, "Origins of the Rivalry," in J.C. Hurewitz, ed., *Soviet-American Rivalry*, p. 3.

27. Text in *The Policy of the Soviet Union in the Arab World: A Short Collection of Foreign Policy Documents* (Moscow: Progress Publishers, 1975), pp. 168–172.

28. Text of Sadat's letter in Anwar Sadat, *In Search of Identity: An Autobiography* (New York: Harper & Row, 1978), appendix 1.

29. Mohamed Heikal, *The Sphinx and the Commisar: the Rise and Fall of Soviet Influence in the Middle East* (New York: Harper & Row, 1978), pp. 253–254.

30. In 1971, for example, a Syrian Communist Party delegation was told by Soviet ideologists that while the USSR was prepared to provide military assistance to the Arab countries, the strategic balance of power in the region and the risk that any Middle East conflict might escalate to East-West confrontation rendered a military solution to the conflict unrealistic. The Soviets also condemned rhetorical threats to "liquidate" Israel, arguing that such threats were unsound both tactically and as a matter of principle. For the minutes of this meeting, see Records of the Syrian Communist Party, "Special Document: The Soviet Attitude to the Palestine Problem," *Journal of Palestine Studies* 2, No. 1 (Autumn 1972): 185–202.

31. Report of the Security Council (16 July 1967–15 July 1968), 23rd United Nations GAOR Supplement 2, UN Doc. A/7202 (1968), pp. 19–20.

32. Text of Soviet statement in *Soviet News* 5708 (London) 9 October 1973, p. 421. (Subsequent statements were even more strongly pro-Arab.)

33. Jon D. Glassman, *Arms for the Arabs: The Soviet Union and the War in the Middle East* (Baltimore: Johns Hopkins University Press, 1975), p. 131.

34. *Washington Post*, November 28, 1973.

35. Muhammad Ibrahim Kamil, *al-Salam al-Dhie'* [The Lost Peace], 2nd ed. (London: al-Sharkah al-Suodiyah lil Abhath wa al-Taswiq, 1984), p. 127.

36. *Ibid.*, p. 26.

37. Seymour M. Hersh, *The Price of Power: Kissenger in the Nixon White House* (New York: Summit Books, 1983), p. 404.

38. Ali E. Hillal Dessouki, "The Primacy of Economics: The Foreign Policy of Egypt," in Bahgat Korany and Ali E. Hillal Dessouki, eds., *The Foreign Policies of Arab States* (Boulder, Colo.: Westview Press, 1984), p. 138.

39. Ibid., p. 141.

40. Ibrahim Karawan, "Egypt and the Western Alliance: The Politics of Westomania," in Steven L. Speigel, ed., *The Middle East and the Western Alliance* (London: George Allen & Unwin, 1982), pp. 174–175.

41. Heikal, *Sphinx*, pp. 275–289.

42. Saad al-Shazly, *The Crossing of the Suez* (San Francisco: American Mideast Research, 1980), p. 50.

43. *al-Mustaqbal* (Paris), June 18, 1983, pp. 53–56.

44. International Institute for Strategic Studies, *The Military Balance 1983–84*, (London: International Institute for Strategic Studies), 1983, pp. 58–59.

45. Galia Golan, *The Soviet Union and the Palestine Liberation Organization* (New York: Praeger, 1980), p. 11.

46. See Michael C. Dunn, "Soviet Interests in the Arabian Peninsula: The Aden Pact and Other Paper Tigers," *Arab-American Affairs* 8 (Spring 1984): 92–98.

47. Hanns Maull, "The Arms Trade with the Middle East and North Africa," *The Middle East and North Africa 1983–84* (London: Europa Publications, 1983), p. 128.

48. George Lenozowski, *The Middle East in World Affairs*, 4th ed. (Ithaca, N.Y.: Cornell University Press, 1980), p. 312.

49. *al-Nahar al-'Arabi wa al-Duwali* (Paris), June 17, 1978, p. 8.

50. Iran "renounced the 1921 Treaty of Friendship, cancelled construction of the second Iran Natural Gas Trunkline, increasingly condemned Soviet regional policies, and took what the Soviets regarded as a number of other hostile actions." These included support for Afghan guerrillas and suppression of the Tudeh (Iranian Communist) Party. From Dennis Ross, "Soviet Views Toward the Gulf War," *Orbis* 28, No. 3 (Fall 1984): 439.

51. *al-Mustaqbal* (Paris), July 28, 1984, p. 5.

52. IISS, *The Military Balance 1984–85* (London: IISS, 1984), p. 22.

53. *al-Mustaqbal* (Paris), June 18, 1983, pp. 53–56; *an-Nahar Arab Report and Memo* (Paris), December 13, 1982, pp. 6–7.

54. Robert O. Freedman, *Soviet Policy Toward the Middle East Since 1970* 3rd ed. (New York: Praeger, 1982), p. 256.

55. The USSR did send private messages of support to Arafat and a private message of criticism to Damascus, but to no effect. One PLO official told the author that the PLO did not expect Moscow to risk offending Damascus or to "drop Syria for the PLO."

56. George Lenczowski, *Soviet Advances in the Middle East* (Washington, D.C.: The American Enterprise Institute for Public Policy Research, 1972), p. 162.

57. See Dawisha, *Soviet Foreign Policy*, pp. 191–197.

58. Quoted in *al-Mustaqbal* (Paris), June 18, 1983, pp. 53–56.

59. In 1973, at the height of Soviet influence in the region, the USSR and Eastern Europe accounted for only 3.7% of the Arab world's exports, compared to 47.9% for the European Community, 12.0% for Japan, and 5.2% for the United States. Similarly, the USSR and Eastern Europe supplied only 7.7% of Arab imports in 1973, compared to 42.3% in the case of the European Community, 10.4% in the case of the United States, and 7.3% in the case of Japan. See Fawziya Issa, "Arab Countries in World Trade," in Ali E. Hillal Dessouki, ed., *International Relations in the Arab World 1973–1982*, Joint Research Program Series No. 39, (Tokyo: Institute of Developing Economies, 1983), pp. 85, 93, 107.

60. The number of millionaires in Egypt reportedly increased from 500 in 1975 to some 17,000 in 1981 as a result of infitah. See Mohammed Heikal, *Autumn of Fury* (London: Andre Deutsch, 1983), p. 185. For an analysis of the attitudes of Egyptian students that shows a significant correlation between class background and support for Sadat's policies, see Raymond A. Hinnesbusch, "Children of the Elite: Political Attitudes of the Westernized Bourgeoisie in Contemporary Egypt," *Middle East Journal* 36, No. 4 (Autumn 1982): 535–561.

The People's Republic of China
and the Middle East

CULTURAL AND COMMERCIAL RELATIONS between the Middle East and China can be traced back at least fifteen centuries: according to the *Hadith* (Prophet's Traditions), the Prophet Muhammad counselled the Muslims to "seek knowledge even unto China." Indeed, Islam was introduced into areas of China around the middle of the seventh century, creating a religious bond between the Middle East and China that spanned culture, time, and distance.

The first diplomatic exchanges between the Islamic state and China occurred during the reign of Caliph Uthman Ibn Affan (A.D. 644–656).[1] Thereafter, political cooperation and conflict ebbed and flowed, but was not of a sustained or vital nature. (For one thing, the great distance between China and the Middle East limited the type and character of the interaction between the two peoples.) Nevertheless, commercial, cultural, and political linkages between the Arabs and China have a long historical tradition. This tradition was severed by the intrusions of the West into both the Middle East and China. Only with the removal of Western domination from both did relations between China and the Middle East begin to evolve anew. This chapter examines the evolving foreign policy of the People's Republic of China in the Middle East.

CHINA'S INITIATIVE

Contacts between the People's Republic of China and the Middle East were initiated at the Afro-Asian Conference convened at Bandung, Indonesia, in April 1955. Prior to that time, China had no diplomatic representation in Africa or the Middle East. The independent Arab states refused to recognize the communist government in Beijing, recognizing instead the Chiang Kai-shek regime in Taiwan. Israel was the only state in the area that recognized the Beijing government, although China did not reciprocate.

By 1954, however, China appeared interested in establishing some contact with the Middle East, and took a tentative step in that direction toward Israel. One report suggests that while David Ha-Cohen was Israeli ambassador to Burma in 1954 China had expressed an "interest in creating commercial and diplomatic ties with us."[2] A conversation with Chou En-lai in Burma in June 1954, reported Ha-Cohen, was followed by an official invitation for a visit by an Israeli delegation. A six-member commission consisting of David Ha-Cohen and his wife, Bracha Chabas; Dr. D. Levin, director of the Asia Department in the Israeli Foreign Office; M. De-Shalit, a senior official in the Israeli foreign ministry; Moshe Bezerano, an industrialist and commercial attache in Moscow; and Yosef Zakin, director of the Export Department, was authorized "to discuss all questions referring to the two friendly nations," and left for a one-month tour of Canton, Beijing, Tientsin, and Sian in February 1955. The delegation met with Chinese Deputy Minister of Commerce Lee-Jin-Min, who expressed China's interest in buying fertilizers, chemicals, drugs, artificial teeth, industrial diamonds, tires, and spare parts from Israel. A memorandum was signed, but no diplomatic exchange occurred. Preparations for the Bandung Conference were already under way, and China, not surprisingly, switched its focus from Israel to the Arab world.

The Bandung Conference offered China the opportunity to establish contacts with the Afro-Asian world. Israel was excluded from the meetings, but it appeared that Gamal Abdel al-Nasser would be there as spokesman for nationalist elements in both Africa and the Middle East. David Ben-Gurion, then Israeli premier, recognized Israel's disadvantage in seeking relations with China, commented years later:

> The Chinese have no grounds for hating Israel, but they have cause for seeking Arab friendship because they are boycotted by the UN, by America and by some European countries. We were one of the first countries to recognize China, but it has not recognized us. Because we have no value for China while the hundred million Arabs have great value for her, as have the hundred million Pakistanis. If

she deliberates with whom to make friends, with Israel or with the Arabs, with Pakistan or Indonesia, she makes the second choice. That is where her interests lie. This is our situation in the world.[3]

It was indeed Nasser that the Chinese decided to court. When Nasser and Nehru arrived at Rangoon Airport in Burma en route to Bandung, Chou En-lai met them at the airport and within five minutes of the meeting Chou En-lai had reportedly invited Nasser to visit China. Nasser was said to be "noncommittal."[4] At Bandung, Chou En-lai and Nasser not only discussed the prospects of increasing the volume of China's purchases of Egyptian cotton, but Chou En-lai also pledged Chinese support of and sympathy for the people of Algeria, Morocco, and Tunisia in their struggle for self-determination and independence—primary issues that Nasser had come to Bandung to win support for. Chou also promised to intercede with the USSR to obtain Soviet arms for Egypt.[5]

In April 1955, Major Salah Salem, Minister of National Guidance, hinted that Egypt might extend recognition to China to increase cotton sales in view of the threatened program of subsidized U.S. cotton exports. *Rose El-Youssief* of Cairo on May 21, 1956, quoted Dr. Abdul Munim Al-Qasioni, Minister of Economics: "Economic relations between Egypt and China were a prelude to political recognition." Other sources emphasized the role played by India's Nehru, reporting that Nehru had urged Nasser to extend recognition to China, and that "Nehru was very successful in establishing cordial and friendly relations [with] President Nasser, the leader of the most powerful state on the Asian continent. Thus, the struggle against imperialism, and the expulsion of the imperialists from both continents, became closely associated with the relations and friendship between Egyptian and Chinese leaders. Both played their roles with great success at Bandung. And each was friendly to the other."[6]

Nasser, however, refrained from extending formal recognition until May of 1956. It was finally extended in retaliation for Western arms shipments to Israel. The Egyptian newspaper *Al-Jumhuriyah* described Egypt's withholding of recognition to Communist China as a diplomatic courtesy to the West, and went on to editorialize: "Probably Egypt's recognition of the People's Democratic Republic of China was a powerful blow to the West. . . . That is actually what it was meant to be."[7] Two months later, Syria also recognized China, followed by Yemen in 1956.

This cordial beginning was buttressed by China's firm support for Egypt during the Suez Crisis. On November 4, 1956, Chou En-lai declared: "China firmly demands that the British and French governments immediately put an end to their aggression against Egypt, that armed provocations against the Arab countries be halted, and that there should be no further delay in carrying out peaceful negotiations on the questions of the Suez Canal."[8] Two days later, the Egyptian ambassador to Beijing announced that a quarter of a million Chinese had volunteered to fight with the Egyptians on Egyptian soil.[9] Egypt declined this offer, but did accept China's gift of U.S. $5 million.

Following the Suez Crisis, China supported the Egyptian proposal for an "Afro-Asian People's Solidarity Conference" to be held in Cairo. Organized at the nongovernmental level, the conference was attended by 577 delegates representing forty-six communist and noncommunist Asian and African countries. Its purpose, as explained by an official Egyptian publication, was to "mobilize the nationalist forces in the Afro-Asian countries to fight imperialism in all its forms throughout the world."[10] The conference, which provided China with the opportunity to make friendly contacts at the party level, established a permanent Afro-Asian Solidarity Council with its secretariat in Cairo. According to the agreements for its establishment, Anwar al-Sadat, president of the Egyptian National Assembly, became president, with a Russian and an Indian as vice-presidents, and Egypt's Yusief al-Sabai, one of the original Free Officers (leaders of the Egyptian coup), as general secretary. Of the other ten secretaries, there were to be one each from the USSR and China. Thus, China now had a permanent channel through which to maintain contacts and funnel propaganda to Afro-Asian nationalist movements.

Other Chinese activities in the area at this time included exhibitions at trade fairs in Morocco and Tunisia, and the opening of a New China News Agency office in Cairo in early 1958. China also recognized the Sudan upon the latter's independence in 1956, although the Sudan failed to respond until after the military coup in October of 1958. Three days after its July 14, 1958, revolution, Iraq recognized China, and Morocco followed suit in November of the same year.

Throughout this early period, the Chinese were acting largely as a supplementary force to the activities of the Soviet Union. In 1959, however, a difference of opinion arose between the two communist states over the proper approach to the Algerian question. On September 16, 1959, President Charles de Gaulle had offered terms of self-determination to Algeria; these were rejected by the Algerian Communist Party, although supported by the French Communist Party.

The Algerian Provisional Government (GPRA) proposed a slate of somewhat cautious terms relative to the initiation of negotiations. Delegations from both Algerian groups attended the celebrations in Beijing marking the tenth anniversary of communist rule, and October 17, 1959, the Chinese announced their opposition to the de Gaulle proposals. Khrushchev shortly thereafter announced his country's approval of the offer. The Chinese, alone of the world communist parties, opposed the Soviet position, going so far as to offer planes and volunteers to the GPRA. Tension mounted, with Khruschev trying to maintain a placid stand in view of the approaching summit meeting in Paris. The issue eventually quieted in light of the failure of the Paris summit, and of the increasing militancy of the Soviet position. (For details of subsequent events in Algeria, see chapter 4).

The dispute stemmed from differing assessments by the two powers of the relative merit and efficacy of two approaches to the West: peaceful coexistence and revolutionary action. The Chinese placed more emphasis upon (and faith in) armed struggle, while the USSR had come to rely upon peaceful competition in its dealings with the West. These differences arose from the national positions and historical experiences of the two states. The USSR feared the escalation of wars of liberation into general war, while the Chinese felt that armed struggle was necessary to weld the kind of communist-dominated united front upon which a successful revolution must, in their estimation, be based. In part, the Chinese position rested upon the tenet that through armed struggle the strength of imperialist powers could be sufficiently reduced to foreclose the possibility of the West's launching a world war. Also, their doctrinal assertion that the imperialist camp is a camp of war while the socialist bloc is the camp of peace naturally leads to the conclusion that a war against imperialism is, in fact, a blow for peace.

China's contact with the Middle East, initiated in 1955, was primarily a ramification of its desire to broaden relations with the new states of Asia and the Middle East. By 1959, however, the level of Chinese involvement had risen substantially to the point that China was establishing itself as an influential factor in Afro-Asian affairs. From 1959 on, competition between the USSR and China would be a dominant factor in the relations of the two states with the Afro-Asian nations. This increased pace of competition between the two largest communist states in the world coincided with the rapid dissolution of the colonial empires in Africa. As W.A.C. Adie noted: "The third period, from 1959 on, is marked by increasingly open struggle in Tropical as well as North Africa and in the Communist International front organizations, which operate in Africa, between orthodox, or Soviet-oriented Communism and what Khrushchev has denounced as 'Mao Tse-tungism.'"[11]

Richard Lowenthal, in a chapter on Chinese policy in Africa, points out that this competition could be seen building from 1959 on, and identifies it with the different concepts of "national democracy" held by the Chinese and the USSR. According to Lowenthal, the Soviet Union considered that the first stage in the development of a revolution is a revolution of the national bourgeoisie. After the success of such a revolution, the communist party can overthrow the nationalist leaders and assume power. The Chinese experience in the 1920s, however, convinced them that the use of this tactic was disastrous in their circumstances, and that the communist party must lead the revolution—albeit in cooperation with a broad united front organization including workers, peasants, national bourgeoisie, and petty bourgeoisie.[12]

The first phase of this on-going disagreement between the Soviet Union and China was not essentially harmful to the communist cause in Afro-Asia. That the two powers supported different countries or different groups had little effect upon their positions, and may have even appeared to perform a useful function from the point of view of a division of labor. The overall effect was to render their efforts more complementary than competitive, ironically enough—although the performers may have been somewhat uncomfortable playing their roles. From 1961 on, however, the issue was carried more to the organizations of the Afro-Asian states, and began to affect and then to disrupt the workings of these organizations. There was a tendency for the Soviets to rely upon the World Peace Council, while China worked through the Afro-Asian machinery itself. However, when the Maoist phases of Chinese foreign policy began to lock into place after the signing of the nuclear test-ban treaty, the Soviet Union defeated China in the Afro-Asian executive committee meeting in Nicosia, Cyprus. China regarded the test ban as a "betrayal"—as trafficking with the imperialist enemy. (The fact that they were at that time developing their own nuclear capacities, and therefore felt that the agreement was directed primarily against them, contributed to China's bitterness.) The Afro-Asians rejected the militant Chinese view, however, and the Soviets were able to gain their support. The metamorphosis of a divergence on tactics into an all-out organizational competition marked the beginning of the real Sino-Soviet split. At that point, the question ceased to be one of tactics, of emphasis, or of priorities, and became rather one of strategy and doctrine.

The extent of Sino-Soviet competition came to light in the course of the preparation (and subsequent cancellation) of the so-called Second Bandung—the second Afro-Asian Conference scheduled for November 5, 1965, at Algiers. In the shadow of the Sino-Soviet dispute, both the People's Republic of China and the USSR sought U.A.R. support. For the Soviet Union, Egyptian support was essential to its candidacy for the conference, while China sought the U.A.R.'s assistance in keeping the Soviets out. One report suggested that Chou En-lai visited Egypt on four occasions in an attempt to secure Egypt's cooperation in the Chinese campaign against the Soviet Union. The first occasion was in April 1965. Then, in June, he visited Nasser on his way to and while returning from Tanzania. Chou En-lai failed to enlist Nasser's support against the Soviet Union, however, and at the conclusion of the third visit relations between the United Arab Republic and China were strained.[13]

Serious and extensive negotiations took place during Chou En-lai's final, twelve-day visit (occasioned by the fall of Ben Bella). The results were that Nasser agreed to maintain neutrality in the Sino-Soviet dispute, but to support China on certain issues of importance to it. In return, China agreed to coordinate its policy in the Arab world with Egypt, to recognize the United Arab Republic's role as spokesman for the neutral nations, and to support the United Arab Republic on other issues of concern. In September 1965, Nasser went to the USSR. In the course of this visit, the Soviet Union agreed not only to step up work on the High Dam at Aswan but also to participate to the amount of 350 million rubles in the construction of a sawmill and in certain prospecting and substructure operations. In return, Nasser supported the USSR's candidacy for the Algiers conference.

The Second Bandung was subsequently cancelled, and a decade of Afro-Asian conference diplomacy ended. That decade had seen China greatly expand its contacts throughout Afro-Asia, but it had also witnessed the consolidation of Soviet ties in the Middle East. With American interests in the area well entrenched on one side of the political spectrum and the Soviet Union on the other, there appeared little room for a Chinese role in the Middle East. Nevertheless, China's strong interest in the area persisted, as testified to by the fact that during the cultural revolution of 1966–68, the number of Chinese top-level diplomatic posts abroad dropped from forty to one— and that one was Cairo.[14] The Chinese ambassador to Egypt, Huang

Hua, was a man with impressive credentials as well as a close friend of Chou En-lai.

China, of course, could not begin to match the massive aid poured into the Middle East by both the United States and the Soviet Union, and therefore could not effectively compete for influence at the governmental level. At the same time, however, China was not committed to the maintenance of a status quo, as were both of the superpowers. Prior to June 1967, there appeared to be no serious challenge to this status quo; American and Soviet spheres of influence seemed to have attained an equilibrium of sorts. The June war, however, introduced a new element into Middle East politics: out of the agony and frustration of defeat and continued Israeli occupation arose a viable and popular Palestinian resistance movement that posed a threat to both American and Soviet interests in the area, and that threatened the delicate equilibrium of the status quo. At the same time, people's wars of liberation broke out on the Arabian Peninsula, and China's local commitment to armed struggle made it the natural ally of such uprisings. Thus, there was suddenly a role in Middle East politics that neither the United States nor the Soviet Union could fill.

The Palestine Issue

The Palestine issue has loomed in the forefront of Middle East politics since the partition of 1948, but by the mid-fifties the rights of the Palestinians to return to their homeland appeared a moot point in international affairs. Israel ignored all United Nations resolutions endorsing this action, and the various Arab regimes recognized their inability to effect such a return by themselves. The issue, however, remained at the very heart of Arab nationalist sentiment, and no Arab leader could safely ignore it. Nor did the Soviet Union, whose increasing support to nationalist Arab governments from 1955 on had by the mid-sixties won it a role in Middle East politics comparable in scale to the American role there, underestimate this burning issue. For Arab governments, however, problems of political stability, modernization, and national sovereignty necessarily took precedence over the Palestine question. And for the Soviet Union, Palestine was an issue, not a cause. The Soviet aim was to win friends and influence in the area, and Soviet support, like the American support at the other side of the political spectrum, was used to buttress the recipient regimes against external and internal threats to their power. Thus, by the mid-sixties, neither superpower (nor many of the Arab regimes, either) took the Palestine issue very seriously, although all conceded its sentimental and emotional impact. Beyond that, the existence of Israel was a fact; the Palestinians, ensconced in refugee camps, appeared relatively pacific; and each Arab regime had its own more pressing problems to reckon with.

Following the Bandung Conference, China vociferously supported "the Arabs in their struggle against imperialism and Zionism" but took no particular note of the Palestine issue. However, the *Yearbook for the Palestine Question for the Year 1964* noted that "Chinese support on the Palestine question went beyond . . . [this] to clearly indicate the *legitimate* rights of the Palestinians to *return* to their usurped land."[15] Indeed, in 1964 China initiated aid to al-Fatah (then a little-known underground Palestinian organization), and China's interest in the Palestine issue became a prominent feature of its Middle East policy. On March 27, 1964, the *Peking Review* reported that a rally was held in Beijing to demonstrate Chinese "support for the Palestinian people's struggle to regain their legitimate rights and return to their homes!"[16] This position was made official in the joint communique issued by Chairman Liu Shao-chi of China and Sudanese President Abboud during the latter's visit to China that month.[17]

When the Second Arab Summit Conference of September 1964 endorsed the establishment of a Palestine Liberation Organization (PLO), almost no one took it very seriously—neither the Arab regimes nor the Soviet Union; neither Israel nor the United States. Its purpose, as envisaged by most observers, was to satisfy popular Arab sentiment, *not* to confront Israel. China, however, hailed the creation of the Palestine Liberation Organization as an advancement of the Palestinian struggle "to new heights."[18] And even more than moral support (which indeed the PLO already received from many corners), China contributed material aid, which the Palestinians were discovering was in short supply, even from their founders. Ahmad Shuqairy, president of the PLO, relates in his memoirs how he went to the Chinese embassy in Cairo for the first time in February 1965 to express his desire to visit Beijing. Within four days of his request, the Chinese ambassador went personally to PLO headquarters to notify Shuqairy that "Comrade Chou En-lai welcomes your arrival at your earliest convenience with a delegation of your choice. This invitation is extended to you both personally and in your capacity as Chairman of the Palestine Liberation Organization."[19]

Highest diplomatic honors were apparently accorded the Palestinian delegation. "As if we were a sovereign, independent state," wrote Shucairy, the Chinese ambassador and his aides were at the Cairo airport to bid the delegation farewell on its departure for Beijing on March 15, 1965. Upon arrival in Beijing, Shuqairy's delegation found "a splendid reception" awaiting them, with a crowd that numbered "in the thousands." The full diplomatic corps resident in Beijing had been gathered in a reception line, and the delegation was met by, among others, Marshal hin-Yi, China's foreign minister and deputy vice-chairman of the State Council.[20]

Of his meeting with Chou En-lai, Shuqairy reports that the premier listened to him "very intently" for a full two hours. The dialogue that followed is well worth repeating verbatim as reported by Shuqairy:

CHOU: Exactly what do you want from us?

SHUQAIRY: In addition to political support we want military aid.

CHOU: And what do you want explicitly?

SHUQAIRY: We need small and medium arms. We also need to send a mission of our officers to train on guerrilla warfare. You have a wealth of experience on this subject.

CHOU: You know we are always ready to support any liberation movement in the world as much as we can. Our responsibilities toward our people are great; we're not rich. But we feel we have a responsibility toward the liberation movements in the world in support of the oppressed nations to fight American imperialism. We will not delay in helping you as much as we can.

SHUQAIRY: Our demands are not great. I leave up to you the amount of aid that you can give us.

CHOU: We're not like everybody else who offers aid and expects payment with interest. This is political payoff. This is not our method.

SHUQAIRY: We don't want planes or tanks. We need the arms that are appropriate for guerrilla warfare.

CHOU: And where do you want the arms to arrive? Have you agreed with any of the Arab governments? Have you talked with President Nasser on the subject?

SHUQAIRY: Really, I did not discuss the subject with anybody, but I believe Cairo will not object to that. We would like the arms to be shipped to the port of Alexandria.

CHOU: We're ready to do this, and we can send you the arms free. We'll ship them on our ships directly to Alexandria. We don't trust other ships for the American fleet is closely watching. Announce what you want. We're not afraid of the Americans, but we do fear the Americans for you.

SHUQAIRY: I can't find the appropriate words to express my great gratitude. As long as your ships are going to Alexandria, is it possible for us to send our officers on it too, to begin their training with you?

CHOU: Of course that's possible. It's better if you keep in close touch with our embassy in Cairo to make all necessary arrangements for the arms and the officers.

SHUQAIRY: I'll never forget this favor. . . .

CHOU: This is our duty. There is no reason to thank us. You want to fight for your land. We can't abandon you, and we can't abandon the Afro-Asian nations. . . . Did the Russians give you anything?

SHUQAIRY: Nothing received till now from Moscow.

CHOU: What aid have you requested from Moscow?

SHUQAIRY: We have asked for military and cultural aid, but nothing has been received till now.

CHOU: I know you are a close friend of the Soviet leadership.

SHUQAIRY: The friendship is still there, but the aid isn't.

CHOU: But from us, friendship and aid. I would like to emphasize that we will be very delighted if the Russians offer you any aid. We do not want our friendship to be at the expense of your friendship with Moscow. If they offer you any aid we will be very happy. What concerns us is that you win your independence and freedom.

SHUQAIRY: This is the revolutionary spirit.

CHOU: Continue your efforts with the Soviet Union, although I think you'll get nothing from them. No political or cultural aid. Moscow recognized Israel and has economic relations with her. In addition, the Soviet Union agreed with America to the partition of Palestine and the creation of Israel.

SHUQAIRY: That is true. The Arab world remembers this stand. . . . Would you allow us to open an office in Peking?

CHOU: Tomorrow morning. We will give you the office space, recognize the PLO, and will give your office diplomatic immunity. We will treat them like any other friendly embassy. . . . We are with you, and we are ready to do whatever we can.[21]

On the eve of the June War—May 15, 1967—a rally for the support of the Palestinian movement was sponsored by the Permanent Afro-Asian Writers' Organization and the Afro-Asian Journalists' Organization. The PLO representative in Beijing, Rashid Jarbou, affirmed the strength of Chinese support: "And from Peking the Arab nation of Palestine finds complete moral and material support for the liberation of its homeland. On this occasion I would like to greet and thank the government and the nation of the Chinese People's Republic and its great leader, Mao Tse-tung, for its positive support of the Palestinian people's struggle."[22]

Why did China alone place such significance on the Palestine liberation movement? The movement certainly did not appear credible in 1965–66. However, in addition to China's strong commitment to support people's wars of liberation, there were few other avenues open for Chinese influence in the Middle East. Perhaps, too, China saw the potential of such a movement. After all, had not Chairman Mao and his embattled comrades marched more than 6,000 miles against incredible odds to ultimate victory? Had not the Chinese alone recognized and supported the Algerian liberation movement when the rest of the world considered it capricious? Whatever the reasons, the Beijing government must have felt vindicated when, in the aftermath of the June War, the Palestine resistance movement arose as a viable force in Middle East politics—one that posed a significant threat to the status quo. Thoroughly opposed to American policy in the area (and disappointed with Soviet policy), the Palestine resistance movement drew heavily upon Chinese support.

Of the eleven principal guerrilla groups, the following five made public their gratitude for Chinese aid: al-Fatah, Palestine Liberation Organization, Popular Front for the Liberation of Palestine, Popular Democratic Front for the Liberation of Palestine, and the Popular Organization for the Liberation of Palestine. These radical groups patterned themselves on the Chinese ideological style, and the thoughts of Chairman Mao, if not actually quoted, were certainly paraphrased in their rhetoric. One need only examine the publications and speeches of the spokesmen of the Popular Front for the Liberation of Palestine and the left-wing of al-Fatah to see the strength of Chinese influence. And while this did not make China exactly a political power in the Middle East, from 1967 onward it was certainly a conspicuous ideological ally of an emergent radical movement in Middle East politics. Thus, following China's admission to the United Nations, *Voice of Fatah* announced on October 29, 1971: "The Palestine Resistance welcomes China's recovery of its lawful rights at the UN, since China is the state closest to the Resistance in its attitude to liberation in strategy and practice."[23] On December 8, 1971, Deputy Chinese Foreign Minister and Chairman of China's delegation to the United Nations Chiao Kuan-hua, in a speech on the Middle East question before a plenary session of the General Assembly, attacked both the United States and the Soviet Union as "colluding with each other" in the Middle East. With America supporting Israel and the Soviet Union supporting several Arab governments, China made the issue triangular by placing her full support behind the Palestinian people. In his speech, Kuan-hua affirmed for the world that "the Chinese Government and people always stand on the side of the Palestinian and other Arab peoples who are subjected to aggression, firmly support their just struggles and give them assistance within the limits of our capability." He rejected the imposed settlement of the Middle East situation proposed in the four-power talks between the United States, the Soviet Union, France, and England, demanding instead that "the destiny of the Palestinian and other Arab peoples must be decided by themselves; their affairs must be handled by themselves. We oppose all conspiratorial activities of aggression, subversion, control, and interference carried out by any superpower against the Arab countries and peoples."[24]

The Dhofari Revolution

On June 9, 1965, an armed struggle was initiated in Dhofar— the western province of the Sultanate of Muscat and Oman on the coast of the Arabian Gulf—by the Dhofar Liberation Front. The Front was formed in 1964 by a coalition of the Dhofari branch of the Arab Nationalist Movement and the Dhofar Benevolence Society (a Dhofari separatist organization), and was primarily a nationalist movement dedicated to the liquidation of the autocratic and repressive Sultanate of Muscat and Oman. Lacking outside material support, the movement remained small and relatively ineffective in its first years, and but for the sultan's heavy-handed treatment of the Dhofari population in the course of dealing with the rebellion, it appears that the insurrection could have been contained. By 1968, however, the sultan had effectively alienated the entire Dhofari population. The rebels drew immediate moral support from the new, radical regime of South Yemen, and—through South Yemen—they began to receive material support from China.

Contingents of rebels were received in Beijing for political and guerrilla training,[25] and these returned to Dhofar with ideological as well as technical fortification.[25] Radicalization of the movement proceeded apace. At its second congress at Himrin in 1968, the Dhofar

Liberation Front became the Popular Front for the Liberation of the Occupied Arab Gulf (PFLOAG), reflecting a strong anti-imperialist position and the expansion of the cause to a people's war of liberation for the entire Arab Gulf. Scientific socialism was adopted as a revolutionary theory, and a People's Army of Liberation was formed.[26]

The Popular Front for the Liberation of the Occupied Arab Gulf received little support from the Arab world. In an interview with *Al-Tali'ah*, a Front spokesman stated: "The Front has had official contacts with the League of Arab States and Arab capitals, to explain the question of the revolution in Dhofar. Effective help was requested by the Front in favor of the revolution, but most replies have been negative."[27] By 1970 primary support for the movement reportedly came from the People's Democratic Republic of Yemen and from China.[28] South Yemen supported the Dhofari movement for both ideological and geopolitical reasons, and has acted as an intermediary between the Dhofari movement and China. China supplied the guerrillas through Southern Yemen, trained guerrillas in Beijing, and had military advisors with the guerrillas in Dhofar.[29]

At its peak, the Popular Front for the Liberation of the Occupied Arab Gulf controlled most of the interior of Dhofar and several cities: Dalkut, Rakhyut, and Sadah. Indeed, the very success of the insurgents had been a major factor in the decision of Qabus Ben Said to overthrow his father in July 1970. Thereafter Sultan Qabus sought to modernize Oman and prosecute the war against the guerrillas more effectively, ultimately calling upon Iran and Jordan for military assistance.

CHINESE POLICY IN THE 1970s AND 1980s

China's staunch support of the Palestine and Arab Gulf liberation movements was the most sensational aspect of its Middle East policy as of the end of the sixties. While this won for China a degree of ideological influence over radical movements in the area, the strong ideological orientation of its Middle East policy constrained China in the diplomatic arena. Except for Morocco, by 1970 China's relations were limited to the nationalist regimes of the Middle East. Egypt, the Sudan, Syria, Iraq, Algeria, and North and South Yemen—and only in the last-named did China effectively compete with the Soviet Union for influence. Furthermore, China had no relations with any of the non-

Arab Middle East governments. In contrast, Soviet relations with Turkey and Iran steadily improved throughout the late sixties, in spite of those countries' close ties with the United States.

By late 1971 and 1972, however, it was evident that China's Middle East policy was undergoing fundamental changes—partly because of power struggles within China, and partly because of the increased emphasis on the dangers of Soviet social imperialism. Conversely, the emphasis on dictation of policy by ideology appeared to be considerably lessened, if not dropped altogether, as China established relations with such incompatible regimes as Kuwait, Lebanon, Iran, and Turkey—countries it had previously classified as the "running dogs of imperialism." Following Kuwait's recognition of China in March 1971, Beijing newspapers and broadcasts beamed to the Middle East praised Kuwait, despite its monarchial regime, as a country using its oil riches "to support the struggle against imperialism and Zionism."[30] Similarly, following Iran's recognition in August 1971, Chou En-lai publicly praised the Shah as a "leader striving for uplift of oppressed masses," and China officially praised Iran's nationalistic oil policy as a "just struggle to safeguard its national independence and sovereignty and to protect its natural resources."[31]

The success of China's new approach was evident also in the General Assembly vote on China's admission to the United Nations. Countries previously considered staunch supporters of American efforts to keep Nationalist China in the United Nations voted now for its expulsion. Only Saudi Arabia among the Middle East states voted with the United States, while Bahrain, Jordan, and Lebanon abstained. By 1979, only five Middle Eastern states—Bahrain, Qatar, the United Arab Emirates, Saudi Arabia, and Israel—did not maintain diplomatic relations with China.[32] Although Israel recognized China, full relations were never established.

Most observers saw China's drive to expand relations as a considerable moderation of Chinese policy. Other events—most notably China's support of Pakistan during the Bengali rebellion—corroborated the view that China was following a more pragmatic foreign policy, one based on national interest rather than ideology. Pragmatism characterized Chinese policy in the Middle East, too, when China supported President Jafar al-Numayri of the Sudan in his extermination of Sudanese Communists in the aftermath of an abortive July 1971 coup. The Soviet Union, on the other hand, supported the coup, which was led by alleged communist party members and sympathizers. The coup was aborted through the concerted action of Libya and

Egypt, and Numeiry returned to power to vent his wrath against both the Sudanese Communist Party and the Soviet Union. Chou En-lai congratulated Sudan for having "smashed a foreign subversive plot" and praised Sudan for its "glorious anti-imperialist tradition." Thus, China's position in the Sudan subsequently improved at the expense of Moscow.[33]

An even surer indication of China's new orientation was provided on the occasion of the visit of the Chinese minister of foreign affairs to Iran in June 1973. With the blessing of the United States and a massive arms arsenal provided by America, Iran had in 1973 undertaken to be the guardian of the Arab Gulf, with the announced intention of insuring stability in the area and guaranteeing the flow of oil to Western markets. China saw Iran's efforts as representing a major obstacle to Soviet expansionism in the area, and favored them accordingly. According to one source, the Chinese Foreign Minister not only expressed his country's support for Iran's policy in the Gulf, but also China's support of Iran's acquisition of American armaments, describing them as "necessary, important, and understandable."[34] Moreover, since continued support for the Dhofar Rebellion inhibited China's efforts to establish good relations with Iran, Kuwait, and other Arab Gulf states, China withdrew its support for PFLOAG in the early 1970s. Iran and Jordan subsequently sent troops to fight the guerrillas, and by 1976 the rebellion had been all but suppressed. In 1978, Oman itself established diplomatic relations with the People's Republic of China—a dramatic indication of the dramatic changes in Chinese foreign policy since the late 1960s.

The 1970s also saw changes take place in China's relationship with the PLO, although to a much lesser extent. In addition to tactical disagreements with the fedayeen over the PLO's chronic lack of unity and predisposition to violence, and strategic differences over the continued existence of Israel, the Chinese accorded less importance to the Palestinians as their relations with Arab states steadily improved. In addition, Beijing was disappointed by the PLO's growing ties to the USSR after 1973, while the Palestinians were undoubtedly disappointed with China's tacit support for Egypt's realignment with the West and Kissinger's step-by-step diplomacy.[35] Such difficulties did not lead to an abrogation of Chinese-Palestinian friendship, however, nor to an end to Chinese support for the PLO, and when Yasser Arafat visited Beijing in 1970 Chou En-lai told the Palestinian delegation that China continued to support the Palestinian struggle and that it understood Soviet-PLO links: "You represent a national liberation movement . . . and it is normal that you should try to get help wherever you can find it."[36] Ideological sympathy for a national liberation movement was doubtless part of the reason for China's continued support for the PLO, but it is also important to recognize that Chinese support for the PLO—unlike its support for the Dhofar Rebellion—was popular throughout the Arab world.

Finally, as Soviet influence in the Middle East receded after 1973, so too did the apparent salience of the region in Chinese eyes. Analysis based on events data reveals a significant decline in the average annual level of Chinese interaction with Egypt, Syria, and Iraq between 1963–73 and 1973–78.[37] The major exception to this pattern appears to have been Iran, where relations flourished until the end of the decade.

Chinese foreign policy vis-à-vis the Middle East in the 1980s has represented a continuation of the pattern established in the 1970s. In other words, Chinese leaders have continued to view the area (particularly the Arab Gulf) as a buffer to Soviet expansionism; China has tacitly supported US diplomacy in the Middle East to the extent that it is directed against Soviet influence; China has continued to grant support to the PLO while calling for an Israeli withdrawal from the occupied territories and the establishment of a Palestinian state; and Chinese diplomacy in the region has continued to be characterized by a moderate tone and the maintenance of friendly bilateral relations with a number of states. The salience of the Middle East in Chinese foreign policy and the international significance of Chinese actions in the region remain lower than they were in the 1960s, however, and may even have declined since the 1970s. With the Vietnamese invasion of Cambodia and the rise of Sino-Vietnamese tensions (and the December 1979 Soviet invasion of Afghanistan), Chinese attentions have become focused elsewhere in Asia.

Furthermore, late 1979 and early 1980 saw a number of developments that severely complicated Chinese foreign policy in the key Arab Gulf region. The first of these was the Iranian revolution. As already noted, China had forged close ties to the Shah in the 1970s. When Teng Ying-chao (widow of Chou En-lai, and vice-chairperson of the Chinese National People's Congress) visited Iran in November of 1977, she noted "that the Iranian Government and people, under the leadership of His Majesty the Shahanshah, are vigilantly safeguarding their country's independence and sovereignty and have obtained remarkable achievements in energetically building their country and culture."[38] Chinese Foreign Minister Huang Hua made an equally friendly visit in June 1978, and in August–September 1978 Chairman Hua Kuo-feng himself travelled to Tehran where he praised the Shah's regional policies.

As it happened, this latter visit coincided with the rapid growth of domestic unrest in Iran that exploded into the revolution that would topple the Shah only a few months later. Needless to say, such past gestures of support for the Iranian monarchy were not appreciated by those who formed the new revolutionary government in 1979. The Ayatollah Khomeini himself is reported to have said of Hua Kuo-feng's 1978 visit: "You stepped over the bodies of thousands of Iranians who were killed by the Shah."[39]

Given Chinese perceptions of the geostrategic importance of Iran as a barrier to the Soviet Union, the Iranian Revolution and the consequent deterioration of Iranian-Chinese relations was a serious matter indeed. Subsequent Chinese efforts attempted to avoid further antagonizing the Islamic Republic, while at the same time emphasizing to Iran's new rulers the seriousness of the Soviet threat—a threat made all the more real by the Soviet invasion of Afghanistan.

China tried to steer a neutral course during the American Embassy hostage crisis, simultaneously stressing the inviolability of diplomatic personnel and the sanctity of the principle of nonintervention in the internal affairs of a host nation. When the Iran-Iraq War erupted, China's policy dilemmas were intensified still further: support for Iraq would anger Iran, and possibly push it closer to the USSR, support for Iran, on the other hand, might strengthen the Soviet position in Iraq, and would in any case almost certainly damage relations with Iraq as well as with the other Arab Gulf states with which China had carefully cultivated diplomatic relations since the early 1970s. Here again, China has sought to limit its losses by adopting a neutral position in the conflict. Chinese statements have assiduously avoided assigning blame for the war to one or the other of the contending parties; instead, China has stressed the need for a negotiated settlement to the conflict, arguing that "the turmoil in the Gulf region cannot do any harm to the oil-exporting Soviet Union; on the contrary, it will only pave the way for the Soviet Union to step in at this sensitive region upon which it has long kept a covetous eye."[40] Chinese Foreign Minister Wu Xueqian did visit Iran in November 1984, following a visit to China by Iranian Foreign Minister Ali Akbhar Velayti the previous year. That same month, however, an Iraqi delegation was invited to Beijing (doubtless to balance Wu Xueqian's trip), and Chinese

Communist Party General Secretary Hu Yaobang was careful to emphasize China's "strict neutrality".[41]

While the Iranian Revolution and the Iran-Iraq War have certainly complicated Chinese policy calculations in regard to the Arab Gulf, they have not totally undermined Chinese foreign policy there. Despite the continuation of the war, China has managed to maintain satisfactory relations with Iraq, and has apparently improved relations with Iran to a similar level. Clear evidence of the latter was provided in June 1985 when the Iranian foreign minister made a second visit to Beijing, this time accompanied by the powerful Speaker of the Iranian *Mailis* (Parliament), Hashemi Rafsanjani.

Beijing has also made some progress in furthering ties with other Gulf states. The United Arab Emirates and the People's Republic of China established diplomatic relations in November 1984, and China has official or unofficial trade relations with all states in the area. In November 1984, Chinese-Gulf trade represented nearly one-quarter of all Chinese trade with the Middle East.[42]

Like its activities in the Arab Gulf, Chinese policy elsewhere in the Middle East has been motivated primarily by a desire to limit and reduce Soviet influence. In the case of Egypt, China hailed Sadat's severance of ties with the USSR in the mid-1970s, and provided Egypt with spare parts for its Soviet-supplied arms as well as some other military equipment. (A formal arms agreement between the two countries was concluded in 1978–79.) When Sadat was assassinated in October 1981, Premier Zhao Ziyang stated that he was "deeply grieved."[43] China has maintained good relations with Sadat's successor, Hosni Mubarak, who made an official visit to Beijing in 1983, and whose armed forces continue to receive equipment and spare parts under a new Sino-Egyptian arms agreement concluded in 1983.

Similarly China has fostered friendly relations with other pro-Western regimes in the area. To the south of Egypt, a military cooperation agreement between China and the Sudan was signed in July 1982. To the east, China concluded trade and cultural agreements with Jordan in 1978–79, and Chinese President Li Xian-nian visited Amman in 1984. Jordan represents China's single most important trading partner in the Middle East, accounting for nearly one-half of all Chinese exports to the region in 1983.

China and the PLO have also remained on good terms in the 1980s, and China has lent both political and material assistance to the cause of Palestinian liberation. China has also steadfastly continued to refuse to establish diplomatic relations with Israel. The position of the People's Republic on the Palestine question and the Arab-Israeli conflict was clearly stated by Foreign Minister Huang Hua in his address to the United Nations General Assembly on 3 October 1982:

> We firmly support the Palestinian, Lebanese, and other Arab peoples in their struggle against Israeli aggression and expansion. The question of Palestine is at the core of the Middle East issue. . . . Any proposal or formula designed to exclude the PLO from the settlement of the Middle East question would be wrong and unworkable. The plan put forward at the 12th Arab Summit Conference held recently in Fez, Morocco, provides a good basis for a fair and reasonable settlement of the questions of Palestine and the Middle East. In our view, to achieve peace in the Middle East, Israel must evacuate the Arab territories it has occupied since 1967, including Jerusalem; the Palestinian people must regain their national rights, including the right to return to their homeland, the right to self-determination and the right to establish their own state; and the rights to independence and existence of all countries in the Middle East should be respected.[44]

Hua Huang also condemned Israel's invasion of Lebanon in the strongest terms. Significantly, this condemnation was extended to cover the United States—Sino-American rapprochement and strategic cooperation against the Soviet Union notwithstanding. In the same speech, Huang observed that "[T]he United States cannot shirk its responsibility for [the Israeli invasion and the Sabra and Shatila massacre of Palestinian civilians] since it has always shielded and abetted the Israeli aggressors."[45]

Since the 1983 rebellion within the ranks of Yasser Arafat's al-Fatah guerrilla organization, the Chinese have supported Arafat's leadership of both Fatah and the PLO. Indeed, during the fighting between pro- and anti-Arafat forces in northern Lebanon in the latter half of 1983, the Chinese supplied Arafat loyalists with arms and ammunition via Egypt. The following year Arafat visited Beijing in May, and personally thanked the Chinese leadership for their "firm support."[46] In return, Deng Xiaoping stressed the importance of Palestinian unity, praised Arafat's leadership, and reminded him of the setbacks suffered by the Red Army as a result of an "erroneous 'Leftist' Line" during the 1930s—indirect but clear criticism of Arafat's own radical opponents within the PLO.[47]

PRINCIPLES AND OBJECTIVES OF CHINESE POLICY

The principles of Chinese foreign policy are based on an ideology that theorizes a world order achieved through revolutionary struggle by oppressed peoples struggling against exploitation. Initially, at least, all policy statements were couched in a revolutionary rhetoric that belied the motivation of national interest. The two concepts are not independent, however, for the pursuit of national interests is conducted in a world perceived through an ideological framework. Without conducting a lengthy discussion of Chinese ideology, we can simply assume that, as with any state, national survival is the immediate goal of both internal and external Chinese policy, while maximization of power is the long-term goal. Ideology provides a view of the world that identifies threats to survival and defines the concept of power. The principles of foreign policy are a reflection of ideology, while the objectives thereof are a function of geopolitical, strategic, and economic motivations mediated by ideology. In China's case, a significant evolution in the interpretation of foreign policy principles and in the specific nature of foreign policy objectives has taken place since the Chinese revolution, largely in response to the increased tempo of Sino-Soviet hostilities and to the rise of China as a major international actor with global interests and responsibilities.

In terms of principles, China views the Middle East as one of the potential revolutionary rural areas of the world, and an area struggling against imperialism; and the theme of the anti-imperialist struggle was and is a prominent aspect of Chinese policy in the Middle East. During his visit to Cairo in 1964, Chou En-lai elaborated five principles of China's relations with Arab countries. These principles were formalized in the joint communique the Chinese and Yemeni heads of state issued on June 15, 1964: (1) China supports the Arab peoples in their struggle to oppose imperialism and old and new colonialism, and to win and safeguard national independence; (2) China supports the pursuance of a policy of peace, neutrality, and nonalignment by the governments of Arab countries; (3) China supports the desire of the Arab peoples to achieve solidarity and unity in the manner of their own choice: (4) China supports the Arab countries in their efforts to settle their disputes through peaceful consultation; and (5) China holds that the sovereignty of the Arab countries should be respected by all other countries and that encroachment and interference from any quarter should be opposed.[48]

When Chou En-lai set forth these principles, the Middle East was an area of some interest to China but of no vital strategic or economic concern. To the Middle Eastern states, too, China appeared a remote state peripheral to their problems and policies. We may recall that from its assumption of power in 1949 until the Bandung Conference of 1955, the Chinese People's Republic showed but little interest in Afro-Asian affairs and no interest in the Middle East. From Bandung until 1959, its policy was one of cooperation with the Soviet Union and development of ties of friendship and cooperation with Afro-Asian states along Bandung lines. From 1959 until 1961, China was involved in a number of tactical disagreements with the Soviet Union, disagreements that created tension between the two states and ultimately led them to compete for influence in Afro-Asia. Throughout this period, the activities of the USSR and China were complementary in their effects, though competitive in nature. Between 1961 and 1963, the dispute took the form of a competition for the dominance of various organizations associated with the Afro-Asian and nonaligned countries. From 1963 onward, finally, it is impossible to separate Chinese policy in Afro-Asia from the ideological dispute within the communist world.

Competition with the Soviet Union, therefore, is the singular most significant factor of China's active Middle East policy. The first priority of Chinese foreign policy, according to one Chinese source, is the struggle against imperialism and revisionism.[49] China's interest in the Middle East relates directly to this principle. When the Soviet attitude toward the West relaxed in 1958–59, it was to the shocked consternation of China. The Chinese viewed coexistence—the new Soviet approach to East-West relations—as an imminent threat to the progress of world communism, and, more particularly, to the advancement of Chinese interests in Asia. Well-entrenched Western interests in Asia in effect circumscribed Chinese relations in their vital sphere, and to acquiesce to Western dominance in the area appeared as much a danger to the security of China as would have been an ideological capitulation to capitalism. China's expanded role in Afro-Asia, therefore, was designed not only to counterpose Western influence but also to undermine the Soviet policy of coexistence and return it to a creed embodying active opposition to the West. Thus, while the Middle East is not at the center of Chinese policy, the issues at stake bear heavily upon the defense of Chinese vital interests.

Prior to 1967, China's ability to influence events in the Middle East was severely restricted due both to its peripheral connections with the area and its inability to compete with the massive amounts of American and Soviet aid. The thrust of its policy was propaganda aimed at exposing American plots and Soviet machinations. Governments of the area, however, responded with suspicion to this Chinese incitement to armed struggle. After all, China's support of Arab issues could hardly counterpose the ties of Arab governments with either the United States or the Soviet Union. The only area outside both American and Soviet spheres of influence was the Palestine liberation movement, and China provided it with aid, propaganda, and technical assistance. This proved to be a timely gesture, for the Palestine liberation movement exploded—to the alarm of both the United States and the Soviet Union—becoming, after 1967, the rallying point of nationalists throughout the Middle East. For its part, the USSR was forced to counter this by stepping up its own support for liberation movements in the region, including the PLO.[50]

In the early 1970s, the nature of Chinese policy in the Middle East and elsewhere underwent substantial alteration as a result of several interrelated factors. Within the Chinese government and Communist Party, the end of the Cultural Revolution and the internal power struggles of the post-Mao period resulted in the formulation and implementation of a revised, less ideological, more pragmatic approach to international relations. The challenge of the Soviet Union, rather than that of the United States, was emphasized. By 1973, China's ideological position on the two superpowers was unequivocally posited:

> Both Soviet revisionism and US imperialism are our arch enemies. At present Soviet revisionism is our most important enemy. After World War II, at first it was US imperialism which lorded it over the world; so we said that US imperialism was the No. 1 enemy. Later, Soviet revisionist, social-imperialism emerged. . . . The present situation is: US imperialism's counterrevolutionary global strategy has met with repeated setbacks; its aggressive power has been weakened; and hence, it has had to make some retraction and adjustment of its strategy. Soviet revisionism, on the other hand, is stretching its arms in all directions, and is expanding desparately. It is more crazy, adventurist and deceptive. That is why Soviet revisionism has become our country's most dangerous and most important enemy.[51]

Increased Chinese pragmatism and emphasis on the Soviet threat created the conditions for improved relations with the West, particularly with the United States. Richard Nixon's much publicized 1972 visit to China dramatized a major transformation of Sino-American relations that had been going on since the beginning of the decade, and the remainder of the 1970s and the 1980s saw the normalization of relations between the two countries and clear signs of their willingness to cooperate in opposing Soviet influence around the world. President Carter recalled the concern expressed by Deng Xiaoping during his 1979 visit to the United States to the effect that over the years China "had begun to realize that the danger to them from the United States was less and less, while the Soviet Union was a greater concern. It was necessary for other nations to unite in opposing hegemony. In his opinion, the United States had not done enough to contain the Soviets, and the situation in the non-Soviet world had not really improved."[52]

In the Middle East, the Chinese generally supported those US actions that weakened or undermined Soviet policy: the arming of the Shah, for example, and the encouragement of Sadat's realignment of Egyptian foreign policy won China's hearty approval. The People's Republic of China has not, however, expressed approval of some American actions. During his discussions with Carter, for example, Deng stressed the need to solve the Palestinian question. Similarly, China was critical of US support for Israel during its 1982 invasion of Lebanon. China, unlike the United States (but like much of Europe) lent its support to the so-called Fahd Peace Plan of 1981–82.

Thus, as already noted, the close nature of the Sino-American relationships since the early 1970s has not diminished China's basic support for the Palestinian cause. There has, however, been a change in China's approach to the Palestinian issue, and in particular to its view of the role of outside powers. Whereas in 1971 China's United Nations representative Chiao Kuan-hua bitterly condemned imposed settlements and "conspiratorial activities," stressing the need for the Arab people to decide their own affairs, thirteen years later Chinese leaders were expressing "firm support for convening an international conference of the five permanent members of the UN Security Council to discuss and settle the Palestinian question."[53] At the same time, China continues to maintain that it is superpower interference—particularly on the part of the Soviet Union—that has, to date, inhibited a peaceful settlement of the conflict in the area.

Finally, it is important to evaluate the role that economic interests play in the People's Republic of China's contemporary policy in the Middle East. As Table 7.1 shows, China's trade with the Middle East has increased dramatically in recent years.

TABLE 7.1

Chinese Trade with the Middle East 1973–1983

(US$ million)

	1973	1978	1983
Imports	196	138	470
% of world	4.5	1.3	2.2
Exports	322	364	3,026
% of world	7.9	3.7	13.7

SOURCE: International Monetary Fund, *Direction of Trade Yearbook* (various), (Washington, D.C.: International Monetary Fund, annual).

In the area of exports, much of this growth is attributable to Jordan, which in 1983 purchased no less than $1,520 million in Chinese goods.[54] Nevertheless, even excluding Jordan, the Middle East has, over recent years, come to represent an increasingly important source of markets for the People's Republic of China. Whereas global Chinese trade increased at an average rate of 16% per year between 1978 and 1983, Chinese-Middle East trade increased by 47% per year (31% excluding Jordan).

At the same time, one should not assign too much importance to economic motives in Chinese Middle Eastern foreign policy. Unlike many of the nations of Western Europe, China is not dependent on foreign trade for a large percentage of its total economic activity.[55] Furthermore, while trade with the region (which in 1983 produced a trade surplus of over $2.5 billion in China's favor) supplies China with hard currency that can later be spent elsewhere, the Middle East generally does not offer those high-technology industrial goods that China wants most. Thus, in the eyes of Chinese foreign policy-makers, trade with the Middle East is most clearly seen as a beneficial by-product of—but not the major reason for—good bilateral relations with the countries of the region.

NOTES

1. Muhammad Mahmoud Zaytun, *al-Sin wa al-Arab Abra al-Tarikh* [The Arabs and the Chinese through History] (Cairo: Dar al-Ma'arif, 1964), p. 42.

2. *Devar Hoshavua* (Tel Aviv) July 30, 1965.

3. Ibid. August 6, 1965.

4. *New York Times*, April 22, 1955; *al-Ahram* (Cairo) April 16, 1955.

5. John K. Cooley, "China and the Palestinians," *Journal of Palestine Studies* 1, No. 2 (Winter 1972): 19–34.

6. *New York Times* , April 22, 1955; *al-Ahram*, May 1, 1955.

7. *al-Jumhuriyah* (Cairo), May 17, 1956.

8. American Consulate General, *Survey of China Mainland Press*, Hong Kong, 1404 (November 5, 1956), p. 33.

9. *al-Abram* (Cairo), November 8, 1956.

10. Muhammad Anis, *Al-Mutamar al-Asyawi al Ifrigie* [The Afro-Asian Conference], We Choose for You Series, No. 44 (Cairo: We Choose for Your Committee, n.d.), pp. 204–205.

11. W.A.C. Adie, "Chinese Policy Towards Africa," in Sven Hamrell and Carl Gosta Widstrand, eds., *The Soviet Bloc, China, and Africa* (Uppsala: Almqvist and Wiksells [for the Scandinavian Institute for African Studies], 1964), p. 46

12. Richard Lowenthal, "The Sino-Soviet Split and its Repercussions in Africa," in Zbigniew Brzezinsky ed., *Africa and the Communist World* (Stanford, Calif.: Stanford University Press, 1963), pp. 142–203.

13. *Est et Ouest* (Paris) November 16–30, 1965.

14. *Christian Science Monitor*, July 18–20, 1970.

15. *al-Kitab al-Sanawi lil Qadhiyah al-Filistiniyah li 'Am 1964* (Beirut: Mussasat al-Dirasat al-Filistiniyah, 1966), p. 318.

16. *Peking Review*, March 27, 1964. p.

17. Ibid., May 22, 1964.

18. Ibid., September 18, 1964.

19. Ahmad Shuqairy, *Min al-Qumah ila al-Hazimah: Ma'a al-Mulok wa al-Rosaa* [From the Summit to the Defeat with Presidents and Kings] (Beirut: Dar Alawaden, 1971), p. 219.

20. Ibid., p. 229–232.

21. Ibid.

22. General Secretariat of the Afro-Asian Journalists' Organization, *Tayyed Hasim Li Nichal al-Sh'ab al-Filistini* [A Decisive Support for the Struggle of the Palestinian Nation] (Beijing, 1967), p. 7.

23. Reported in *Free Palestine* (London), December 1971–January 1972.

24. American Consulate General, Hong Kong, *Survey of China Mainland Press*, 5037–40 (20–23 December 1971), pp. 32–33.

25. *Times* (London), August 3, 1970.

26. *Al-Thawri* (Aden), June 8, 1971.

27. *Al-Talivah* (Kuwait), July 17, 1968.

28. *New York Times*, July 12, 1970.

29. *Times* (London), August 3, 1970.

30. *Christian Science Monitor* April 9, 1971.

31. *Christian Science Monitor*, September 23, 1971.

32. Yitzhak Shichor, *The Middle East in China's Foreign Policy, 1949–1977* (Cambridge: Cambridge University Press, 1979), p. 177.

33. Nigel Disney, "China and the Middle East," *MERIP Reports* 63 (1977): 11.

34. *Al-Muhrer* (Beirut), June 16, 1973.

35. On the latter, see Shichor, *The Middle East in China's Foreign Policy, 1949–1977*, p. 185.

36. Abu Iyad, *My Home, My Land: A Narrative of the Palestinian Struggle* (New York: Times Books, 1981), p. 67.

37. Edward E. Azar, "Soviet and Chinese Roles in the Middle East", *Problems of Communism* 28, No. 3 (May–June 1979): 22–23.

38. *Hsinhua Weekly* 49 (10 December 1977), cited in A.H.H. Abidi, *China, Iran, and the Persian Gulf*, (Atlantic Highlands, NJ: Humanities Press, 1982) p. 148.

39. For his part, the ex-Shah later remarked on Chinese support for his leadership: "I must also pay homage to the loyalty of the Chinese leaders when Mr. Hua Kuofeng visited me, at a time when the Iranian crisis was reaching its peak. I had the impression that the Chinese alone were in favour of a strong Iran." (Quoted in *ibid.*, p. 174.)

40. *Xinhua News Agency*, September 24, 1980, cited in *ibid.*, p. 190.

41. *Beijing Review* 27, No. 48 (26 November 1984), p. 6. The limited Chinese role in supplying arms to the combatants has been similarly balanced. In 1980, it was widely reported that the PRC was allowing North Korean aircraft to transit its airspace en route to Iran with arms deliveries. Chinese agreements to supply Iran with F-6 fighters and to supply Iraq with T-69 tanks and spare parts have also been reported, although as of the end of 1985 no such deliveries of major Chinese military equipment appear to have taken place.

42. Of Chinese exports to the region, 32% were textiles, 20% light manufactures, 8% foodstuffs, and 7% tools and appliances. See *al-Mustaqbal* (Paris) 33, June 25, 1983, pp. 41–45.

43. Yasser Arafat, who was visiting China at the time, caused some difficulty for his hosts by openly applauding Sadat's death.

44. *Beijing Review* 25, No. 41 (October 11, 1982), pp. 16–17.

45. Ibid.

46. *Beijing Review* 27, No. 20 (May 14, 1984), pp. 8–10.

47. Ibid.

48. *Peking Review*, June 19, 1964.

49. Lin Piao, quoted in ibid., September 3, 1965.

50. *New York Times* January 1, 1972. As noted in chapter 6, the late 1960s and early 1970s saw the first signs of improvement in Soviet-PLO relations.

51. "Soviet Revisionism Is Our Country's Most Dangerous and Most Important Enemy," Outline of Education on Situation for Companies (Lesson 2), *Reference*

Materials Concerning Education on Situation 42 (Kunming Military Region: Propaganda Division, Political Department, 1973), in *Issues and Studies* 10, No. 9 (June 1974), p. 98.

52. Jimmy Carter, *Keeping Faith: Memoirs of a President* (Toronto: Bantam Books, 1982), p. 204.

53. *Beijing Review* 27, No. 20 (May 14, 1984), p. 9.

54. Other major Chinese export markets in the region in 1983 included Iran ($267 million); Egypt ($205 million); Syria ($196 million); Saudi Arabia ($149 million); Morocco ($147 million); Algeria ($100 million); Kuwait ($99 million); Yemen Arab Republic ($81 million); United Arab Emirates ($68 million); and the People's Democratic Republic of Yemen ($53 million). China's imports, on the other hand, came primarily from Egypt ($68 million), Yemen Arab Republic ($50 million), Kuwait ($50 million), Qatar ($43 million), Mauritania ($49 million), Morocco ($35 million), and Libya ($34 million).

55. China's total foreign trade (imports and exports) is equivalent to less than 13% of China's declared GNP.

Africa and the Middle East

RELATIONS BETWEEN THE VARIOUS STATES and empires of the Middle East and their counterparts in Africa are ancient. The fall of the Western Roman Empire, and the disorders thereof, diminished these connections as well as destroyed most of the historical records. Until the rise of Islam, the great barbarian invasions focused the attention of Egypt and Mediterranean Africa on local affairs. Only a few Arab traders crossed the Red Sea and negotiated the coastal waters in their small vessels to maintain a hazy Middle Eastern–African contact.

Of this period, actually, little is known with certainty. In the centuries between the Hejira and the onslaught of European colonialism, the Arabs held a virtual monopoly on economic and cultural exchange with sub-Saharan Africa. This well-developed trade faltered as both Islam and Sudanic empires lost their cohesion and autonomy, but it never disappeared completely, not even at the height of European colonial dominance. The nature of contemporary African–Middle Eastern relations and the patterns of that interaction are the subjects of this chapter.

Of the several Middle Eastern countries, neither Turkey nor Iran has participated in interregional or cross-regional efforts to the same extent as the Arabs; nor does either have the comparable historical, cultural, or geographical linkages with Africa. This chapter, therefore, concentrates primarily on the Arab world and its relations with Africa, for it is the Arabs who provide the main thrust for regional interaction. However, Israel also invests considerable effort in

African relations; consequently, the Arab-Israeli dispute is a significant aspect of Middle Eastern-African interaction.

THE ARABS AND AFRICA

When in the middle of the twentieth century the colonial powers lost their dominion over both Arab and African lands, the various governments of the two regions *ipso facto* became a part of the anticolonial, anti-imperialist movement. The commonality of viewpoint extended beyond foreign policy to common problems of economic and political development. Although great diversity of opinion characterizes the politics of these regions, a degree of cooperation has proceeded through the media of international conferences, diplomatic and trade relations, and the United Nations. In addition, there have been attempts by both Arab and African nations to enlist the support of their counterparts on matters of regional interest—the Arab-Israeli dispute on the part of the Arabs, for example, and the South African problem on the part of the black African states.

Historical and Cultural Ties

The impetus given Arab expansion in the seventh century by the rise of Islam carried Arab armies into Egypt in 649, and into the rest of North Africa by the end of the century. However, the spread of Islam into the Sudanic lands of Africa was a long, slow process. Islam did not replace Christianity in the Nile Valley until the thirteenth century, for example—although Berber converts had carried Islam across the Western Sudan by the eleventh century, and there were notable centers of Islamic civilization on the Niger at Jinna and Timbuktu by the fourteenth century. On the East African coast, trading stations became permanent settlements at various points, the largest of which—Zanzibar—became the official residence of the ruler of Oman. Thus Islam diffused from the northern and eastern coasts of Africa into the center, although the rate at which the faith was adopted by the natives may have been less rapid than it appears, due to the tendency of the upper classes to adopt Islam as a badge of association with the highly regarded Arab culture.

The religious connection between the Arab world and Africa

is an important cultural bond, however much modification the tenets of Islam have undergone in the process of adaptation to the African environment. Nonetheless, Islam has provided the motive for such cultural exchanges as the visits of Arab travelers to the cities and universities of the Sudan, the education of Africans at al-Azhar in Cairo, the ritual pilgrimages to Mecca (by those Africans who could afford them), and the movements of itinerant marabouts throughout Muslim Africa. One of the major foci of cooperation between Arab and African governments is the base of understanding provided by a common religious background, however variant. It must be stated that although religion does not seem to be a controlling factor in international relations, it has often provided a tool for developing cooperation in those contexts where friendship between governments already exists.

The basis of cooperation was not created by religion alone, however. The ancient trade routes—those down the east coast forged by the Arab traders of Yemen and Oman, those up the Nile first opened by the Pharaohs, and those across the Sahara pioneered by the Phoenicians and Romans—all fell under the control of the Arabs of North Africa (or under the control of their allies among the converted tribesmen of the Sahara). Traffic in slaves, gold, and salt moving north, and in cloth and such manufactured goods as weapons moving south, provided the base for extensive trade. Again, this trade should not be overrated as a source of cooperation, however. Under the economic systems prevalent throughout Africa and Arabia during the period of Arab dominance, trade was necessarily limited. The economies of the day operated on a subsistence basis, and only essential primary goods and certain luxuries were exchanged—and then only by rulers and members of the upper classes. Furthermore, trade was controlled by various private merchants operating under the aegis of various regimes. For much of this period, the Arab world was divided among a variety of such regimes, and the internal instability of some of them often disrupted trade—seriously, at times.

This same shifting political situation also had an effect upon the political intervention of Arabs into Africa. Although there had been an increasingly important pattern of trade up the Nile and from the east coast for centuries, it was not until the nineteenth century that Egypt, under the leadership of the Khedive Ismail and his British advisors, attempted to take advantage of the shorter distance to the interior (what is now Uganda) by the coastal route. An expedition was sent, but the landing on Zanzibari territory led to protests from the

British government sufficient to halt the expedition. Shortly afterward, the division of African territory among the European powers prevented any further attempts to consolidate an Egyptian empire in Africa.

Political relations were not always advantageous to the reputation of the Arabs in any event. The slave trade and the trade in arms had extremely damaging effects among the population of Africa. In West Africa, the spread of Islam was often accomplished with the sword rather than by peaceful conversion. In the Nile Valley, for example, it was Arab armies, not missionaries, that took Islam up to the mountain kingdom of Ethiopia. Altogether, the African experience with the Arabs was not a happy one. However, the intervention of European powers not only prevented the Arabs from acquiring imperial possessions but also subjected the Arabs to the experience of colonization. Under these circumstances, the Arabs, instead of conquerors, became fellow-sufferers of imperialism. Nevertheless, the experience of the Africans who were subjected to European rule—especially in the Belgian Congo and the Portuguese territories, but to a lesser degree in the French, Spanish, and German colonies—made the misdeeds of the Arabs seem mild by comparison.

THE BASES OF INTERACTION

The common experiences of the Africans and Arabs—the subjection to colonialism, the training of nationalist politicians in Europe, the diffusion of feelings of unity over areas transcending the tribe or traditional village—gave them objective and subjective bases for common action. Until imperialism began to recede, the opportunities for communication across colonial boundaries were limited, however, so that it was not until the end of World War II that a common front could begin to form. Even then, the states of the Arab East were primarily interested in establishing their own political identities and solving their domestic problems, and in the case of North African Arab states were involved in a long struggle for independence. The significance of the independence of Egypt from foreign control (and of the fact that the Egyptian revolution occurred as early as it did: 1952) should not be underrated in assessing the reasons for the pivotal role Egypt has played in Africa.

The chief basis of Arab-African interaction is ideological and subjective; however, a set of problems of foreign and domestic policy is common to the two regions, and it is within this framework that the nationalist-neutralist ideology has developed. The problem of the relationship of former colonies to the former colonizer has been serious, perhaps especially among the former French territories. Among both African and Arab states colonized by France, the relationship to France has always been an important question. These states are generally more dependent upon France for economic aid and for trade than former British colonies are upon Britain, for example. In some cases—notably that of Chad—the French have utilized military forces to enforce domestic stability; only on one occasion—in 1964 in East Africa—have the British taken a similar action, and then only briefly. The material dependence of African states upon France is not matched among the Arab states, even those of North Africa (although Tunisia's economy is based on the French connection to a significant degree).

Perhaps more important on a continuous basis than material connection has been the union engendered by the French assimilationist policy. Although the policy failed to turn Africans into Frenchmen, and thus to make African territories into integral parts of France—just as the policy failed in Syria, Lebanon, and Southeast Asia—it is nevertheless true that many leaders of African states were educated in France and received their first political training there. The former union of African parties in the Rassemblement Democratique Africaine was predicated largely on the fact that the African territories required a unified delegation at the National Assembly in Paris, where one African leader—Felix Houphouet-Boigny—even served in several ministries. The reluctance to sever the French connection is evident from the fact that only Guinea voted "no" in the 1958 referendum—although it has to be added that within the next two years the other French territories opted for a much looser form of association with France.

Related to the problem of the relationship to the metropolitan power has been the problem of the cold war and subsequent East-West competition. For those states that had to struggle violently for their independence, foreign assistance was essential. And because the French, British, Belgians, Portuguese, and Spanish were all formal or de facto members of the Western alliance, it was difficult for liberation movements to obtain any support from the states of the Western bloc. A turn to the communist states was the obvious and, in some cases, essential course. After independence was obtained, the decision had to be made to continue the association with the communist states, or to return to some form of negotiated association with the metropolitan power and its allies (or some combination of the two). The need to make this decision also presented itself, albeit in a somewhat different form, to those states whose independence was achieved without a violent revolution, but who likewise disapproved of the methods employed by the colonial powers and hence felt a sense of fellowship for those nationalists who had turned to the East.

However, most African states, faced with the prodigious problems of economic development, have had no wish to be drawn into the competition of the Western and the Eastern blocs unless they could benefit their participation. This has led to the position of nonalignment, the principal tenets of which are anti-imperialism, disassociation from any blocs or alliances, and the presentation of something of a united front for peace.

In addition to these problems of foreign policy, the chief problems of domestic policy were two, and in these matters there was considerable similarity between the problems of the Arabs and those of the Africans. The problem of economic development was and is crucial for these new states; it is not only common to them, but may be alleviated by common action. As evidence of this fact, there have been numerous attempts—some more successful than others—to establish various forms of economic unions, customs unions, common markets, and cooperative enterprises.

The problem of internal stability is not so easily solved through common action, but it has been widely felt that some form of political union, aside from its economic advantages, could provide the basis for progress in politics and in social life. The Mali Federation of the Soudan (now Mali) and Senegal (1960–62); the United Arab Republic of Egypt and Syria (1958–61); the proposed Egyptian-Iraqi-Syrian unions of 1963 and 1964; the numerous Libyan merger offers or agreements with Egypt, the Sudan, Morocco, and others since 1969; the Federation of Tanganyika, Uganda, and Kenya into an East African entity; the Conseil d'Entente of Niger, the Ivory Coast, Upper Volta, and Dahomey; and the union of Tanganyika and Zanzibar into Tanzania in 1964—all are examples of attempts to gain advantages from political unity in the areas of political stability and national development.

Aside from the possibilities of united action in international relations—at the United Nations, for example—objective circumstances do not provide as great a motive for cooperation as an ideological agreement that was, ironically enough, fostered by the objective conditions created by colonial rule. During the period between 1950 and 1960, there were few places in Africa that could serve as centers of African nationalist activity. The most important of these was Cairo, where the Egyptian government maintained support for the offices of many African liberation movements, facilities for radio broadcasts and publishing, secretarial help, and other services. This generosity left many African nationalists with favorable impressions of Egypt, and led to an interchange of views that no doubt created a viable area of agreement between the Egyptian regime and many of the leaders of the independent states of Africa.

Gamal Abd al-Nasser, more than any other Arab leader (until Ben Bella in Algeria), believed in a strong connection between the Arabs and the Africans. In his 1954 book, *Egypt's Liberation: The Philosophy of the Revolution*, Nasser devoted considerable space to Egypt's role in the African circle. He observed that Egypt, because of its location in Africa, could not "remain aloof from the terrible and sanguinary conflict going on there," and that Egypt had a responsibility in Africa that could not be surrendered.[1]

The feeling of unity with Africa common to the Egyptian leadership was not shared by all Arab politicians, of course, but the North Africans—whose own struggles for liberation had been supported by Egypt—shared in this feeling at least in part. It is difficult in retrospect to be sure whether anti-imperialism was a cause or a consequence of cooperation, but the two were probably interdependent. As the states cooperated in the solution of their particular problems with colonialism, they came to see imperialism per se as an evil they must combine to combat. The Bandung Conference of 1955, which provided an opportunity for President Nasser to meet the leaders of the anti-imperialist movement and to discover the truly global scale of its activities, added to his perceptions of the importance of African liberation the idea of a consistent framework for pursuing not only the winning of liberation but its perpetuation as well.

During the 1950s and 1960s, this anti-imperialistic theme continued to be central not only to Egyptian policy under Nasser but also to the policies of such states as Algeria, Iraq, Syria, Ghana, Guinea, and Mali. In pursuit of this policy, Egypt involved herself in the Congo, nationalizing Belgian property in Egypt as an indicator of her position; and, when it was found that Egypt was over-involved, President Nasser participated in the Casablanca Conference in 1961 as a means of presenting a united front on the side of anti-imperialism. After gaining independence from France (1962), Algeria also became a leading anti-imperialist state, perhaps even more ready than Nasser's Egypt to support violent revolutionary actions. A few years later (1969), revolutionary Libya under Colonel Muammar Qaddafi began to assume a similar role. Both Algeria and Libya have provided aid and training to a number of southern African liberation movements, as well as to the Polasario in the formerly Spanish Western Sahara.

Although there has been a significant degree of ideological agreement—especially on nonalignment, anticolonialism, anti-imperialism, and cooperation through the United Nations and other joint endeavors of the nations of Africa—and although this agreement has been linked to the domestic ideal of socialism and development, the extent of disagreement has also been significant. Again, the francophone states, which depend more heavily upon European assistance, have not been willing to go as far in cooperating with the leaders of the anti-imperialist movement as have the former British colonies. While Ghana, Kenya, Tanzania, Egypt, and Iraq have been notably anti-imperialist at one time or another, only Algeria and Guinea among French-speaking African states have been active.

The problem here has been one of priorities. Although some states find that their first priorities are political and economic independence, others consider that political stability and economic development are imperative, even at the expense of independent foreign policies. For developing countries, the pursuance of an anti-imperialist foreign policy can be a costly affair, since there is the risk of alienating potential benefactors in the developed world, of increasing the possibility of covert or overt destabilization attempts by foreign powers, and of maintaining a more expensive foreign policy apparatus than would otherwise be necessary.

International Conferences

At the Bandung Conference in 1955, the first Afro-Asian People's Solidarity Conference at Cairo in 1957, and the All-African People's Conference at Accra in December 1958, the basis was laid for three important trends. The first was the use of the international conference as a means of resolving questions among the nations of Afro-Asia, and of providing at least the semblance of a united front. The second was the pressure exerted by Russia and China upon the conferences and the permanent secretariats they established. The third was the inability of the Afro-Asian states to go beyond generalities to identify specific measures.

After Bandung, the international conference became important as a means of gathering together statesmen from Africa, Asia, and Latin America. Some of these conferences were for nonaligned nations, others for all Afro-Asians. The problems of membership became acute at times, as at the Cairo preparatory conference before the Belgrade meeting of 1961, and the Algiers meeting in 1965.

The communist states attempted throughout the period of conference diplomacy to gain control of representation at various conferences and on various secretariats. The Afro-Asian People's Solidarity movement was a communist initiative, but was taken over by the Egyptians when the communist states failed to maintain lasting control. Eventually, at Algiers, the efforts of China and the USSR to outdo each other in seeking influence in Afro-Asia not only led to the disruption of the conference but also diminished the usefulness of conferences in general.

The problem of international conferences that eventually proved insoluble, however, was that of unity. After Bandung, it became virtually an article of faith that a high degree of agreement be reached, and that no rifts remain that might provide the imperialist states with a handhold wherewith to further divide Afro-Asia. The real divisions among Afro-Asian states on ideological grounds and for reasons of national interest, as well as the extent to which common interest in some matters was simply lacking, meant that every attempt to get beyond platitudes ended in failure. The Casablanca group of five states was able to maintain solidarity for only about two years after its creation in 1961; larger groups collapsed even more quickly. Any attempt to involve significant numbers of states involved some dilution of principles, and—given the diversity among these states—getting agreement among all of them required that there be little or no content to the matter under discussion.

The United Arab Republic participated in a number of conferences, including many hosted in Cairo. The permanent organs of various groups were also located in Cairo. A major exception to Egyptian initiative in conference diplomacy was the effort of Prime Minister Ahmed Mohammed Mahgoub of the Sudan to sponsor a conference of Asian and African leaders in Khartoum after the 1967 war with Israel. Algiers, too, was the seat of several conferences. However, until the early 1970s the Arab states proved unable to sustain any African interest in condemning Israel, and except for the Organization for African Unity (OAU), few of the organizations linking Arabs and sub-Saharan Africans proved effective.

Within the framework of the OAU, the Arab states of Africa

have maintained continuing relations with the non-Arab African states in both the political and functional spheres. Egypt, Libya, Algeria, and Morocco have all been very active within the organization, and four other Arab states (Djibouti, Mauritania, Somalia, Sudan) are also members. Moreover, progress towards a formal Afro-Arab dialogue between the Organization of African Unity and the League of Arab States was made soon after the 1973 Arab-Israeli war, when a meeting of the OAU Council of Ministers in Algiers in November passed a resolution calling for "Cooperation Between African and Arab States" in light of "the common objectives between African and Arab people."[2] President Mobutu of Zaire attended the Arab Summit Conference later that month as an observer. The OAU also formed an Afro-Arab Relations Coordination Committee of seven (later twelve) members to further the process of interregional cooperation, particularly on issues of economic development. This committee met with its Arab League counterpart in Cairo in July 1975, paving the way for a meeting of African and Arab states at the ministerial level in Dakar in April 1976. At this last meeting, a joint program on Afro-Arab cooperation was drafted.

The Afro-Arab conference reached its peak the following year, when sixty African and Arab heads of state and government and the representatives of eighteen African and Arab organizations and six liberation movements held a summit conference in Cairo on March 7–9, 1977. At the Cairo conference agreement was reached on four declarations, which collectively made up the so-called Afro-Arab Cooperation Charter:[3]

1. *Political Declaration of the Afro-Arab Summit Conference*, in which those assembled upheld the importance of nonalignment, peaceful coexistence, the establishment of a just economic order, respect for sovereignty and territorial integrity; noninterference in the internal affairs of other states; self-determination; and the peaceful settlement of disputes. The Arab and African representatives also condemned aggression and occupation, imperialism, racism, racial segregation, and Zionism, and pledged their support for liberation movements, for the front line/confrontation states, and for efforts to isolate Israel, South Africa, and Rhodesia. (This document closely followed the draft prepared at Dakar a year earlier.)

2. *Declaration and Action Program for Afro-Arab Cooperation*. In this declaration the summit called for specific interregional cooperation in four areas: (1) political and diplomatic; (2) economic and financial (including mining and industry, agriculture, energy, water,

communication, and finance); (3) trade; and (4) education, culture, science, technology, and information.

3. *Declaration on Economic and Financial Cooperation*, in which a number of particular priorities and programs were detailed.

4. *Decision on Organization and Method of Action*. The summit agreed to formalize the existing 26-member coordinating committee (12 members from each side, plus the secretary-generals of the League of Arab States and the OAU), and called for the establishment of an Afro-Arab court or arbitration committee to settle differences arising from Afro-Arab cooperation, as well as an Arab League–OAU fund to finance these institutions.

Soon after the 1977 Summit, however, Sadat's peace initiative and the signing of the Camp David accords halted further progress on the Afro-Arab dialogue. Egypt was expelled from the League of Arab States, and Arab states opposed Egyptian participation in the coordination committee and Afro-Arab meetings as a member of the OAU. Other Afro-Arab differences over oil pricing, economic aid, and Arab involvement in various African disputes also fractionated the dialogue. As a result, the dialogue has only really existed since 1977 in a nonofficial form, as meetings between individuals and nongovernmental organizations, rather than between ambassadors, ministers, or heads of state and governments.

A final organization linking Africa and Asia is the Islamic Conference Organization (ICO). As of 1984, all the Arab countries and fourteen black African countries were members, together making up more than two-thirds of the ICO's total membership.[4] Although the political scope of the ICO is limited in comparison to that of the League of Arab States or the Organization of African Unity, it has furnished a medium through which Muslim Africa has been able to express its strong and continuing support for the liberation of Palestine and Jerusalem. Moreover, with the growing importance of Islam in the political processes of both Middle East and African states in recent decades, it may be that Islam, the ICO, and Islamic missionary work in sub-Saharan Africa will together play an increasingly important role as a link between the two regions.[5]

Diplomatic Relations

The extent of bilateral diplomatic relations (measured not only by the number of permanent missions but also by the size and apparent importance of these missions, the status of their personnel, the extent of their activities, and their success creating a climate in which trade can flourish and heads of states can meet constructively) is exceedingly important. The intermittent and occasional nature of international conferences, compounded by the limitations placed upon participants by the requirements of parliamentary diplomacy, limits their effectiveness for the long-run coordination of the policies of any two states. Further, as in the United Nations, the resolutions of international conferences seldom carry any pressure for their enactment by participants, as distinct from treaties between states, which are ordinarily enacted into law and implemented through legislative or executive action. But even if treaties are not enforced, they at least signal an indication of a change in the relations of the states involved; and while they remain in force, they provide a basis for the exchange of goods and ideas.

As might be expected from Egypt's early involvement in Africa, the United Arab Republic had the largest diplomatic corps among the Arab states operating in Africa in the 1950s and 1960s, with embassies in sixteen African countries as of 1964 and twenty-four by 1966. In 1967 Iraq had eight embassies serving ten African countries; Syria was represented in five African countries, and had accepted representatives of four; Lebanon had diplomatic relations with twelve African nations; and Jordan was represented in eight. Although Algeria only became independent in 1962, by 1967 Algerian ambassadors or *charges d'affaires* were in fifteen other African countries.

During this period the United Arab Republic had relations with most African states and with the Middle Eastern states as well, and so formed something of a link between the two regions. This linkage was sometimes more than indirect, as several countries maintained embassies in the U.A.R. accredited to Ethiopia and Guinea, while both Ethiopian and Guinean ambassadors to Iraq resided in the U.A.R. The other Middle Eastern countries were more limited in their activities. Of the countries in which Iraq was represented, for example, six are either completely or dominantly Arabic (Algeria, Morocco, the Sudan, UAR, Libya, and Tunisia), and three others (Guinea, Nigeria, and Ethiopia) have large Muslim communities. Only Ghana is preponderantly non-Muslim.

Syria's more limited representation included Guinea, Somalia, the Sudan, Tunisia, and the UAR—all nations with a Muslim majority. The embassies of Algeria, Libya, Morocco, and Tunisia (all of them Arab-Islamic states) were in Syria. Jordan was in a similar position.

Algeria's representatives resided in all of the Islamic states of Africa, but only in five or six states without large bodies of Muslims. If we consider two African states, both dominated by non-Muslims but with substantial Islamic communities, Chad had relations with Lebanon, Saudi Arabia, and Israel in the Middle East, but with Libya, Morocco, and the Sudan of the smaller community of Arab African states. Ethiopia had relations with Morocco, Somalia, the Sudan, and the U.A.R. among African Arab states, as well as with Israel. Ghana and Guinea were also widely represented in the Arab states of Africa and Asia.

Thus in the 1960s diplomatic relations, while extensive through the area, tended to fall into patterns of affinities: with some exceptions, Asian Arab states tended to concentrate their efforts on Arab Africa and to a lesser extent Islamic non-Arab Africa, while African states tended to decrease their involvement east of Suez. This pattern continued, amid a general expansion of African-Arab relations, in the 1970s. By 1972 there were, in addition to virtually universal ties among Arab states, some 92 Arab diplomatic missions in 33 sub-Saharan African states—an average of 2.8 missions per capital.[6] In those four non-Arab countries with a Muslim majority (Guinea, Mali, Niger, Senegal) the average rose to 5.5; in those countries with a sizeable but non-majority Muslim population, the average stood at 3.7. Ghana and Nigeria—the former with a legacy of radical foreign policy and pan-Africanism left over from Nkrumah; the latter the most powerful black African state and an important OPEC member, with a Muslim near-majority—had the greatest representation, with eight Arab missions each. The black African states had 93 missions in Arab countries.

As Table 8.1 indicates, by 1984 the number of Arab diplomatic missions had grown still further—to a total of 151 in 43 non-Arab African states, or an average of 3.5 per capital. Once again, greater representation is found in those black African states with a sizeable Muslim population (or with a noticeable "Islamic" tinge to their foreign policy): for those 14 states that are members of the ICO the average rises to 4.1, while for those four states with a Muslim majority the average stands at 7. Senegal (11), Kenya and Nigeria (10), Guinea and Ethiopia (8) have the greatest Arab representation. (Seven states have none.) Most Arab missions in black Africa (71%) belong to Arab African states. Egypt has the most diplomatic posts (31), followed by Algeria (21), Libya (18), Iraq (14), and Morocco and Saudi Arabia (10 each). Only Bahrain, Jordan, Qatar, and the United Arab Emirates have no permanent diplomatic representatives in black Africa. The PLO operates an additional 14 offices in countries on the continent.[7]

Aside from those relations that may be properly called diplomatic, in the sense of permanently established missions or embassies there has been a considerable amount of bilateral exchanges among heads of state of the African and Arab regions. Personal diplomacy has been effective in two senses. When preliminary work has been completed by professional foreign office or embassy staffs, the heads of state may place the final seal of approval on the matter as a sort of ritual. When, on the other hand, the purpose is not the implementation of a policy but the creation of a mood or the plotting of a general strategy of action, then the meetings of presidents, prime ministers, and kings seem to have some effect. It may seem that a simple agreement of two states might be expressed as easily by an exchange of notes as by a meeting of the leaders of the nations. But a meeting of, say, President Nasser and President Julius Nyerere may have a greater impact than could be achieved by impersonal diplomacy. In the underdeveloped world, where charismatic leadership is almost a political necessity, simple agreements often have more political than economic significance. Where communication between states is at best tenuous, the more traditional diplomacy of direct, especially private, meetings of heads of state and government can dissolve feelings of distrust, misunderstanding, and bias and create impressions of goodwill, commonality, and respect. In this connection, the loss of many of the prominent leaders of the 1950s and 1960s (Nasser, Ben Bella, Nkrumah, et al.) may have seriously inhibited the development of African-Arab relations in recent years.

The United Nations

For most of the first fifteen years of the existence of the United Nations, only four African states were members—Ethiopia, Egypt, Liberia, and South Africa—and the latter is an African state only in the geographic sense. During the early years of the United Nations, eight Middle Eastern countries were members: Turkey, Iran, and Israel (which are outside the focus of this chapter), and Iraq, Saudi Arabia, Lebanon, Yemen, and Syria, which are all Eastern Arab states. Other African states became members in time, and in 1960 seventeen African states joined the United Nations upon gaining their independence from various European powers.

TABLE 8.1

Arab Diplomatic Representation in Africa, 1984

	MAURITANIA	MOROCCO	ALGERIA	TUNISIA	LIBYA	SOMALIA	DJIBOUTI	SUDAN	EGYPT	SOUTH YEMEN	NORTH YEMEN	BAHRAIN	OMAN	SAUDI ARABIA	UNITED ARAB EMIRATES	QATAR	KUWAIT	LEBANON	JORDAN	SYRIA	IRAQ	TOTALS
TOTALS	7	10	21	5	18	7	1	9	31	2	2	0	1	10	0	0	2	7	0	4	14	151
ZIMBABWE		●	●	●					●												●	5
ZAMBIA					●				●					●							●	4
ZAIRE	●	●	●	●					●												●	6
UPPER VOLTA			●						●													2
UGANDA			●		●	●		●	●					●							●	7
TOGO				●					●									●				3
TANZANIA		●	●			●		●	●	●											●	7
SWAZILAND																						0
SIERRA LEONE									●								●					2
SEYCHELLES					●																	1
SENEGAL	●		●	●	●	●		●	●					●				●		●	●	11
SAO TOME and PRINCIPE																						0
RWANDA									●													1
NIGERIA	●		●		●	●		●	●					●				●		●	●	10
NIGER		●							●													2
MOZAMBIQUE			●		●				●													3
MAURITIUS					●				●													2
MALI	●		●		●				●					●				●			●	7
MALAWI																						0
MADAGASCAR			●		●				●					●								4
LIBERIA		●	●						●								●					4
LESOTHO																						0
KENYA			●		●	●		●	●		●		●	●				●		●		10
IVORY COAST	●	●	●	●				●	●												●	7
GUINEA-BISSAU			●		●				●													3
GUINEA			●		●	●			●					●				●		●	●	8
GHANA		●	●		●				●					●								5
GAMBIA	●																				●	2
GABON	●	●							●													3
ETHIOPIA			●		●	●	●	●	●	●	●											8
EQUATORIAL GUINEA																						0
CONGO			●		●				●												●	4
COMOROS																						0
CHAD								●	●												●	3
CENTRAL AFRICAN REPUBLIC			●					●	●												●	4
CAPE VERDE																						0
CAMEROON		●	●		●				●					●								5
BURUNDI									●									●				2
BOTSWANA					●																	1
BENIN			●		●				●													3
ANGOLA		●							●													2

A major source of Arab-African interaction in the United Nations is the joint membership of several states in the African, Afro-Asian, and Arab caucusing groups. Although these groups do not bind their members to vote in a certain way, they provide a valuable opportunity for discussion of issues, and it would be strange indeed if mutual membership did not lead to a certain amount of interchange of views. The cohesion of the African group between 1946 and 1962 was relatively high as shown by Thomas Hovet, Jr., in *Africa in the United Nations*.[8] During this period the members of the group were divided on 24.5 percent of the votes, voted identically on 47.1 percent of the votes, and were voting identically or abstaining in 28.4 percent of the votes. In other words, on nearly half of all roll-call votes taken in the first sixteen sessions of the United Nations, all African members of the organization voted yes or no, or abstained, without dissent. During this period, the numbers of members of the caucusing group grew from three (through the ninth session) to thirty-two. Identical and solidarity votes tended to become fewer as the group grew. From the thirteenth through the sixteenth sessions, the African members of the Arab caucusing group voted identically on 61.8 percent of the roll-calls, and divided on only 8.7 percent.

The divisions in the Arab faction during this period were generally between Libya, the Sudan, and Tunisia on the one hand, and Morocco and the U.A.R. on the other. (Algeria was not yet a member.) Until the formation of the Organization for African Unity in 1963, the Casablanca group included Algeria, Ghana, Guinea, Mali, Morocco, and the U.A.R.; these were considered the radical states of Africa. The Casablanca group voted identically on 78.6 percent of the issues between 1958 and 1962, and were divided on only 4.9 percent. They divided on only three votes on African questions during this period; in each case, Guinea dissented from the choice of the other members. The African Arab states not only formed a cohesive group, uniting with some of the African states; the members of this group still maintained a high degree of cohesion with the rest of the African group. From the session of 1958 through that of 1961–62, the Sudan's percentage of identical votes with the majority of the caucus ranged from 71.4 to 86.4; Morocco ranged from 69.2 to 78.6 percent; Tunisia from 68.9 to 75.8 percent; Libya from 67.5 to 88.6 percent; and the U.A.R. from 69.8 to 79.2 percent.

During the 1960s it was evident that the Arab countries in the United Nations were more supportive of Black African struggles against racism and colonialism in southern Africa than were black

African states of the Arab position in the Arab-Israeli conflict. Olawayi Abegunrin has shown that on five important General Assembly resolutions regarding southern Africa between 1961 and 1966, the Arab states supported the African position 92% of the time and abstained or were absent for the remainder.[9] In contrast, Fouad Ajami and Martin Sours have found that during the 1967 Arab-Israeli War, only 17.4% of the votes cast by sub-Saharan African states were pro-Arab, while 41.4% were pro-Israeli and a similar proportion were abstentions.[10] Still, the Arab countries continued to lend political support at the UN to the cause of national liberation in southern Africa, although not without seeking reciprocation of their efforts through African support on the Palestine issue.

An analysis of African voting on Arab-Israeli issues during the period 1967–1972 made by Kochan, Gitelson, and Dubeck shows that for 39 UN General Assembly roll-call votes during this period, several distinct groupings of African states can be identified. Eight black African states (Botswana, Dahomey, Ivory Coast, Lesotho, Liberia, Malawi, and Madagascar) generally supported Israel; ten other states (Burundi, Congo-Brazzaville, Equatorial Guinea, Guinea, Mali, Nigeria, Senegal, Tanzania, Uganda, and Zambia) generally voted with the Arab countries. The remaining fifteen states tended to abstain or absent themselves from such votes, although pro-Arab (Cameroon, Chad, Ethiopia, Kenya, Mauritius, Niger), pro-Israel (Gabon, Gambia, Ghana, Swaziland), and genuinely neutralist or ambivalent (Central African Republic, Sierra Leone, Togo, Upper Volta, Zaire) leanings could be discerned.[11] African states were most likely to vote with the Arab states on resolutions calling for Israel's conditional withdrawal to its pre-1967 borders, and less likely to do so on resolutions dealing with the restoration of Palestinian rights or which singled out Israel for condemnation.[12]

Afro-Arab cohesion in the United Nations General Assembly reached its highest level during 1973–74, when African countries began casting the greatest proportion of their votes on Arab-Israeli resolutions with the Arab countries. In 1973, General Assembly resolution 3151, which condemned the "unholy alliance between Portuguese colonialism, South African racism, Zionism and Israeli imperialism," was supported by all Arab countries and by all black African states except ten (all of which abstained or were absent). The following year, only two black African states abstained on General Assembly resolution 3236, which reaffirmed the "inalienable rights of the Palestinian people," including the right to self-determination, national independence, and the return to their homes and property. The resolution further recognized the legitimacy of Palestinian armed struggle. African states also lent bloc support to resolution 3237 (1974), which granted UN observer status to the PLO.

A number of possible explanations for this convergence have been suggested. Some have argued that African support for the Palestinian cause was the product of Arab economic blackmail—a combination of African fear for continued access to the oil supplies of the Arab countries and Arab promises of economic aid in exchange for political support. Others have argued that the voting agreement reflected a genuine ideological sympathy arising from Islam or from a common anti-imperialist orientation. A third view has seen this development as the result of a diplomatic *quid pro quo* whereby Arab support for the African struggle against apartheid and South Africa was reciprocated by African support for the Arab struggle against Zionism and Israel. The best explanation, however, is a combination of all of these. Arab use of the "oil weapon" during and after the 1973 Arab-Israeli War certainly forced some African leaders (like other leaders around the world) to reevaluate their positions. At the same time, Arab support for African liberation struggles, the parallels drawn by some between the settler regimes of Israel and Southern Africa (and the close collaboration between the two), and African acceptance of the legitimacy of the Palestinian struggle were at least as important.[13]

Unfortunately, no comprehensive examination of Afro-Arab voting in the United Nations General Assembly has been published for the period since 1973. At first glance, General Assembly resolution 3379 (1975) classifying Zionism as a form of racism seems to indicate a weakening of African UN support for the Arab cause. That resolution was supported by 20 black African states and opposed by five, with 12 abstentions.[14] Similarly, African states were less than enthusiastic about Arab attempts to expel Israel from the General Assembly in the mid-1970s, and about similar Iranian attempts after 1979. In the former case, however, the examination of African voting on 36 General Assembly roll-call votes on the question of Palestine recorded by the Institute for Palestine Studies between 1976 and 1978 shows continued highs levels of black African support for the Arab position on the Palestine Question. In 1976, black Africa cast 73% of their votes with the Arab countries, 3% with Israel, and abstained or were absent for the remainder. In 1977 and 1978, support stood at 86% and 84%, with *no* votes cast with Israel.[15] With regards to Israel's UN membership, African reluctance to expel Israel was heavily influenced by Egyptian ambivalence on the subject—not to mention U.S. hostility.

For their part, Arab countries have maintained their support for the struggle against apartheid in southern Africa in the UN and before other international organizations. While it is true that African-Israeli relations have improved since the mid-1970s, and that the division in the Arab world since the mid-1970s has created occasional splits within Arab voting at the UN (a condition under which African confusion is only natural), it is certainly safe to say that on southern African and Palestinian resolutions Afro-Arab voting cohesion at the UN has continued into the 1980s as a general rule.

Trade and Economic Assistance

Although trade between African and Arab countries has been carried on for millennia, it is not an important part of their contemporary interaction. With the exception of the sub-Saharan Arab Somalia and Djibouti, in no case does the trade of a black African state with an Arab state represent a major portion of either country's total global trade. Similarly, those trading agreements that are signed between Arab and African countries are more often gestures of friendship and cooperation than attempts to foster significant economic links. In 1978, exports to the Arab oil-exporting countries totaled around $200 million, or 0.2% of the total exports of the sub-Saharan African countries, while exports to sub-Saharan Africa were worth only $700 million, or 0.7% of the total exports of Arab oil exporting countries.[16] Most of this small level of trade takes place along the Red Sea/Indian Ocean region, and represents the modern continuation of age-old patterns of trade and commerce. Since both regions are primarily producers and exporters of primary products and importers of manufactured goods, there will be little likelihood of any increase in interregional trade until such time as fundamental restructurings of their internal economies occur.

One aspect of Arab-African trade that has been significant is that of African oil imports from the Arab world. In particular, many Africans (and non-African analysts) have claimed that the rapid increase in world oil prices after 1973 was a major blow to developing African economies. Of the 33 countries described as most seriously affected by the 1974 oil crisis, 21 were African. The proportion of total African imports taken up by oil rose from 4.6% in 1973 to 8.8% one year later, with the oil import bills of some African countries growing by as much as 440% (Ivory Coast). This added burden was said to have caused a downward deflection of African economic growth rates of 2.3% in 1974 and 3.1% in 1975.[17] Other analysts have observed, however, that even after 1973–74, oil imports represented only a small portion of African imports, and that inflationary prices of Western manufactured goods had an equal or even greater impact on the Third World.[18] Also, it is only fair to note that it was OPEC, rather than the Arab countries per se, that oversaw the increase in world oil prices during this period, and that those African countries that exported oil (notably Nigeria) gained considerable benefit from the additional revenues that resulted.

Regardless of the exact direct and indirect effect of the oil crisis on Africa, the important point to be noted here is that African oil consumers saw the rise of world oil prices as a serious threat to their development plans. As early as November 1973, the OAU Council of Ministers expressed concern over the issue, and the Afro-Arab Relations Coordination Committee was mandated upon its formation to "study the effects of the oil embargo on African Countries" and to "discuss with Arab crude oil producing countries how best to alleviate the effects of this impact."[19] Arab oil producers subsequently refused to supply Africa with oil at concessionary rates, but did agree at their November 1973 Summit conference to alleviate the impact of higher oil prices through greater levels of economic aid. Three major multilateral Arab aid institutions were later set up: the Special Arab Assistance Fund for Africa (SAAFA), with an initial $200 million; the Fund for Arab-African Technical Assistance, with an initial $15 million; and, in January 1975 (nearly a year after first announced), the Arab Bank for Development in Africa (BADEA) with $231 million in initial capitalization. (In 1977 the Special Arab Assistance Fund was integrated into BADEA.) By the end of 1983, BADEA had paid-up stock of $985.5 million, and had approved (with SAAFA) loans and grants to African countries totaling $812.1 million. All OAU members not members of the League of Arab States are theoretically eligible for BADEA assistance.[20]

In addition to BADEA, Arab economic aid has reached black Africa through a number of other channels. These include the IMF, the OPEC Special Fund, the Islamic Development Bank, and North African contributions to the OAU-sponsored African Development Bank (ADB). In addition, a number of Arab countries provide substantial quantities of bilateral aid to Africa; in 1974 the Saudi Development Fund, the Kuwait Fund for Arab Economic Development, the External Iraqi Fund for Development, and the Abu Dhabi Fund were all made available to non-Arab countries. According to Dr. Chadli Ayari of BADEA, Arab aid to Africa between 1973 and 1980 totaled some $5,707 million.[21]

Despite such levels of aid, there have been persistent African criticisms of Arab oil pricing and economic assistance. The earliest aid institutions were slow in forming and were initially undercapitalized, with the League of Arab States at first offering only $200 million in assistance. Furthermore, while the oil-exporting Arab countries allocate a greater proportion of their GNP to foreign aid than any other group of countries, Arab aid to Africa continues to pale in comparison to Arab aid to other Arab countries. Also, many Arab pledges of aid have not been fulfilled. African states also resent the Arab use of aid as an instrument of foreign policy, a practice evident in both the unofficial but clearly observable preference given to those African countries that either have a significant Islamic element or which have granted maximum support to the Palestinian cause. (The political manipulation of Arab foreign aid was also clearly evident in BADEA's decision to cut off aid to Zaire upon that country's resumption of diplomatic relations with Israel in 1982.) Because of these dissatisfactions, African countries have repeatedly requested, to no avail, that Arab aid be disbursed through the ADB.

Developments in the world oil market played a major (although far from exclusive) role in bringing Africa and the Arab world closer together in the early 1970s. Since then, however, the impact of high oil prices and the tension between rich and poor have served to keep them apart.

ARAB, AFRICAN, AND AFRO-ARAB ISSUES

Having described the major forms of interaction between the Arab world and Africa, the specific scope and nature of that interaction is perhaps best explored within the context of specific issues. Numerous issues of importance have arisen in recent years: the Western Sahara dispute; Libyan intervention in Chad (and involvement elsewhere in Africa); the continuing conflict in the Horn of Africa over the Ogaden, Tigre, and Eritrea; and economic tensions arising from dramatic rises in the price of oil since 1973. The constraints of available space make it necessary, however, to focus our attention on the two issues that are perhaps most salient and enduring in the respective foreign relations of the Arab world and Africa. The first of these is the question of Palestine; the other is the struggle against colonialism, racism, and apartheid in southern Africa.

Africa and the Arab-Israeli Conflict (1948–1967)

While certainly not the only factor, Arab-Israeli competition is perhaps the most significant aspect of Middle East–African interaction. While the Arabs have sought Third World support in their struggle with Israel, the thrust of Israeli policy has been to counterbalance Arab influence in the Third World and to break out of the isolation created by the hostility of its immediate neighbors. Africa has long been a primary target of this policy.

Israel's African policy has been implemented through three channels: diplomatic relations, trade, and aid. Soon after the establishment of the state and amid the decolonization of Africa, Israel conducted an intense diplomatic effort south of the Sahara to counteract the long-established ties of the Arabs with Africa. Between 1957 and 1967, Israel established diplomatic representation in twenty-nine African countries.

Israel's diplomatic effort in Africa was complemented by a small but steadily increasing volume of trade relations. Although trade with Africa accounted for less than 4 percent of Israel's total world trade, it increased some 42 percent between 1966 and 1969. Israeli exports to Africa, which in 1967 amounted to $24.44 million, reached $34.26 million in 1969. Similarly, there was a slow but continued rise in imports, from $27.39 million in 1967 to $31.30 in 1969.[22]

Although the volume of Israeli-African trade was not so great that Israel or the various African countries could not do without it, the figures may have belied its importance. Israeli-African trade relations were (and are) nascent relations between infant economies. In addition to seeking influence in Africa, Israel was laying the groundwork for its young industry, which, as it grows, would require increasing volumes of raw materials and markets for its products—markets that are difficult to find among the industrialized nations. Israel, in fact, made an effort to establish trade relations, however minimal, with almost all of the African countries south of the Sahara. By 1967 only Botswana, Burundi, Gambia, Lesotho, Mauritius, and Swaziland did not have some measure of trade with Israel (although all of them had diplomatic relations). This effort is particularly striking when we note that 56 percent of all Israeli trade with Africa was concentrated in only five countries (listed in the order of importance): Republic of South Africa ($14.6 million in trade), Central African Republic ($6.6 million), Ethiopia ($6 million), Uganda ($5.1), and Gabon ($4.4). As the figures show, Israel's major trading partner in Africa during this period was the Republic of South Africa.[23] Yet no African country stopped trading with Israel because of this—a testimonial, perhaps, to the adroitness of Israel's diplomacy.

In the field of foreign aid, Israel's budget was quite modest compared to those of the Soviet Union, the United States, China, or France. In 1966, according to one observer, Israel's Technical Assistance Department had a budget of $5 million, or 26 million francs, compared to the corresponding French department's budget of 1,120 million francs that year.[24] During the 1960s, Israeli aid represented only about 0.05 percent of the total aid received by black Africa. But figures again distorted the significance, for Israeli aid to Africa was its most effective tool in support of its diplomatic effort. The program created goodwill for Israel throughout black Africa. Because Israel could not compete with the aid programs of the big powers, it concentrated its aid on small, delineated, and specifically practical projects designed to be immediately profitable or beneficial to the receiving country. In addition, the program was well dispersed throughout Africa: thirty of the thirty-eight countries in tropical Africa signed technical-assistance agreements with Israel between 1960 and 1966.

Israeli aid to Africa assumed three forms: the sending of experts to interested countries, the organization of internships (training programs), and the creation of joint Israel-African enterprises. (In addition, Israel engaged in a military aid program in Africa.) The importance Israel attached to Africa was clear. Out of thirty-three bilateral aid agreements concluded with the Third World, twenty were signed with African countries. Sixty percent of the Israeli experts working abroad in the 1960s worked in Africa, while 50 percent of the foreign trainees receiving professional training in Israel were Africans. Between 1958 and 1966, some 5,000 Africans were trained in Israel. In addition, of some 4,237 itinerant on-the-job training courses provided by Israel, 3,649 were lavished on Africa.

The test of Israeli diplomacy in Africa came during the Arab-Israeli war of 1967. During the war the majority of African states opted to remain silent. Only seven states openly took sides: Guinea, Mali,

Somalia, Burundi, Zambia, and Tanzania in support of the Arabs; Malawi in support of Israel. The voting at the Fifth Emergency Special Session of the United Nations General Assembly in the aftermath of the war on major resolutions pertaining to the conflict gave a more complete picture. On the Yugoslav resolution (co-sponsored by thirteen Afro-Asian states, and generally considered to be a compromise between the Soviet and American positions), sub-Saharan African voting broke down accordingly: twelve in favor, eight against, and eleven abstentions. Because the resolution was opposed by Israel and supported by the Arabs, votes in favor were generally considered to be pro-Arab, while those against were seen as pro-Israel. The high percentage of abstentions reflects the difficulty of many African states to come to grips with the problem of taking a stance on the Arab-Israeli issue. Thus, it appears that by 1967 neither the Arabs nor Israel had gained the upper hand in Africa; rather, Arab-Israeli competition had effectively neutralized the continent.

The Arab-Israeli Conflict (1967–1974)

After the 1967 war, the relative strengths of Israel and the Arab countries began to change. One cause of this was the war itself: previous African perceptions of its "correct" borders notwithstanding, Israel was now clearly an aggressor occupying large portions of Arab territory, including that of an African state (Egypt). In addition, the growth of a Palestinian liberation movement seeking to free its land from occupation struck a chord with many African leaders who saw a parallel with their own past liberation struggles, or with the continuing struggle for liberation in Southern Africa. Other factors, including some dissatisfaction with specific Israeli aid projects and Arab policy, were also important.

Commencing in the early 1970s, the Israelis suffered a series of setbacks in their program of cementing closer relations with sub-Saharan Africa. In November 1971, several moderate African leaders visited Israel as part of an Arab-Israeli mediatory effort carried out on behalf of the Organization for African Unity. Headed by Senegalese President Senghor, the group encountered considerable inflexibility on the question of the repatriation of lost Arab lands and stated that this was a "definite impediment in the growth of smooth relations with African countries."[25] This setback was underscored by a more serious incident the following April, when a 470-man Israeli technical team was expelled from Uganda and diplomatic relations severed by President Idi Amin. Israel's relations with Uganda had been very close during the 1960s under the regime of Amin's predecessor, Milton Obote, and Israel is reported to have assisted Amin in his own rise to power.[26] Amin's action occurred only a few months after his meeting with Libya's President Muammar Qaddafi, and the vacuum created by the Israeli departure was soon filled by Libyan aid and advisors.

While the Ugandan realignment was the most spectacular reversal, changes also occurred in the tier of countries immediately south of the Sahara. Chad broke off relations with Israel in October 1972, and the Congo Republic and Niger followed suit two months later. In both cases, Israeli assistance teams left along with the diplomatic contingent, and Egyptian and Algerian advisors supplanted them.[27] Energetic diplomatic and propaganda efforts by Arab countries, notably Libya, were in large measure responsible for these changes.

An important direct channel of Afro-Asian contact denied to the Israelis was the OAU. At the council of ministers conference in Morocco in June 1972, African leaders passed a resolution pledging "all possible support for Egypt" in her struggle with Israel.[28] In the same connection, Israel was condemned unanimously for her "obstructive and negative attitude" as far as preconditions for a peace settlement were concerned. Nevertheless, African support for the Arabs was still not solid. Although strongly worded, the Moroccan document left the nature of the "support" for Egypt indefinite. Moreover, numerous signatories, including Zaire, Kenya, and the Ivory Coast, expressed reservations about the document, fearing it would force them to choose between Arab and Israeli aid.[29] The 1973 OAU Summit Conference held at Addis Ababa, however, not only condemned Israel and demanded her withdrawal from occupied Arab territory, but also passed a resolution demanding that African countries consider collective or individual political or economic steps against Israel if it continued to refuse to evacuate occupied Arab territories.[30]

Israel reacted to these changes in her relations with Africa by stepping up her assistance efforts elsewhere on the continent. The main redeployment was in the far south: Israeli missions in Swaziland, Lesotho, and Botswana were upgraded considerably. These three states have been closely associated with the white regimes in Southern Africa since they obtained independence. By contrast, Arab countries have made no effort to build relations with Southern Africa.

Closer identification of Israel with countries unwilling to take a strong position on the South African question further reinforced the tendency of black African states to align with the Arabs. Indeed, the similarity of the position of South Africa vis-à-vis black African states to Israel's own situation in the Arab World suggested the polarization of the continent along these lines. Israel tried to forestall this by maintaining an active role among black African moderates. However, this role became more and more difficult to sustain, and by 1973 was impossible. The Non-Aligned Nations Conference, held in Algiers in September 1973, passed a strongly worded resolution condemning continued Israeli occupation of Arab lands, after which two more African countries broke relations with Israel.

The decisive move of black Africans behind the Arab position, however, occurred during the October 1973 Arab-Israeli War. At this time, a variety of factors—African anti-imperialism, Islamic sympathies, Israel's flouting of UN ceasefire resolutions and occupation of African-Arab territory, Arab diplomatic and economic pressure, and the ripple effect of the first few suspensions of diplomatic relations—resulted in a triumph of Arab over Israeli policy as one African state after another broke off relations with Tel Aviv. Between the outbreak of the fighting and November 13, twenty black African states had broken relations with Israel, bringing the total to twenty-nine.[31] Thus, except for Malawi, Lesotho, and Swaziland, Israel continued to maintain relations with only the racist regimes of South Africa and Rhodesia.

After the war, African support for the Arab cause continued. In November 1973, sixteen Central and East African states condemned Israel's ties with the racist and colonial regimes of southern Africa, affirmed support for the Palestinian struggle, and called for economic ties with Israel to be broken.[32] That same month, a meeting of the OAU Council of Ministers called for the severance of diplomatic relations with Israel until the Palestinian people found fulfillment of their legitimate national rights. Subsequent meetings of the OAU (and the 1977 Afro-Arab Summit) also expressed solidarity with the Palestinian struggle and condemned Zionism, and African states lent their support to the Arab cause in resolutions before the United Nations and other international bodies—although not often to Arab attempts to bring about Israel's expulsion from the U.N.

The Arab-Israeli Conflict (1974–   )

From a high point in 1973–74, the pattern of African support for the Arab cause and shunning of Israel blurred slightly in the following decade. Increased oil prices and dissatisfaction with the level of Arab aid to Africa were major causes, creating some resentment against the Arab countries in sub-Saharan Africa. African unhappiness with Arab political involvement in several African disputes also generated some negative fallout. Many black African nations were resentful of Arab support for Somalia and for Eritrean guerrillas in the Horn of Africa, seeing these actions as unwelcome foreign interferences in African affairs. Libya's intervention in Chad (and the real or perceived Libyan support for opposition groups in Niger, Mali, Uganda, Zaire, and elsewhere) also damaged Arab relations with Africa, as did Libyan and PLO support for the dictatorship of Idi Amin in Uganda. Also, the Western Sahara dispute and the question of whether to admit the "government" of the Saharwi Arab Democratic Republic into the OAU has created multiple crises for that organization, and has done little to improve Afro-Arab relations.

Egypt's breaking of Arab ranks and its move toward the negotiation of a separate Egyptian-Israeli peace treaty exacerbated the deterioration of Afro-Arab solidarity (particularly on the Palestine issue), since it not only destroyed Egypt's earlier role as a link between the Arab and African political communities but also created a situation in which there was no longer a single, unified Arab position on the Arab-Israeli conflict around which African countries could rally their support. The fact that Egypt, a leading Arab and African state, had concluded a treaty and opened diplomatic relations with Israel had a significant impact on many African leaders, who saw no reason why their countries too should not now renew their ties with Tel Aviv.

Finally, the impact of Israel's continued attempts to maintain and expand its influence in Africa should not be underestimated. Israel's declared trade with black Africa had grown from $55.1 million in 1973 to $137.2 million in 1981—and according to one unnamed Israeli official, such published figures considerably understate the dimensions of Israel's African trade.[33] In 1981, Israeli companies were said to have a further $2 billion in contracts in Africa. Four thousand Israelis work south of the Sahara, and between 1973 and 1981 some 900 African students were said to have received training at Israel's Afro-Asian Institute.[34] Furthermore, numerous prominent Israelis have made visits to Africa, or have met with African leaders in third countries. The most important of these in terms of furthering Israeli influence in the region have perhaps been the "secret" visits to Africa by the Director of Israel's Foreign Ministry, David Kimche, in 1980 and by Ariel Sharon in 1981. In addition to its few embassies, Israel maintains diplomatic "interest" sections, trade representatives, or technical assistance offices in most of the African countries that severed relations with it in the early 1970s.

All of these developments have resulted in a significant improvement in African-Israeli relations. According to another anonymous Israeli official cited by the Toronto *Globe and Mail*, only Angola, Benin, Congo, Madagascar, Mali, Mozambique, Tanzania, and Uganda still refuse to have any contact with Israel.[35] At the same time, however, only two of those states that severed ties in 1972–73 have since normalized relations. The first to do so was Zaire, which reestablished diplomatic relations in May 1982. In exchange, it received military assistance from Israel, including training, intelligence data, and arms captured from the PLO in Lebanon. The Israeli Embassy and Zionist lobby organizations in Washington also intervened on Zaire's behalf during Congressional debates on U.S. foreign aid.[36] In August 1983, President Samuel Doe of Liberia visited Israel—the first African Head of State to do so since 1971—after announcing his country's intention to also reestablish formal relations. Because of these actions, Israeli Foreign Minister Yitzhak Shamir visited Zaire in 1983, and Israeli President Chaim Herzog visited both Zaire and Liberia in January 1984.

There are a number of reasons why more African countries have not followed the example of Zaire and Liberia. Fear of Arab countermeasures certainly plays a part—and not without reason: in response to Zaire's decision to reestablish relations with Israel,

> Qatar and Saudi Arabia [also Kuwait and the UAE] promptly broke off their diplomatic relations with Kinshasa; Algeria and Tunisia recalled their ambassadors for 'consultations.' Syria called for a special meeting of the Arab League to discuss the situation. . . . Arab States also took immediate steps to cut their aid to Zaire. The Arab Bank for the Economic Development of Africa (BADEA), for example, suspended all its projects in Zaire. It argued that by reestablishing diplomatic relations with Israel, Kinshasa had rejected 'one of the fundamental principles on which Afro-Arab cooperation is based.' BADEA's chairman also addressed a stern warning to other African states that under no circumstances would the Bank assist any country which maintained relations with Israel.[37]

For other countries, the issue is an ideological and moral one. Such states as Mozambique, Angola, and Tanzania support the struggle for Palestinian national rights, and see no reason to reestablish relations unless by doing so progress on that issue would be made. Furthermore, many African states find Israel's close political, economic, and military ties to South Africa a major obstacle to normalization.[38] Israel's invasion and occupation of Lebanon and its complicity in the massacre of Palestinian refugees at Sabra and Shatila created an additional obstacle after June 1982. Finally, since many of the technical and economic benefits of trade with Israel can be obtained without taking the difficult and costly decision to formally renew ties, there is little incentive to do so.

Because of these factors, no dramatic change in Africa's position on the Arab-Israeli conflict or in its relation with the respective parties is to be expected in the near future. It is also important to place the changing balance of Arab-Israeli influence in Africa in perspective. While Israel has made significant gains since the mid-1970s, almost all black African states have continued to support the Palestinian cause bilaterally—through the OAU and ICO, and in the United Nations.

Southern Africa

As already noted, the Arab countries have been unanimous in their condemnation of racism, colonialism, and apartheid in southern Africa. Moreover, such support, far from being the exclusive product of a political quid pro quo for African support on the Palestinian question, extends back to the days when much of sub-Saharan Africa was ambivalent on this issue (or even pro-Israeli). Thus, Arab support for national liberation in southern Africa flows from a commitment to anti-imperialism and decolonization.

Such a view is supported by an examination of the historical development of Arab support for African liberation struggles. In the years immediately following World War II, almost all Arab countries were either under direct colonial control themselves or were closely tied to colonial powers; in either case, they were in no position (or had no inclination) to pursue an anti-imperialist policy at home or abroad. In 1952, however, the revolution in Egypt changed all this, simultaneously marking both the transformation of political power in the Middle East and the beginnings of Arab involvement in the decolonization of north, central, and southern Africa. Later, in the mid- and late-1960s respectively, Egypt was joined in its support for African national liberation forces by revolutionary Algeria and Libya.

Indeed, after Nasser's death in 1970 and Anwar al-Sadat's subsequent deradicalization of Egypt and alignment with the West, it was these latter regimes, rather than Egypt, that assumed the leading Arab role on the issue of southern Africa.

Arab involvement in the problems of southern Africa has taken many forms, the first and most obvious of which has been direct material aid to local national liberation forces. Under Nasser, the United Arab Republic provided training, arms, and radio facilities to nationalist movements in Angola, Kenya, Rhodesia, and South Africa.[39] Similarly, Libya and particularly Algeria have lent direct assistance to numerous liberation movements, including FRELIMO in Mozambique, the MPLA in Angola, ZAPU in Rhodesia, SWAPO in Namibia, and the ANC in South Africa itself. Moreover, the Algerians are said to have played an important role in the formation of the OAU Liberation Committee in 1963.[40] Through the Liberation Committee, Algeria, Egypt and Libya as well as other Arab-African states (Mauritania, Morocco, Somalia) have also made material or political contributions to liberation groups. During the March 1977 Afro-Arab Summit Conference, Arab countries pledged $11 million ($2 million each from Libya, Qatar, Saudi Arabia, and the United Arab Emirates; $1 million each from Egypt, Jordan and Kuwait) in additional support.

A second mechanism of Arab involvement with the southern African problem has been through international forums and organizations, especially the United Nations. As already noted, an examination of the Arab voting record on UN General Assembly resolutions dealing with southern Africa reveals strong support for decolonization and the struggle against apartheid. Arab countries have also played an important role in bringing about South Africa's exclusion from this and other world bodies.

A third aspect of Arab involvement in this question has concerned the Arab world's use of economic weapons (embargoes and boycotts) against colonial Portugal, Rhodesia, and South Africa. Here Arab support has been less than total. According to a 1973 report by OAU Secretary General Nzo Ekangaki, 90% of South Africa's oil supplies between 1964 and 1970 originated from the Arabian Gulf, with two-thirds of these coming from Arab states—Arab rhetorical support for African and OAU calls for economic sanctions against South Africa notwithstanding. Arab countries also were said to supply the bulk of Portuguese oil imports, with two-thirds of these coming from Iraq and Saudi Arabia alone.[41] Although much of this flow was attributable to a lack of Arab concern and the domination of Western oil companies over the production and distribution of Middle East oil rather than to deliberate Arab policies, the fact remains that such exports played a major role in maintaining the South African economy.

The initiation of an Arab oil embargo in 1973 promised to change this situation. At their November 1973 meeting, the OAU Council of Ministers called upon Arab countries to "impose a total economic embargo, and in particular an oil embargo" against Portugal, Rhodesia, and South Africa. On November 28, Arab oil producers responded by announcing that they would indeed halt all oil shipments to these countries. This decision was widely hailed in Africa as a major blow against racism and colonialism.[42]

It soon became apparent, however, that most Arab oil producers were unwilling to implement the controls—monitoring of oil transfers; punishment of sanction-busting vessels and companies—needed to enforce their declaration, much to the dismay of the African countries. In 1975 an OAU report claimed that Arab states continued to provide South Africa with 72% of its oil.[43] Six years later, another report prepared for the OAU revealed the extent of illicit tanker traffic between the Arab world and South Africa.[44] Recognizing the shortcomings of the embargo, the Organization of Arab Petroleum Exporting Countries (OAPEC) passed a resolution in May 1981 calling for tighter monitoring and control of petroleum exports in an effort to reduce the quantity of Arab oil reaching South Africa.

CONCLUSION

In sum, there has been a considerable interchange of ideas between the Middle East and Africa. Historical, cultural, geographical, and political interplay affects both regions (though neither uniformly nor consistently). Historical and cultural ties between the Arab and the African states extend back over many centuries, and were augmented in the latter half of the twentieth century with an incomplete ideology based upon anticolonialism, anti-imperialism, and nonalignment. This channel of interaction was expressed through the media of international conferences, diplomatic relations, and the United Nations, in a variety of contexts. Although both the early conferences and the Afro-Arab dialogue of the 1970s raised the hope that the African states could join with the Arab states to forge a common approach to issues of concern and a positive force in world politics, this hope has proved illusory. In diplomatic and trade relations, as in international conferences, the importance of leaders and national policies—as opposed to comprehensive and institutional mechanisms of regional cooperation—has been evident. Even in the United Nations, where cooperation has been clearest, agreement is based more upon parallel action stemming from common views than on any coordination of effort in an institutional sense.

If Afro-Arab interregional cooperation has not been achieved on a lasting and institutional basis in the past, what can we expect of the future? Although prediction is difficult at the best of times, three things can be stated almost with certainty. First, the cultural, economic, political, and ideological ties between the Arab and African worlds will continue as they have for millennia. At the same time, numerous interregional disputes (arising from the unequal distribution of wealth, and from Arab involvement in "African" issues and vice versa) will continue to plague relations, although never to the point of open rupture. Second, Arab African countries will continue to be the linchpins of the interregional relationships, able to unite (as in the case of Algeria or Nasser's Egypt) or divide (as in the case of contemporary Libya or Sadat's Egypt) the two. In this respect, Egypt's recent attempts under President Hosni Mubarak to revitalize its African policy are highly significant. Third and finally, unity in the Arab world, and hence the ability to speak in a reasonably unified voice on Afro-Arab issues, will remain a sine qua non of a useful, formal Afro-Arab dialogue. In other words, the fragmentation of the Middle East regional system described in chapter 3 has had a severe and negative impact on Afro-Arab interregional relations. Since cohesion on the Middle East regional system requires Egypt's reacceptance into the Arab world, the revitalization of focussing elements such as Arab nationalism, the attenuation of differences between the Damascus-Tripoli and Baghdad-Riyadh-Amman-Cairo axes, and perhaps even the end of the Iran-Iraq war, progress in this area may be long in coming.

NOTES

1. Gamal Abdel Nasser, Egypt's Liberation: The Philosophy of the Revolution (Washington D.C., Public Affairs Press, 1955).

2. OAU Council of Ministers (November 1973), Resolution on "Cooperation Between African and Arab States," in Colin Legum, ed., Africa Contemporary Record 1973–1974, (London: Africana Publishing, 1979), p. A11.

3. Text in *Africa Contemporary Record 1976-1977*, pp. A98-A107.

4. The fourteen black African members are Benin, Cameroon, Chad, Comoros, Gabon, Gambia, Guinea, Guinea-Bissau, Mali, Niger, Senegal, Sierra Leone, Uganda, and Upper Volta.

5. On the other hand, the 1985 coup in the Sudan may put this process "on hold." Up until President Numeiry's overthrow, Sudan had supported a major Islamic missionary effort in Africa, thus performing the function of an Islamic-Arab-African link between Africa and the Middle East. The Sudanese coup and the deemphasis of Islam that will almost certainly follow it, however, jeopardize this function. More important, the downfall of Numeiry has demonstrated the limitations of Islam as a political legitimizing device, and hence could possibly presage a decline in its importance in domestic and interstate policy.

6. Figures from Table 6 in Ran Kochan, Susan Aurelia Gitelson, and Ephraim Dubeck, "Black African UN Voting Behavior on the Middle East Conflict," in Michael Curtis and Susan Aurelia Gitelson, eds., *Israel in the Third World* (New Brunswick, N.J.: Transaction Books, 1976), p. 307.

7. Nzongola-Ntalaja, "Africa and the Question of Palestine," in Ibrahim Abu-Lughod, ed., *Palestinian Rights: Affirmation and Denial* (Wilmette, Ill.: Medina Press, 1982), p. 208. The figure is for 1980.

8. Thomas Hovet, Jr., *Africa in the United Nations* (London: Faber and Faber, 1963).

9. Olawayi Abegunrin, "The Arabs and the Southern Africa Problem," *International Affairs* (London) 60, No. 1 (Winter 1983/84), pp. 103-104 (Table 1).

10. Fouad Ajami and Martin H. Sours, "Israel and Sub-Saharan Africa: A Study of Interaction," *African Studies Review* 13, No. 3 (December 1970), p. 412.

11. Kochan, Gitelson and Dubeck, "Black African UN Voting Behavior," pp. 300-303.

12. In the first case (resolutions calling for a return to the *status quo ante*), 63% of black African votes were cast with the Arab states and only 1% with Israel (the remainder being abstentions or absences). On resolutions dealing with Palestinian rights the respective figures were 30% pro-Arab, 11% pro-Israeli; on one-sided resolutions condemning Israel, 14% and 45%. (Calculated from *Ibid.*, p. 298.)

13. Analyses of African voting behavior on the Arab-Israeli issue by Gitelson and by Kochan, Gitelson, and Dubeck have found the strongest correlation between ideological factors (radical foreign policies; Islam) and support for the Arab cause, and little or no correlation between aid and voting. Nor is there any clear connection between the Arab "oil weapon" and UN voting behavior: in 1973, for example, those countries most dependent on oil imports, in both absolute terms and as a percentage of all imports (Kenya, Tanzania, Zambia, the Ivory Coast, and Ethiopia) did not become noticeably more pro-Arab than states that consumed little oil (Burundi, Guinea-Bissau, Equatorial Guinea, Upper Volta, Rwanda), or which had significant domestic supplies (Nigeria, Angola, Congo). See Susan Aurelia Gitelson, "Unfulfilled Expectations: Israeli and Arab Aid As Political Instruments in Black African United Nations Voting Behavior," *Jewish Social Studies* 38 (Spring 1976), pp. 159-175, and Kochan, Gitelson, and Dubeck, "Black African UN Voting Behavior," pp. 304-310.

14. The Central African Republic, the Ivory Coast, Liberia, Malawi, and Swaziland opposed the resolution.

260 INTERNATIONAL RELATIONS

15. Calculated from *International Documents on Palestine 1976–1978* (Beirut: Institute for Palestine Studies, annual), appendix F.

16. Frank A. Ocwieja, "Patterns of Trade and Prospects for Growth in a Tri-regional System: Arab Oil Exporters, Sub-Saharan Developing Africa, and the OECD," in Dunstan M. Wai, ed. *Interdependence in a World of Unequals: African-Arab-CECD Economic Cooperation for Development* (Boulder: Westview Press, 1982), pp. 138–139.

17. Ernest J. Wilson III, "Africa, the Energy Crisis, and the Triangular Relationship," in Wai, *Interdependence*, pp. 111. See also Victor T. LeVine and Timothy W. Luke, *The Arab-African Connection and Economic Realities* (Boulder: Westview Press, 1979), pp. 35–39.

18. Ibrahim F. I. Shihata, *The Other Face of OPEC: Financial Assistance to the Third World* (London: Longman, 1982), pp. 251–253.

19. OAU Council of Ministers (November 1973), "Resolution on Cooperation Between African and Arab States," p. A11.

20. "Arab Bank for Economic Development in Africa/Banque Arabe pour le Developpement Economique en Afrique," *Africa South of the Sahara 1984–1985* (London: Europa Publications, 1984), pp. 169–170.

21. Colin Legum, "African-Arab Relations: 'A State of Quasi Lethargy,'" *Africa Contemporary Record 1981–1982*, p. A253.

22. *Le Moniteur Africain* (Dakar), July 23, 1970.

23. The figures do not reveal the full extent of Israeli-South African trade in this or any other period, as the huge diamond trade between the two countries was usually conducted through intermediary organizations based in London or elsewhere.

24. J. C. Froelich in *Revue Militaire Generals* (Paris), February 1968.

25. *New York Times*, November 3, 1971.

26. Oye Ogunbadejo, "Black Africa and Israel: Towards a Rapprochement?" *Africa Contemporary Record 1982–1983*, p. A122.

27. *New York Times*, December 25, 1972.

28. Ibid., June 27, 1972.

29. Ibid.

30. *Le Monde*, May 30, 1973.

31. The twenty-nine were Zaire (6 October 1973); Rwanda (9 October); Cameroon and Equatorial Guinea (15 October); Upper Volta and Tanzania (18 October); Malagasy Republic (20 October); Central African Republic (21 October); Sierra Leone (22 October); Ethiopia (23 October); Nigeria, Zambia, and Gambia (25 October); Ghana and Senegal (27 October); Gabon (29 October); Kenya (1 November); Liberia (2 November); Ivory Coast (8 November); and Botswana (13 November). For a discussion of African motivations in 1973 see Jake C. Miller, "African-Israeli Relations: Impact on Continental Unity," *Middle East Journal* 29, No. 4 (Autumn 1975), pp. 393–408.

32. *New York Times*, November 25, 1973.

33. *Globe and Mail* (Toronto), August 23, 1983.

34. S. K. B. Asante, "Africa in World Politics: The Case of the Organization of African Unity and the Middle Eastern Conflict," *International Problems* (Tel Aviv) 20, No. 2–4 (Summer 1981), p. 123. See also Ogunbadejo, "Black Africa and Israel," p. A123, and International Monetary Fund, *Direction of Trade Yearbook* (various) (Washington, D.C.: International Monetary Fund, annual).

35. *Globe and Mail* (Toronto), August 23, 1983.

36. Ogunbadejo, "Black Africa and Israel," p. A125.

37. *Ibid.*

38. For details of these see Richard P. Stevens and Abdel M. Elmessiri, *Israel and South Africa: the Progression of a Relationship* (New York: New World Books, 1976), and James Adams, *The Unnatural Alliance* (London: Quartet Books, 1984).

39. For details, see T. Y. Ismael, *The U.A.R. in Africa: Egypt's Policy Under Nasser* (Evanston, Ill.: Northwestern University Press, 1971).

40. Olusola Ojo, "The Role of the Arab World in the Decolonization Process of Black Africa", *International Problems* (Tel Aviv), 20 No. 2–4 (Summer 1981), p. 77.

41. *African Research Bulletin* (Economical and Financial Series), November 15–December 14, 1973, p. 2936.

42. Ojo, "Role of the Arab World," p. 79.

43. OAU Doc. ECM/2 (ix), Annex II, cited in *ibid.*

44. Shipping Research Bureau of Amsterdam, *How They Break the Oil Embargo: Oil Tankers to South Africa 1980–81* (OAU, 1982), cited in Abegunrin, "Arabs and Southern African Problem," pp. 101–102.

BIBLIOGRAPHY

CHAPTER 1: *The Middle East in Global Politics*

Binder, Leonard. "The Middle East as a Subordinate International System." *World Politics* 10, No. 3 (1958).

Brecher, Michael. "The Middle East Subordinate System and its Impact on Israel's Foreign Policy." *International Studies Quarterly* 15, No. 2 (June 1969).

Brown, L. Carl. *International Politics in the Middle East: Old Rules, Dangerous Games.* Princeton: Princeton University Press, 1984.

Cantori, Louis J., and Speigel, Steven L. *The International Politics of Regions: A Comparative Approach.* Englewood Cliffs, N.J.: Prentice-Hall, 1970.

Evron, Yair. *The Middle East: Nations, Superpowers and Wars.* New York: Praeger, 1975.

Feld, Werner J., and Gavin Boyd. *Comparative Regional Systems: West and Eastern Europe, North America, the Middle East and Developing Countries.* New York: Pergamon Press, 1980.

Haas, Michael. "International Subsystems: Stability and Polarity." *American Political Science Review* 64 (March 1970).

Ismael, Tareq Y. *The Middle East in World Politics.* Syracuse, N.Y.: Syracuse University Press, 1974.

Korany, Bahgat, and Dessouki, Ali E. Hillal, eds. *The Foreign Policies of Arab States.* Boulder: Westview Press, 1984.

Russett, Bruce M. *International Regions and International System.* Chicago: Rand McNally, 1967.

Said, Edward W. *Orientalism*. New York: Pantheon, 1978.

Thompson, William R. "Delineating Regional Subsystems: Visit Networks and the Middle East Case." *International Journal of Middle East Studies* 13, No. 2 (May 1981).

CHAPTER 2: *The Regional System and Foreign Policy*

Ajami, Fouad. *The Arab Predicament: Arab Political Thought and Practice Since 1967.* Cambridge: Cambridge University Press, 1981.

Brown, L. Carl. *International Politics in the Middle East: Old Rules, Dangerous Games.* Princeton: Princeton University Press, 1984.

Damis, John. "Prospects for Unity/Disunity in North Africa." *Arab-American Affairs* 6 (Fall 1983).

Dessouki, Ali E. Hillal, ed. *International Relations in the Arab World.* Joint Research Program Series No. 39. Tokyo: Institute of Developing Economies, 1983.

Kazziha, W. *Palestine in the Arab Dilemma.* London: Croom Helm, 1980.

Kerr, Malcolm H. *The Arab Cold War: Gamal 'Abd al-Nasir and His Rivals, 1958–1970.* 3rd ed. London: Oxford University Press, 1971.

————— and El Sayed Yassin, eds. *Rich and Poor States in the Middle East: Egypt and the New Arab Order.* Boulder: Westview Press, 1982.

Korany, Bahgat, and Dessouki, Ali E. Hillal, eds. *The Foreign Policies of Arab States.* Boulder: Westview Press, 1984.

MacDonald, Robert W. *The League of Arab States: A Study of the Dynamics of Regional Organization.* Princeton: Princeton University Press, 1965.

Seale, Patrick. *The Struggle for Syria: A Study of Post-War Arab Politics 1945–1958.* Oxford: Oxford University Press, 1965.

al-Sowayegh, Abdulaziz. *Arab Petro-Politics.* London: Croom Helm, 1984.

Taylor, Alan R. *The Arab Balance of Power.* Syracuse, N.Y.: Syracuse University Press, 1982.

CHAPTER 3: *Domestic Sources of Foreign Policy*

Bill, James A., and Leiden, Carl. *Politics in the Middle East.* 2nd ed. Boston: Little, Brown and Company, 1984.

Brecher, Michael. *The Foreign Policy System of Israel: Setting, Images, Process.* Oxford: The Clarendon Press, 1972.

al-Chalabi, Fadhil J. *OPEC and the International Oil Industry: A Changing Structure.* Oxford: Oxford University Press, 1980.

Dawisha, Adeed I. *Egypt in the Arab World: The Elements of Foreign Policy.* London: Macmillan, 1976.

———, ed. *Islam and Foreign Policy.* Cambridge: Cambridge University Press, 1984.

Dekmejian, R. Hrair. *Islam in Revolution: Fundamentalism in the Arab World.* Syracuse, N.Y.: Syracuse University Press, 1985.

Esposito, John. *Islam and Politics.* Syracuse, N.Y.: Syracuse University Press, 1984.

El Azhary, M. S., ed. *The Impact of Oil Revenues on Arab Gulf Development.* London: Croom Helm, 1984.

Hudson, Michael. *Arab Politics: The Search for Legitimacy.* New Haven: Yale University Press, 1977.

Ismael, Jacqueline S. *Kuwait: Social Change in Historical Perspective.* Syracuse, N.Y.: Syracuse University Press, 1982.

Ismael, Tareq Y. *Governments and Politics of the Contemporary Middle East.* Homewood, Ill.: The Dorsey Press, 1970.

———. *The Arab Left.* Syracuse, N.Y.: Syracuse University Press, 1976.

——— and Ismael, Jacqueline S. *Government and Politics in Islam.* London: Frances Pinter, 1985.

Issawi, Charles. *An Economic History of the Middle East and North Africa.* New York: Columbia University Press, 1982.

Korany, Bahgat, and Dessouki, Ali E. Hillal, eds. *The Foreign Policies of Arab States.* Boulder, Col.: Westview Press, 1984.

McLaurin, R. D.; Mughisuddin, Mohammed; and Wagner, Abraham. *Foreign Policy Making in the Middle East.* New York: Praeger, 1977.

McLaurin, R. D., Peretz, Don; and Snider, Lewis W. *Middle East Foreign Policy: Issues and Processes.* New York: Praeger, 1982.

Owen, Roger. *The Middle East in the World Economy 1800–1914.* London: Methuen, 1981.

Proctor, Jesse Harris, *Islam and International Relations.* New York: Praeger, 1965.

Ramazani, Rouhallah. *Iran's Foreign Policy, 1941–1973.* Charlottesville, Va.: University of Virginia Press, 1975.

Sayigh, Yusif A. *The Economics of the Arab World: Development Since 1945.* London: Croom Helm, 1978.

———. *Arab Oil Policies.* London: Croom Helm, 1983.

CHAPTER 4: *Western Europe and the Middle East*

Allen, David, and Smith, Michael. "Europe, The United States, and the Middle East: a Case Study in Comparative Policy Making." *Journal of Common Market Studies* 22, No. 2 (December 1983).

Anderson, M. S. *The Eastern Question 1774–1923*. New York: Macmillan, 1966.

Antonius, George. *The Arab Awakening*. New York: H. Hamilton, 1938.

Artner, Stephen J. "The Middle East: A Chance for Europe?" *International Affairs*. (London) 56 (Summer 1980).

Bar-Zohar, Michel. *Suez Ultra Secret*. Paris: Fayard, 1964.

Beaufre, Andre. *The Suez Expedition, 1956*. New York: Praeger, 1969.

Bielenstein, Dieter, ed. *Europe's Future in the Arab View*. Saarbrucken: Verlag Breitenbach, 1981.

Brown, L. Carl. *International Politics and the Middle East: Old Rules, Dangerous Games*. Princeton: Princeton University Press, 1984.

Bullard, Reader. *Britain and the Middle East from the Earliest Times to 1963*. 3rd rev. ed. London: Hutchinson University Library, 1964.

Busch, Briton C. *Britain and the Persian Gulf, 1894–1914*. Berkeley: University of California Press, 1967.

———. *Britain, India, and the Arabs, 1914–1921*. Berkeley: University of California Press, 1971.

Calvocoressi, Peter, et al. *Suez Ten Years After*. Anthony Moncrieff, ed. New York: Pantheon, 1967.

Carothers, Thomas. "Mitterand and the Middle East." *The World Today* 38, No. 10 (October 1982).

Childers, Erskine B. *The Road to Suez: A Study of Western-Arab Relations*. London: McGibbon & Kee, 1962.

Chubin, Shahram. "La France et le Golfe: opportunisme ou continuité?" *Politique Etrangère* 4 (1983).

Cummings, Henry H. *Franco-British Rivalry in the Post-War Near East*. London: Oxford University Press, 1938.

al-Dajani, Ahmad Sidqi. "The PLO and the Euro-Arab Dialogue." *Journal of Palestine Studies* 35 (Spring 1980).

Eden, Anthony. *Full Circle*. Boston: Houghton Mifflin, 1960.

Fontaine, Andre. "What is French Policy?" *Foreign Affairs* 45 (October 1966).

Fullick, Roy, and Powell, Geoffrey. *Suez: The Double War*. London: Hamish Hamilton, 1979.

Garfinkle, Adam. *Western Europe's Middle East Diplomacy and the United States.* Philadelphia: Foreign Policy Research Institute, 1983.

Glubb, John Bagot. *A Soldier with the Arabs.* New York: Harper, 1957.

Great Britain. *Parliamentary Papers.*

Greilsammer, Ilan. "Failure of the European 'Initiatives' in the Middle East." *Jerusalem Quarterly* 33 (Fall 1984).

Hallala, Saadallah. "The Euro-Arab Dialogue: An Assessment 1973–1983." *Arab-American Affairs* 10 (Fall 1984).

Hirszowicz, Lukask. *The Third Reich and the Arab East.* Toronto: University of Toronto Press, 1966.

Hodges, Troy. *Western Sahara: The Roots of a Desert War.* Westport, Conn.: Lawrence Hill & Co., 1983.

Holden, David. "The Persian Gulf: After the British Raj." *Foreign Affairs* 49, No. 4 (July 1971).

Horne, Alistair. *A Savage War of Peace: Algeria 1954–1962.* London: Macmillan, 1977.

Howard, Michael. "Britain's Strategic Problem East of Suez." *International Affairs* (London) 42, No. 2 (April 1966).

Hurewitz, J.C. *The Middle East and North Africa in World Politics: A Documentary Record.* New Haven: Yale University Press, 1979.

Institute for Palestine Studies. *International Documents on Palestine.* Beirut: Institute for Palestine Studies, annual.

Ismael, Tareq Y. *The Middle East in World Politics: A Study in Contemporary International Relations.* Syracuse, N.Y.: Syracuse University Press, 1974.

Kelley, J. B. *Britain and the Persian Gulf, 1795–1880.* Oxford: The Clarendon Press, 1968.

Khedourie, Elie. *In the Anglo-Arab Labyrinth: the McMahon Correspondence and its Interpretations 1914–1939.* Cambridge: Cambridge University Press, 1976.

King, Gillian. *Imperial Outpost—Aden: Its Place in British Strategic Policy.* London: Oxford University Press, 1964.

Knapp, Wilfrid. *A History of War and Peace, 1939–1965.* London: Oxford University Press, 1967.

Klieman, Aaron. *Foundations of British Policy in the Arab World: The Cairo Conference of 1921.* Baltimore: The Johns Hopkins Press, 1970.

League of Nations. *Treaty Series.*

Lonrigg, Stephen. *Syria and Lebanon Under French Mandate.* Oxford: Oxford University Press, 1958.

Love, Kenneth. *Suez: The Twice-Fought War*. New York: McGraw-Hill, 1969.

al-Mani, Saleh. *The Euro-Arab Dialogue: A Study in Associative Diplomacy*. London: Francis Pinter, 1983.

Marlowe, John. *A History of Modern Egypt and Anglo-Egyptian, Relations 1800–1953*. 2nd ed. Hamden, Conn.: Anchor, 1965.

Moisi, Dominique. "L'Europe et le conflit israelo-arabe." *Politique Etrangère* No. 4 (1980).

_____. "La France de Mitterand et le conflit du Proche-Orient: comment concilier emotion et politique?" *Politique Etrangère* No. 2 (1982).

Monroe, Elizabeth. *Britian's Moment in the Middle East, 1914–1956*. Baltimore: Johns Hopkins Press, 1963.

Nevakivi, Jukka. *Britain, France, and the Arab Middle East 1914–1920*. London: The Athlone Press, 1969.

Nutting, Anthony. *No End of a Lesson: The Story of Suez*. New York: Potter, 1967.

Paget, Julian. *Last Post: Aden 1964–1967*. London: Faber and Faber, 1969.

Robertson, Terence. *Crisis: The Inside Story of the Suez Conspiracy*. London: Hutchinson, 1964.

Rouleau, Eric. "French Policy in the Middle East." *World Today* 24, No. 5 (May 1968).

Sachar, Howard M. *Europe Leaves the Middle East 1936–1954*. New York: Alfred A. Knopf, 1972.

Segre, Claudio G. *The Fourth Shore: The Italian Colonization of Libya*. Chicago: University of Chicago Press, 1974.

Sicherman, Harvey. "Europe's Role in the Middle East: Illusions and Realities." *Orbis*, 28, No. 4 (Winter 1985).

Speigel, Steven L. *The Middle East and the Western Alliance*. London: George Allen & Unwin, 1982.

Steinbach, Udo. "Germany's Attitude Toward the Middle East." *Arab-American Affairs* 10 (Fall 1984).

Sus, Ibrahim. "Western Europe and the October War." *Journal of Palestine Studies* 3, No. 4 (Winter 1974).

Taylor, Alan R. "The Euro-Arab Dialogue: Quest for an Interregional Partnership." *Middle East Journal* 32, No. 4 (Autumn 1978).

Tibawi, A. L. *Anglo-Arab Relations and the Question of Palestine 1914–1921*. London: Luzac & Company, 1977.

Trumpener, Ulrich. *Germany and the Ottoman Empire 1914–1918*. Princeton: Princeton University Press, 1968.

Volker, Edmond, ed. *Euro-Arab Cooperation*. Leyden: A. W. Sijthoff, 1976.

Weber, Frank G. *Eagles Over the Crescent: Germany, Austria, and the Diplomacy of the Turkish Alliance 1914–1918.* Ithaca, N.Y.: Cornell University Press, 1970.

Williams, Ann. *Britain and France in the Middle East and North Africa, 1914–1967.* London: Macmillan, 1968.

CHAPTER 5: *The United States and the Middle East*

Acheson, Dean G. *Present at the Creation: My Years in the State Department.* New York: Norton, 1969.

Aruri, Naseer H; Moughrabi, Fouad; and Stork, Joe. *Reagan and the Middle East.* Belmont, Mass.: AAUG Press, 1983.

Badeau, John. *The American Approach to the Arab World.* New York: Harper and Row, 1968.

Baker, R.S., and Dodd, W.E. *The Public Papers of Woodrow Wilson.* New York: Harper, 1927.

Carter, Jimmy. *The Blood of Abraham.* Boston: Houghton Mifflin, 1985.

Chomsky, Noam. *The Fateful Triangle: The United States, Israel, and the Palestinians.* Boston: South End Press, 1983.

Daniel, Robert L. *American Philanthropy in the Near East, 1820–1960.* Athens, O.: Ohio State University Press, 1970.

De Novo, John A. *American Interests and Policies in the Middle East, 1900–1939.* Minneapolis: University of Minnesota Press, 1963.

Ennes, James J., Jr. *Assault on the Liberty: The True Story of an Israeli Attack on an American Intelligence Ship.* New York: Random House, 1979.

Evans, Laurence. *United States Policy and the Partition of Turkey, 1914–1924.* Baltimore: Johns Hopkins University Press, 1965.

Field, James A. *America and the Mediterranean World, 1776–1882.* Princeton: Princeton University Press, 1969.

Finnie, David H. *Pioneers East: The Early American Experience in the Middle East.* Cambridge, Mass.: Harvard University Press, 1967.

Francher, Michael. *The United States and the Palestinian People.* Beirut: Institute for Palestine Studies, 1970.

Freedman, Robert, ed. *The Middle East Since Camp David.* Boulder: Westview Press, 1984.

Garfinkle, Adam. *Western Europe's Middle East Diplomacy and the United States.* Philadelphia: Foreign Policy Research Institute, 1983.

Grabill, Joseph L. *Protestant Diplomacy and the Near East: Missionary In-*

fluence on American Policy, 1810–1927. Minneapolis, Minn.: University of Minnesota Press, 1971.

Green, Stephen. *Taking Sides: America's Secret Relations with a Militant Israel.* New York: William Morrow, 1984.

Harris, George. *Troubled Alliance: Turkish-American Problems in Historical Perspective, 1945–1971.* Stanford, Calif.: The Hoover Institution, 1972.

Heller, Mark. *The Iran-Iraq War: Implications for Third Parties.* Cambridge, Mass.: Harvard University Center for International Affairs, Paper No. 23, January 1984.

Hurewitz, J.C., ed. *Soviet-American Rivalry in the Middle East.* New York: Praeger, 1969.

Jones, Joseph M. *The Fifteen Weeks.* New York: Viking, 1955.

Jureidini, Paul, and McLaurin, R.D. *Beyond Camp David: Emerging Alignments and Leaders in the Middle East.* Syracuse, N.Y.: Syracuse University Press, 1981.

Kerr, Malcolm, ed. *The Elusive Peace in the Middle East.* Albany, N.Y.: State University New York Press, 1975.

Khadduri, Majid. *Major Middle Eastern Problems in International Law.* Washington, D.C.: American Enterprise Institute, 1972.

Kissinger, Henry. *Years of Upheaval.* Toronto: Little, Brown, 1982.

Korany, Bahgat, and Dessouki, Ali E. Hillal, eds. *The Foreign Policies of the Arab States.* Boulder: Westview Press, 1984.

Lall, Arthur. *The UN and the Middle East Crisis, 1967.* New York: Columbia University Press, 1968.

Laqueur, Walter. *Confrontation: The Middle East and World Politics.* New York: Quadrangle, 1974.

Legum, Colin, and Shaked, Haim, eds. *Middle East Contemporary Survey,* 5 vols., New York: Homes and Meier. 1976–83.

Lenczowski, George. *The Middle East in World Affairs.* 4th ed. Ithaca, N.Y.: Cornell University Press, 1980.

———. *Russia and the West in Iran, 1914–1918.* Ithaca, N.Y.: Cornell University Press, 1972.

Lukacs, Yehuda, ed. *Documents on the Israeli-Palestinian Conflict, 1967–1983.* Cambridge: Cambridge University Press, 1984.

Moore, John, ed. *The Arab-Israeli Conflict.* 3 vols. Princeton: Princeton University Press, 1974.

Peck, Juliana. *The Reagan Administration and the Palestine Question: The First Thousand Days.* Washington, D.C.: Institute for Palestine Studies, 1984.

Polk, William. *The Arab World*. 4th ed. Cambridge, Mass.: Harvard University Press, 1980.

Quandt, William. *Decade of Decisions: American Policy Toward the Arab-Israeli Conflict, 1967–1976*. Berkeley: University of California Press, 1977.

———. *Saudi Arabia in the 1980's: Foreign Policy, Security, and Oil*. Washington, D.C.: Brookings Institution, 1981.

Ramazani, Rouhallah. *Beyond the Arab-Israeli Conflict: New Directions for U.S. Policy in the Middle East*. Cambridge, Mass.: Institute for Foreign Policy Analysis, 1977.

———. *U.S.-Iranian Relations since 1971*. New York: Praeger, 1981.

Reich, Bernard. *Quest for Peace: United States-Israeli Relations and Arab-Israeli Conflict*. New Brunswick, N.J.: Transaction Books, 1977.

Saunders, Harold. *The Middle East Problem in the 1980's*. Washington, D.C.: American Enterprise Institute, 1981.

Shaked, Haim, and Rabinovich, Itamar, eds. *The United States and the Middle East: Perceptions and Policies*. New Brunswick, N.J.: Transaction Books, 1980.

Sheehan, Edward. *The Arabs, Israelis, and Kissinger*. New York: Crowell, 1976.

Speigel, Steven, ed. *The Middle East and the Western Alliance*. London: Allen & Unwin, 1982.

———. *The Other Arab-Israeli Conflict: America's Middle Eastern Policy from Truman to Reagan*. Chicago: University of Chicago Press, 1985.

Stebbins, Richard P. *Documents on American Foreign Relations 1966*. New York: Harper and Row, 1967.

Thomas, Hugh. *The Suez Affair*. New York: Harper and Row, 1967.

Tibawi, A.L. *American Interests in Syria, 1800–1901: A Study of Educational, Literary and Religious Work*. London: Oxford University Press, 1966.

Tillman, Seth. *The United States in the Middle East*. Bloomington, Ind.: Indiana University Press, 1982.

Touval, Saadia. *The Peace Brokers: Mediators in the Arab-Israeli Conflict, 1948–1979*. Princeton, N.J.: Princeton University Press, 1982.

Udovich, A.L., ed. *The Middle East: Oil, Conflict, and Hope*. Lexington, Mass.: Lexington Books, 1976.

United States Department of State. *The Quest for Peace: Principal U.S. Public Statements and Documents Relating to the Arab-Israeli Peace Process, 1967–83*. Washington, D.C.: U.S. Government Printing Office, 1983.

———. *Anglo-American Committee of Inquiry: Report to the United States Government and His Majesty's Government in the United Kingdom.* Lausanne, Switzerland, April 20, 1946; Washington, D.C.: U.S. Government Printing Office, 1946.

U.S. Foreign Policy for the 1970's, a New Strategy for Peace. A Report to the Congress by Richard Nixon, President of the United States. February 18, 1970. Washington, D.C.: U.S. Government Printing Office, 1970.

Vali, Ferenc A. *Bridge Across the Bosphorus: The Foreign Policy of Turkey.* Baltimore: The Johns Hopkins Press, 1966.

Wainhouse, David, et al. *International Peace Observation: A History and Forecast.* Baltimore: The Johns Hopkins Press, 1966.

Weisband, Edward. *Turkish Foreign Policy, 1943–1945: Small State Diplomacy and Great Power Politics.* Princeton, N.J.: Princeton University Press, 1973.

Whetton, Lawrence. *The Arab-Israeli Dispute: Great Power Behavior.* (Adelphi Paper 128). London: International Institute for Strategic Studies, 1977.

———. *The Canal War: Four-Power Conflict in the Middle East.* Cambridge, Mass.: MIT Press, 1974.

Zinner, Paul E. *Documents on American Foreign Relations 1958.* New York: Harper, 1959.

CHAPTER 6: *The USSR and the Middle East*

Dawisha, Karen. *Soviet Foreign Policy Towards Egypt.* London: Macmillan Press, 1979.

———. "Soviet Policy in the Arab World: Permanent Interests and Changing Influence." *Arab Studies Quarterly* 2, No. 1 (Winter 1980).

——— and Dawisha, Adeed, eds. *The Soviet Union and the Middle East.* London: Heinemann Educational Books, 1982.

Dunn, Michael. "Soviet Interests in the Arabian Peninsula: The Aden Pact and Other Paper Tigers." *Arab-American Affairs* 8 (Spring 1984).

Freedman, Robert O. *Soviet Policy Toward the Middle East Since 1970.* 3rd ed. New York: Praeger, 1982.

Glassman, Jon D. *Arms for the Arabs: The Soviet Union and the War in the Middle East.* Baltimore: Johns Hopkins University Press, 1975.

Golan, Galia. *Yom Kippur and After: The Soviet Union and the Middle East Crisis.* Cambridge: Cambridge University Press, 1977.

———. *The Soviet Union and the Palestine Liberation Organization.* New York: Praeger, 1980.

Heikal, Mohamed. *The Sphinx and the Commisar: the Rise and Fall of Soviet Influence in the Middle East.* New York: Harper & Row, 1978.

Hopwood, Derek. *The Russian Presence in Syria and Palestine, 1843–1923: Church and Politics in the Near East.* London: Oxford University Press, 1969.

Hurewitz, J.C., ed. *Soviet-American Rivalry in the Middle East.* New York: Praeger, 1969.

Jargy, Simon, *L'Orient Déchiré: entre l'Est et l'Ouest.* Geneva: Editions Labor et Fides, 1984.

Kappui, Mark V., and Nation, R. Craig, eds. *The Soviet Union and the Middle East in the 1980s: Opportunities, Constraints, and Dilemmas.* Lexington, Mass.: D. C. Heath, 1983.

[Kennan, George F.] "X." "The Sources of Soviet Conduct." *Foreign Affairs* 25, No. 4 (July 1947).

Laqueur, Walter Z., ed. *Communism and Nationalism in the Middle East.* New York: Praeger, 1956.

———. *The Soviet Union and the Middle East.* New York: Praeger, 1969.

———. *The Struggle for the Middle East.* New York: Praeger, 1969.

Lederer, Ivo, and Vucinich, Wayne, eds. *The Soviet Union and the Middle East: The Post-World War II Era.* Stanford, Calif.: Hoover Institution Press, 1974.

Less, Christopher D. "The Soviet Contribution to Iran's Fourth Development Plan." *Mizan* 11, No. 5 (September–October 1969).

Lenczowski, George. *Russia and the West in Iran, 1918–1948: A Study in Big Power Rivalry.* Ithaca, N.Y.: Cornell University Press, 1949.

———. *Soviet Advances in the Middle East.* Washington, D.C.: American Enterprise Institute, 1972.

McLane, Charles B. *Soviet-Middle East Relations.* (Soviet-Third World Relations Volume I). London: Central Asian Research Centre, 1973.

McLaurin, R. D. *The Middle East in Soviet Policy.* Lexington, Mass.: D. C. Heath, 1975.

Morrison, David. "The Middle East: The Soviet Entanglement." *Mizan* 11, No. 3 (May–June 1969).

———. "Soviet Involvement in the Middle East: The New State." *Mizan* 11, No. 5 (September–October 1969).

Riad, Mahmoud. *The Struggle for Peace in the Middle East*. London: Quartet Books, 1981.

Ross, Dennis. "Soviet Views Toward the Gulf War." *Orbis* 28, No. 3 (Fall 1984).

Smolansky, Oles M. *The Soviet Union and the Arab East Under Kruschev*. Lewisburg, Pa.: Bucknell University Press, 1974.

"Special Document: The Soviet Attitude to the Palestine Problem." *Journal of Palestine Studies* 2, No. 1 (Autumn 1972).

Spector, Ivan. *The Soviet Union and the Muslim World*. Seattle: University of Washington Press, 1959.

Stavrou, Theofanic George. *Russia: Interests in Palestine, 1882–1914: A Study of Religious and Educational Enterprises*. Salonika: Institute for Balkan Studies, 1963.

CHAPTER 7: *China and the Middle East*

Abidi, A. H. H. *China, Iran, and the Persian Gulf*. Atlantic Highlands, N.J.: Humanities Press, 1982.

Behbahani, Hashim. *China's Foreign Policy in the Arab World 1955–1975*. London: Routledge and Kegan Paul, 1981.

Brzezinsky, Zbigniew, ed. *Africa and the Communist World*. Stanford, Calif.: Stanford University Press, 1963.

Cooley, John K. "China and the Palestinians." *Journal of Palestine Studies* 1, No. 2 (Winter 1972).

Disney, Nigel. "China and the Middle East." *MERIP Reports* 63 (1977).

Documents on International Affairs. *The Bandung Conference*. London: Oxford University Press, 1955.

Hamrell, Sven, and Widstrand, Carl Gosta, eds. *The Soviet Bloc, China, and Africa*. Upsalla: Almqvist and Wiksells, 1964.

Harris, Lillian Craig. "China's Relations with the PLO." *Journal of Palestine Studies* 25 (Autumn 1977).

Jansen, G.H. *Non-alignment and the Afro-Asian States*. New York: Praeger, 1966.

Khalili, Joseph E. *Communist China's Interaction with the Arab Nationalists Since the Bandung Conference*. New York: Exposition Press, 1970.

Rubenstein, Alvin, ed. *Soviet and Chinese Influence in the Third World*. New York: Praeger, 1975.

Shichor, Yitzhak. *The Middle East in China's Foreign Policy 1949–1977*. Cambridge: Cambridge University Press, 1979.

CHAPTER 8: *Africa and the Middle East*

Abegunrin, Olawayi. "The Arabs and the Southern Africa Problem." *International Affairs* (London) 60, No. 1 (Winter 1983/84).

Abu-Lughod, Ibrahim. *Palestinian Rights: Affirmation and Denial.* Wilmette, Ill.: Medina Press, 1982.

Adams, James. *The Unnatural Alliance.* London: Quartet Books, 1984.

Ajami, Fouad, and Sours, Martin H. "Israel and Sub-Saharan Africa: A Study of Interaction." *African Studies Review* 13, No. 3 (December 1970).

Asante, S. K. B. "Africa in World Politics: The Case of the Organization of African Unity and the Middle East Conflict." *International Problems* (Tel Aviv) 20, No. 2–4 (Summer 1981).

Baulin, Jacques. *The Arab Role in Africa.* Baltimore: Penguin, 1962.

Chibwe, E. C. *Afro-Arab Relations.* New York: St. Martin's Press, 1977.

Curtis, Michael, and Gitelson, Susan Aurelia, eds. *Israel in the Third World.* New Brunswick, N.J.: Transaction Books, 1976.

Gitelson, Susan Aurelia. "The OAU and the Middle East Conflict." *International Organization* 27, No. 2 (Summer 1973).

———. "Why Do Small States Break Diplomatic Relations with Outside Powers? Lessons from the African Experience." *International Studies Quarterly* 18, No. 4 (December 1974).

———. "Unfulfilled Expectations: Israeli and Arab Aid As Political Instruments in Black African United Nations Voting Behavior." *Jewish Social Studies* 38 (Spring 1976).

Haseeb, Khair El-Din, ed. *The Arabs and Africa.* London: Croom Helm, 1985.

Hovet, Thomas Jr. *Africa in the United Nations.* London: Faber and Faber, 1963.

Ismael, Tareq Y. "The United Arab Republic in Africa." *The Canadian Journal of African Studies* 2, No. 2 (Fall 1968).

———. *The U.A.R. in Africa: Egypt's Policy Under Nasser.* Evanston, Ill.: Northwestern University Press, 1971.

———. "Arab-African Relations." *The Arab Historian* 20 (1980).

Jansen, G. H. *Nonalignment and the Afro-Asian States.* New York: Praeger, 1966.

Legum, Colin, ed. *Africa Contemporary Record.* London: Africana Publishing, annual.

LeVine, Victor T., and Luke, Timothy W. *The Arab-African Connection and Economic Realities.* Boulder: Westview Press, 1979.

Mertz, Robert Anton and Pamela McDonald Mertz. *Arab Aid to Sub-Saharan Africa.* Munich: Kaiser, 1983.

Miller, Jake C. "African-Israeli Relations: Impact on Continental Unity." *Middle East Journal* 29, No. 4 (Autumn 1975).

Nasser, Gamal Abdel. *Egypt's Liberation: The Philosophy of the Revolution.* Washington, D.C.: Public Affairs Press, 1955.

Ojo, Olusola. "The Role of the Arab World in the Decolonization Process of Black Africa." *International Problems* (Tel Aviv) 20, No. 2–4 (Summer 1981).

Shihata, Ibrahim F. I. *The Other Face of OPEC: Financial Assistance to the Third World.* London: Longman, 1982.

Stevens, Richard P. and Elmessiri, Abdel M. *Israel and South Africa: the Progression of a Relationship.* New York: New World Books, 1976.

Wai, Dunstan M., ed. *Interdependence in a World of Unequals: African-Arab-OECD Economic Cooperation for Development.* Boulder: Westview Press, 1982.

INDEX

International Relations of the Contemporary Middle East

was composed in 10-point Trump Medieval and leaded two points
on Digital Compugraphic equipment by Metricomp;
with display type set in Lydian on a Linotron 202
by Dix Typesetting Company, Inc.;
printed by sheet-fed offset on 50-pound, acid-free Warren's Old Style,
Smyth sewn and bound over binder's boards in Holliston Roxite B,
also adhesive bound with paper covers
by Thomson-Shore, Inc.;
with dust jackets and paper covers printed in two colors
by Thomson-Shore, Inc.;
and published by

SYRACUSE UNIVERSITY PRESS
SYRACUSE, NEW YORK 13244-5160